STOKES CARSON

Stokes Carson at Inscription House beside a pile of saddle blankets. 1960

STOKES CARSON

Twentieth-Century Trading on
the Navajo Reservation

Willow Roberts

University of New Mexico Press
Albuquerque

Design by Milenda Nan Ok Lee

Library of Congress Cataloging-in-Publication Data

Roberts, Willow, 1943–
  Stokes Carson: twentieth-century trading on the
Navajo Reservation.

  Bibliography: p.
  Includes index.
  1. Carson, Orange Jay, 1886–1974. 2. Navajo Indians
—Trading posts. 3. Indians of North America—
Southwest, New—Trading posts. 3. New Mexico—
Biography. I. Title.
E99.N3C367   1987   978.9'00497   86-19207
ISBN 0-8263-0916-X
ISBN 0-8263-0917-8 (pbk.)

Dedicated to
Jo Drolet
In Memoriam

Contents

Contents

Illustrations

Illustrations

Acknowledgements

I would like to thank every member of the Carson family, and their friends, without whose help and trust this book could not have been written. In particular, Jo and Sam Drolet provided the inspiration, as well as the framework of family history, for all that follows. I like to think that, had she lived, Jo would have been pleased to see her parents' story in print for others to read. But in reality I am sure that it would have been a pleasure secondary to real things: visits of her sisters, of her son, daughter-in-law, and grandson, of her friends, secondary even to her own vivid memory of people and events which she and Sam kept alive in conversation with those who remembered them or those who were interested.

Jo and Sam were joint muses, but I owe gratitude to many others for help and information: Mildred Heflin, for, among many other things, her contribution of ledgers, newspaper clippings, letters, and comments that filled in the period of 1950 and 1960; Marie Leighton, who gave me crucial details of Stokes and the FTC hearings; and Chin and Ed Smith for information on Oljato in general and stock reduction in particular. Raymond and Melissa Drolet let me live and occasionally work at Shonto to observe the workings of a modern-day trading post. Wy and Al Townsend contributed similar details for Inscription House. Edie Jo Yogurst and Sharon Heflin added details of growing up at Shonto, and Nina Heflin gave much useful information on businesses on the reservation. Walter Scribner gave me hours of his time, describing Stokes and Jessie Carson and his own work at different trading posts. C. E. Purviance provided an outsider's point of view as well as a wealth of data: he not only saved all correspondence from Shonto but also collected information for a novel on trading posts. Although he did not live to complete his project, this material was invaluable to me since it was collected at an earlier date and contained fresh and vivid accounts by each of the Carson sisters of a typical day at the various posts. I am indebted to his daughter, Grace P. Brown, of Sacramento, California for permission to use this material. Richard Mike gave me very useful information and insights on the period of the 1970s on the reservation. While at Shonto I was helped in various ways by Grace Brown, Mary and Bill Brown, Ruby Clitso, Floyd Talker, Sr., and Floyd Talker, Jr. During the summer of 1979 I had conversations with many traders, all of whom contributed insights and information: Doug and Barbara Anderson, Kay Ashcroft, Bruce Barnard, Harry Bachelor, Bob and Theta Cooke, Chuck Dickens, Harry and Mike Goulding, Luther Manning, Maurice Tanner, and Dean Winn.

I would like to thank those who read and critiqued the various drafts of the manuscript: Garrick and Roberta Bailey, Dick Barrett, Dave Brugge, Jim Chisholm, Charlotte Frisbie, Donald Parman, and Britt Perez. I have tried to incorporate all of their corrections and many of their suggestions; any remaining errors are mine. I am also indebted to Beth Hadas, my editor, for her encouragement and patience.

Last but by no means least, I would like to add that without the years of moral support, encouragement, criticism, advice, and friendship of Nancy Sommerschield, intellectual godmother without par, none of this endeavor would have been possible.

Preface

The spring of 1979 was an unusually wet one in Chaco Canyon. I had moved to Albuquerque that March to study at the University of New Mexico, but before turning to academic pursuits I wanted to explore the Southwest. The National Park Service had accepted me as a volunteer and, unprepared for the cold gray skies and slick mud, I settled into the excellent library in the park headquarters and began to read intensively about the prehistory, history, archaeology, and ethnology of the area. The library contained the early superintendents' reports from Chaco, and it was in these reports and in the accounts of Richard Wetherill and the archaeological excavations in the canyon that I encountered the first mention of traders.

Later on that spring I undertook to compile an oral history of people who had lived and grown up in the area. The idea had the blessing of the superintendent at Chaco, Walter Herriman, who also gave me introductions with which to begin requesting interviews. The first interview was with Mr. and Mrs. Drolet of Carson's Trading Post. The project was at this point very loosely conceived, for I believed that it would acquire a framework from the interviews. The focus came far sooner than I expected. My interview with the Drolets was an introduction to trader history, for both Jo and Sam knew the details of trading post life from their families' as well as their own experience. Mrs. Drolet's interest in the history of trading posts rubbed off on me, and the stories she told of her parents, Stokes and Jessie Carson, made the history vivid. The subject of traders and trade with the Navajo soon became the focus of the oral history.

I talked to other traders in the area, and I went back many times to visit the Drolets, who gave me introductions to Jo Drolet's sister at Oljato and son and daughter-in-law at Shonto. From the Checkerboard region of New Mexico, I moved to Arizona and the heart of the Navajo Reservation.

The distances on the Navajo Reservation are immense, the landscape dramatic. There are few towns, few stores, no neon signs, and many dirt roads. Finding trading posts that were not on main roads became a challenge; it was not that they were hard to recognize (the gas pump gave them away), but that the network of dirt roads was confusing to a newcomer. Another fact became obvious as I drove about the reservation: there were few whites here. Those I saw, other than the tourists, were government employees—school teachers, Public Health Service employees—or storekeepers and occasionally miners. The Navajos to whom I gave rides from place to place as I traveled were polite and usually silent. One woman drove several miles with me, and we discovered we were the same age; she, however, had had ten children and I none, and so different were our lives that the conversation was driven by curiosity on both sides. Cultural immersion is an important part of anthropology. Living in an alien culture, knowing it from the inside, led to understanding, as well as to new insights into one's own culture. The traders spent most if not all of their lives among the Navajo. Jo Drolet's father built Carson's Trading Post in 1918, when she was three years old, and she lives there still. One of the differences between traders and anthropologists lies in intent, but there might also be similarities in situations, in understanding, in the stresses and strains. This continual daily contact between cultures interested me.

The beginning of Indian trade goes back to the fur trade. Traders created an entrepreneur's niche between the expanding European-American population and the Native American groups they encountered as they moved into the forests, down the rivers, and across the plains and deserts. In the beginning, traders bartered for beaver, mink, and other pelts, taking advantage of the difference in value between the skins and the goods for which they were traded.

The Spaniards built trading networks in the Southwest that extended from Mexico to Santa Fe and included the different Southwestern tribes.[1] Later settlers, from other parts of Europe and North America (often referred to as Anglos), followed the acquisition of the territory by the United States and encroached on Spanish lands and Spanish trade. Anglo traders in the Southwest were less colorful than the trapper-traders of the northern region; they were more akin to adventuresome peddlers who wandered off with a wagon full of buttons and bows and an entrepreneur's eye for whatever might constitute the medium of exchange. Most of the pelts (at least south of Santa Fe and the Rocky Mountains) were those of sheep, and the people who had sheep were the Navajo. Furthermore, the Navajo wove gorgeous blankets, which had been highly sought after as trade items since the 1700s, both by Spaniards and by Indians of other tribes, and which became equally popular with Anglo traders.[2]

Eventually local men, born and bred in the area, replaced the itinerant traders, though a few "outsiders" were always among their ranks. The trading post became an institution on the Navajo Reservation, supplying necessities in the vast distances of the reservation from small stores that, over time, became central points of contact between Anglos and Navajos. Trading posts existed in the Hopi, Zuni, and other Pueblo villages, but these were smaller and more concentrated settlements easily served by one store, in contrast to the dispersed Navajo camps, which needed many.

Stokes Carson was not one of the pioneer traders selling out of a wagon. Rather, he was one of the generation of traders that grew up in the Southwest. He was born in 1886 in Farmington, New Mexico, and heard about trading from friends and family members at a time when it was becoming one of the possible means of livelihood. He built his own trading post, known as Carson's, in 1918, just off the eastern border of the Navajo Reservation. Because of the post's off-reservation location, Stokes could and did own sheep (grazing on reservation land was strictly reserved for Navajos) to supplement his income from the store.

The life of the trader was closely connected to that of the Navajo. If Navajos did well, so did the trader. Improving economic conditions was the aim of many traders, and to this end they tried to find jobs for Navajos, obtain markets for their crafts, and improve their sheep. Most traders had to know or learn something about sheep. Stokes experimented with different breeds and loaned out rams to local Navajos for breeding purposes. He trailed his herd up to public lands in Colorado in the summer; he built sheep dips at Carson's for his own herd as well as for those of other local ranchers and of the Navajo. He exchanged knowledge of sheep with his customers and neighbors, and he traded for their lambs in the spring. Sheep constituted a common interest (and, for off-reservation traders, a mutual enterprise) between traders and Navajos.

I returned to Albuquerque and the University of New Mexico in January 1980, after transcribing tapes of interviews with traders and completing the project. But the story seemed unfinished, and two years later I decided to write a detailed account of more recent events. One of the topics that was mentioned by every trader interviewed was a series of hearings that had occurred in 1972, a reservation-wide investigation of traders and trading operations by the Federal Trade Commission, the Bureau of Indian Affairs, and the Navajo Tribe. The hearings had been dramatic and for a brief time vied with the war in Vietnam and university sit-ins as front-page news in western papers. The traders had bitter memories of the investigation. They had had to answer for a life that they felt had been difficult, and hard to describe, and the trial-like atmosphere had been an ordeal. These hearings were sufficiently unknown that an examination of the background and a description of the events would, I thought, be of interest, and an account of the life of one trading family—the Carsons, whom by then I knew well—would illustrate the details of trading. Further, the account could describe the context of the cross-cultural contact that underlay the hearings, and it could give a broader perspective to the tale. My work was not intended as a full-fledged social science study, nor was it written by a trader (or by a trader's wife, as so many of the best were). I hoped to describe, and clarify, the last twenty-five years of trading from a historical as well as a cross-cultural point of view.

The book was written at Shonto, where other accounts of trading had also begun. Raymond and Melissa Drolet, Stokes's grandson and granddaughter-in-law, had agreed to let me live there for the summer. From May until August 1982, I observed the daily routine of the store, occasionally worked in it, and continued to ask questions and write. The observation of every aspect of Shonto Trading Post, from the daily sales to the bookkeeping, from the delivery of milk to the collecting of cash from the bank, filled out my picture of present-day trading and added to my understanding of recent history. In addition, I had access to the correspondence of Jo Drolet's sister, Mildred Heflin, who had traded at Shonto in the 1950s with her husband. Mildred had kept letters both to and, by a lucky stroke, from herself, and these covered the period during which the Heflins were traders, not only at Shonto, but at two other posts as well. Mildred's own letters were invaluable, for she is one of those people who writes with vivid detail. Her descriptions of weather, work, newspaper reports, Navajo neighbors, and the activities of her family were my best source of what life was like. More than anything else, these letters gave me the feel of trading; they also revealed the things that changed, and those that remained virtually the same, across the years.

One of the interesting events of the summer was the arrival of the truck that came to collect the bales of wool that the trading post had purchased that spring. The hill into Shonto Canyon is steep and unpaved, and the lane to the wool barn narrow and lined with big, old cottonwoods. The large truck negotiated the way with difficulty. The bales of wool that were piled in the barn weighed around two hundred pounds each and were a little over five feet long when filled. There were about a hundred of them to be loaded onto the trailer. Raymond Drolet hired five young Navajo men, and with some help from the two Mormon missionaries who lived nearby, a preschool teacher, Melissa, and me, they rolled the bales out of the barn and up the ramp to the truck bed. At the top of the ramp, the bales had to be maneuvered—half lifted, half pushed—so that the whole trailer was filled from floor to roof with no wasted space. The driver had come for the wool from both Inscription House Trading Post and Shonto, and he came only once a year. The sacking and the wool were rough and dusty and seemed to fill eyes, throat, and clothes with fiber. The odor of lanolin was sickly and pervasive. Sheep, Raymond assured me when the job was finished and everyone was drinking soda pop and resting, were worse. The Navajos laughed and nodded. Once, several years earlier, when Raymond was new to Shonto, the truck that came to collect the sheep and lambs was late; it had to be loaded in the dark. The animals balked at every shadow, ran into corners, refused to climb the ramp. It was midnight before the last lamb was loaded. Sheep meant business and survival, but few traders really liked them. That fall, I attended a livestock auction held by the tribe at the chapter house behind Carson's Trading Post and began to see why. The loading and unloading of sheep, goats, and cows required constant surveillance and strength to make sure the animals went where they should. Each family's livestock for sale was put in a separate pen, weighed, and bid on. As one vehicle after another unloaded its animals, I realized that not every creature survived the journey: sheep trampled each other in fright and a few were dead on arrival; a cow herded into a pen had one eye hanging from its socket. Since the inauguration of auctions by the Navajo tribe, traders have been able to discontinue dealing in livestock. The old sheep corrals at Shonto are full of grass and tall bee weed. Stokes was one of the generation of traders who knew sheep because they had to, but he liked them, and the quality and condition of sheep around Carson's Trading Post, both Stokes's and those of his customers, was a source of pride.

This account is both a biography of Stokes Carson and his family and a history of the trade between Anglos and Navajos, especially in recent years. It is not a history of the Navajo, nor a sociological, economic, or political account. Some details are given to illuminate the situation of trading posts and traders (for a more extensive background, the reader is referred to the bibliography). It is in part a defense of traders, though I hope an objective one. Traders have acquired a dubious reputation, and those traders I knew led me to think that the reputation was frequently undeserved. After some research I have come to the conclusion that the events of the last fifteen years have a more complex background than might be realized. Certainly not every trader was a moral businessman, concerned as much with his customers' welfare as with his own profit. For every Stokes Carson, there was a trader who was not cooperative in his community, who may have been irascible, arrogant, even violent. Cross-cultural situations can be either a license for the worst behaviors of humans or an opportunity for shared conditions and familiarity to inspire deeper understandings.

The term *Indian trader* describes those who, not being Indian themselves, exchange manufactured goods with Native Americans for raw materials and crafts, usually on the latter's home ground. It carries a connotation of a whole way of life and livelihood, with overtones either romantic or pejorative, depending on the speaker. Some understanding of these overtones can be found in Stokes Carson's story, for he and his wife, Jessie, traded off and on the Navajo Reservation for fifty years, and his family still trades there. To understand the world of the Carson family, the reader must know something of life on the Navajo Reservation, past and present, of the history of both the Navajo and the Anglos who moved into their area, of their economy—both that which the two groups shared and that which they did not—and of the history of trade in the region. The chapters that follow will fill in some of these details of the life and times of a twentieth-century Indian trader.

STOKES CARSON

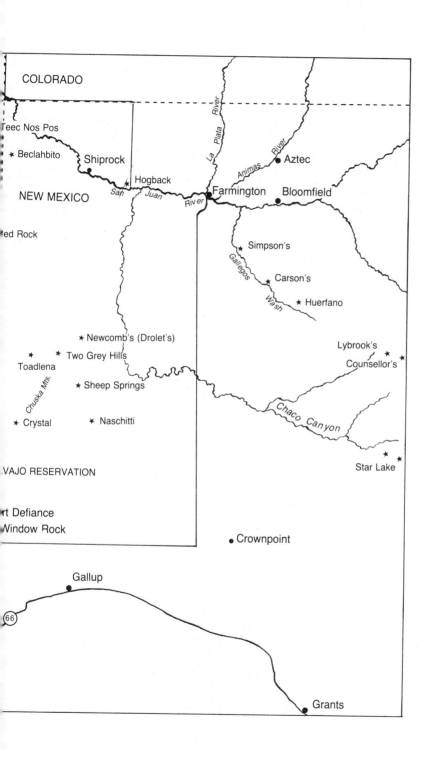

COLORADO

Teec Nos Pos

★ Beclahbito   Shiprock ●   ★ Hogback   ● Aztec   Aztec

NEW MEXICO   San   Juan   River   ● Farmington   Bloomfield ●

La Plata River

Animas River

ed Rock

★ Simpson's

Gallegos

★ Carson's

Wash   ★ Huerfano

★ Newcomb's (Drolet's)

Lybrook's   ★

★   ★ Two Grey Hills   Counsellor's   ★
Toadlena

Chuska Mts.

★ Sheep Springs

Chaco Canyon

★ Crystal   ★ Naschitti

★   ★
Star Lake

VAJO RESERVATION

rt Defiance
Window Rock   ● Crownpoint

Gallup ●

(66)

● Grants

Part I

1886–1918

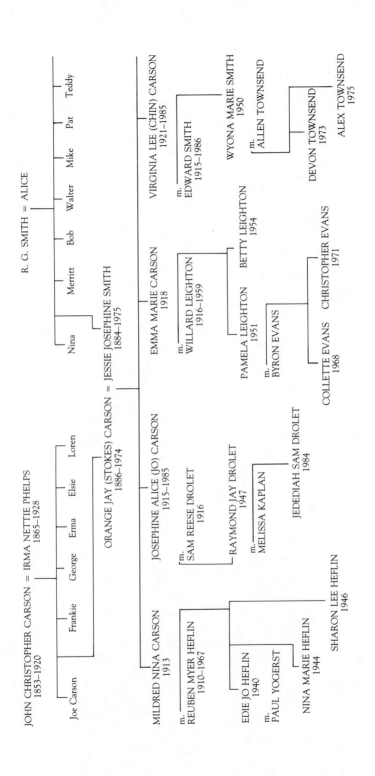

THE CARSON FAMILY

1

Stokes Carson
and Jessie Smith

Stokes Carson was born on April 2, 1886, on a ranch just outside Farmington, a small frontier settlement on the San Juan River, in northwestern New Mexico. His name was in fact Orange Jay Carson, after his maternal grandfather. "Stokes" was a nickname that came from a local cartoon character, a small-time badman, and stuck. Carson never used his given name even as as adult, except as initials on his wool sacks and his stationery: O. J. CARSON. He was the second child of John Christopher Carson and Nettie Phelps, both of whom came to the Southwest in the 1800s—Carson as a young man, Nettie as a baby, moving, like others on the North American continent, into emptier spaces. So typical—and so typically unique—were Nettie Phelps and John Christopher Carson that their travels to and settlement in Farmington should be described.

Sometime in the late 1860s or early 1870s, John Christopher Carson, known as Kit Carson after the famous Indian scout (to whom he was not related), came to the United States from eastern Canada. He reached Iowa and was hired by the Union Pacific Railroad, which was constructing the railroad to the west in the period immediately following the Civil War. John Carson's job was to shovel coal for the engineer, a man named Joe Starrett, as the supply train followed the laborers along the newly laid tracks. The work was tedious, and when the construction crew reached the Great Plains and the herds of buffalo, John exchanged the job of shoveling coal for that of shooting game. He was a good shot and became the supplier of meat for the crew.

According to Carson family history, Joe Starrett was fired following a train wreck; in any event, he and John Carson left the Union Pacific when it reached Colorado and headed for the mining towns of the Rockies. They moved between the mining camps, earning their keep by supplying game. John Carson eventually staked a claim, somewhere between Lake City and Silverton, north of Durango. He was joined by a brother, William, and they worked the claim together, attracted prospectors, and sold it for $5,000. Carson's, the camp, prospered for a short time, and wooden shacks still stand there, surrounded by pine trees and overgrown tracks. The Carson brothers moved south to the San Juan River valley in the territory of New Mexico, looking for land to homestead. Other settlers had already recognized the junction of the Animas, San Juan, and La Plata rivers as a verdant valley in the desert, and five or six small adobe houses on the north bank of the San Juan constituted the beginnings of Farmington. The Carson brothers homesteaded adjacent plots to the east of what was to become the town. John invested his money in an irrigation company that was building the Bloomfield ditch and other channels for supplying water to the homesteaders' fields—and he began to court Nettie Phelps.

Nettie Phelps was the daughter of Orange Jay Phelps and Elizabeth Hazelton, who had settled on land across the river from the Carson homestead. O. J. Phelps was a shoemaker who had come west from Michigan with his wife, Elizabeth, lured by California gold. Theirs was, however, a very domestic outfit when they set out for the glittering and spacious West. Behind the wagon and ox team trailed several head of cattle, and chickens shared the wagon with Elizabeth. It took them about three months to get to California, and wherever they stopped along the journey, Phelps made or mended shoes to keep the family, lacking gold, in groceries. Shoemaking was, if not more profitable, certainly more reliable a livelihood than mining. Eventually the Phelpses settled down in New Mexico. Phelps dug ditches, battling the sandy soil and the fluctuation of arroyos, and raised cows. He sold milk and once a year took a ten-gallon crock of butter to Alamosa, Colorado (it was reputed to take him thirty or forty days for the whole trip) to sell for provisions.

Of the ten children born to Elizabeth and Orange Jay, five girls and three boys survived and grew up on the ranch: Effie, Frank, Nettie, Janie, George, Maggie, Clara, and Wesley. Nettie and Janie married the Carson brothers in a double wedding sometime after 1880 and moved to the Carson ranch. Shortly afterward, the rest of the Phelps family moved to Fort Wingate to supply the army post with milk and butter.

John and Nettie Carson stayed on the homestead, raising cattle, planting fruit trees, alfalfa, and wheat, and bringing up their seven children:

Joe, Stokes, Frankie, George, Erma, Elsie, and Loren. In 1890, Carson was elected sheriff of San Juan County.

Stokes Carson grew up in the atmosphere of self-reliance, hard work, and stoicism typical of frontier settlements. He helped with chores around the ranch, walked to Junction City Elementary School two and a half miles away, and rode to Sunday school. Farmington grew up, too. It had been settled in 1876 by five men, William Hendrickson, Charley Virden and his brother Milton, Albert Pruett, and Henry Wood, all of whom had come down from Colorado looking for land in the lower altitudes to farm. In 1880, the area was opened to the settlers, who began to cultivate the area near the junction of the Animas, Plata, and San Juan rivers, a place called by the Navajo Tota' ("Between Rivers").[1] The valley was green with cottonwoods along the river banks, but in the arid climate and fierce sun the new fields needed irrigation. Digging irrigation ditches to bring water from the rivers was a cooperative activity of the community, which continued to attract people. Later on, companies were formed to raise money for these essential arteries of an agricultural community. Other settlements also sprang up along the valley: Kirtland, Fruitland, Bloomfield, predominantly agricultural also, and partly Mormon.

As he grew older, Stokes fished, hunted rabbits, and shot duck. Occasionally he went with his maternal grandparents to Gallup in the wagon, a trip of about six days, to sell fruit. The journey to Gallup followed a cart track called the Togay Trail, which connected Fort Wingate in the south with Fort Lewis, in Colorado, and was used to haul freight between communities. Sand and sagebrush filled the landscape, broken by outcrops of sandstone, occasional small canyons, arroyos, and shaley badlands eroding slowly into rainbow-colored dunes.

Stokes turned twenty. His father gave him an acre of his own on the homestead to cultivate and, if he could, to make a small income from. Life was not all work, however. The social life of Farmington was provided to a large extent by the churches. In small towns, like Farmington, Bloomfield, or Aztec, local churches not only held the religious services, Sunday schools, baptisms, weddings, and funerals but also the picnics and other gatherings at which the old could talk and the young could get together. It was at one of these picnics that Stokes met Jessie Smith, though since their parents were neighbors it was presumably not for the first time. At the picnic an auction was held for the bag lunches made by each young woman; Stokes bid for Jessie's lunch, saying that anyone who made deviled eggs the way she did deserved more attention.

Jessie's family lived on land across the river from the Carson ranch. Her father, R. G. Smith, had come to the territory from Mississippi with his wife, Alice. Alice herself came from Virginia and found the hard life of the western territories unfamiliar and difficult. Her oldest child, Nina, died of scarlet fever, and two younger children also died, leaving Jessie, Merritt, Bob, Walter, Howard (known as Mike), Taylor (known as Pat), and Teddy. R. G. Smith was a religious man, which perhaps influenced Jessie, who went to work at the Methodist mission when she was about seventeen.

Catholic and protestant missions set up hospitals and schools to provide practical aid to the Native Americans. In New Mexico, two major afflictions, especially of the Navajo, were tuberculosis and trachoma, a serious infection of the eyes. Communicable diseases such as measles, diphtheria, smallpox, and influenza were spread by whites, who had acquired greater immunity to them, and struck Native Americans hard. Mission hospitals provided beds, nurses, and medicines and encouraged the Indians to turn to this novel way of curing.

In 1891 two women working under the auspices of the Missionary Society of the Methodist Church established a mission twenty-five miles west of Farmington, on the eastern slope of the Navajo Reservation at a place called Hogback. The older of the two, Mrs. Eldridge, also served as a government field nurse, riding out among Navajo hogans to attend to the needs of whoever might accept her help. She expanded the mission to include a hospital and a school for Navajos, for which she recruited a nurse, teachers, and young women from the surrounding area to help her. It was at the Hogback mission that Jessie came to work.

The mission was a two-story adobe building between the San Juan River and a bony ridge of sandstone running north-south that gave the place its name. A small post, the Hogback Trading Post, had also been built below the ridge at the point where the river cut through the hogback. Floods from spring thaws and cloudbursts occurred frequently in the days before dams and irrigation ditches lowered the water level of the San Juan, and the mission, built on lower ground than the trading post, caught them all.[2]

Jessie worked at the mission for several years. A photograph—it must have been taken a few years after the turn of the century—shows a young woman, slender and tall in the long skirts of the period, serious-faced. The details of the print are very clear and give her a certain elegance. She leans back in a white cane rocker, her arms lying along the chair's arms, a handkerchief in one hand. Her eyes are large, and she gazes directly and very calmly at the camera.

Stokes and Jessie were married July 25, 1908, at the Aztec Hotel, a handsome brick building on the main street of Aztec. Stokes had saved some money from his one acre to take Jessie on a honeymoon; they went to Denver, a great city of gas lights, horse-drawn trams, crowded streets, and women in silk skirts—an extravagant trip and a treat for Jessie, before she got down to the life of hard work that Stokes was offering her.

2

Navajos, Traders, and Sheep

Here it is necessary to leave Stokes and Jessie Carson on the ranch in Farmington, where they stayed for the next eight years, and give some history of the surrounding territory and of the Navajos who lived there, for it is important to the tale.

Farmington lies a couple of miles east of the Navajo Reservation, in an area now known as the Four Corners, the only spot in the United States where the corners of four states—Colorado, Utah, New Mexico, and Arizona—meet. In 1876, the year Farmington was first settled, only Colorado was a state, having just been admitted; ten years later Utah also gained statehood.

The San Juan River runs through the Four Corners area from southeast to northwest and is joined by the Las Animas and La Plata rivers flowing down from the Rocky Mountains. The Spanish had traversed the region, and fur trappers, so it was said, had found beaver on the San Juan River. Spanish, Indian, and Anglo trading parties had passed through. The major activity in the nineteenth century after U.S. acquisition of this Spanish territory had been to the north, when silver and gold were discovered in the Colorado Rockies.

The Spanish, the earliest European settlers, had come to the region in 1598 and had encountered the inhabitants of pueblos along the Rio Grande, as well as the peoples of the more distant pueblos, Hopi, Zuni, Acoma, and Pecos. Spanish accounts mentioned the Apache in the eastern part of New Mexico, and later the name Navajo, or Nabahu, appeared.[1]

By 1898 (when Stokes was twelve years old), New Mexico was still a relatively undeveloped territory, though a territory battling for statehood. The population was something less than 195,000 (the census figures give 195,310 for 1900), and the number of sheep, as counted by the census, something less than 3,334,000. Before 1860, sheep were raised mostly in the Eastern states, particularly Vermont, New York, Pennsylvania, Virginia, and Kentucky; but the East was filling with people fast, and by the 1890s over 50 percent of all the sheep in the United States were grazing in the West. Cattle, too, became important. Railway lines were beginning to cross the state; more important for Farmington (which got a spur line of its own only in 1902), the Denver and Rio Grande Railroad reached Denver, opening new supply lines and market outlets.[2]

The public issues of territorial politics involved religion, language, taxes, and land. The territory was to a large extent Catholic and Spanish-speaking. Land titles from Spanish and Mexican grants had been a problem for some time. Though the 1848 treaty of acquisition recognized land grants of the Spanish settlers, disputes brought to territorial courts interpreted Spanish deeds and claims by American laws. Land grabbing was a successful method of acquiring land, and the earlier Spanish settlers (as well as Native Americans) were slowly losing out. Such problems created hostility and fraud, and statehood was thought of as a solution to these difficulties.[3]

The white settlers who came to the Southwest were used to hardships, and they admired the fortitude and endurance of the Navajo because they themselves were familiar with cold, hunger, and other difficulties. What they understood less well was the Navajo way of life, which the settlers perceived as a meager living without goods. The Anglo homesteaders had an ideal of how things ought to be and, most of all, of comfort. The Declaration of Independence promised for Americans what no earthly polity had ever thought to secure, in writing, for its citizens, namely, happiness, or at least the pursuit of it. Life on earth did not have to be a continual bitter struggle, and this new land could provide a test of the idea. Material comfort seemed the obvious place to begin. The energy, courage, and hard work that the settlers put toward bringing their ideal to life, and the extremes they suffered to nurture it, extremes of physical hardship and mental strain, constitute a kind of paradox. Well-being was thought to be gained from activity rather than from resting. The plough could not stand still, nor could the house remain unroofed or the surplus unexchanged. In the end, it seemed as though action, rather than comfort in the possession of goods, became the goal.

The Navajos of the Spanish period had been moving slowly west, raiding the Utes, sometimes even the Comanches who boldly ventured into New Mexico, and, as they reached Arizona, the Hopi. Despite the raids on the Hopi, there was some intermarriage between Navajos and Hopis. There was also contact and cooperation between the Navajos and the Eastern Pueblo groups, and after the Pueblo uprising against the Spanish in 1680, Pueblos and Navajos took refuge together in the west, and the Navajo learned spinning and weaving, planting and cultivation.

The Navajos (as well as the Pueblos) obtained horses and then sheep from the Spanish by trade and also by raids, and through trade with other Indian tribes. The sheep that Navajos began to own in some quantity kept them moving from place to place according to the seasons, and gradually the cyclic migration necessitated by summer and winter grazing settled down into consistent patterns determined by local conditions, knowledge of the area, and precedence.

Contact with the Pueblos had introduced the Navajos to building in stone. White settlers in the San Juan Basin were familiar with the round stone hogans with mud-covered log roofs that appeared across the landscape, never very close together. The Navajos also used the older, traditional forked-stick hogan. A Navajo camp usually consisted of stone hogan, forked-sticked hogan, corrals for sheep and horses, and, in summer, a ramada of poles with a brush-covered roof for shade. Navajos not only kept sheep but farmed, wherever it was possible, and their camps, which they moved with the seasons, were placed according to need, close to good soil, pastures, or water.[4]

The Anglos followed the Spanish into the area, slowly throughout the eighteenth century, in greater numbers in the nineteenth. The clashes between the Anglo-Americans and the Navajo, in particular, became fierce as the Navajo grew more hostile to the encroachment on their space and bolder in their raids. In 1863, the United States government decided to gather up this determined group of Native Americans, "contain" them in an area in southeastern New Mexico, and teach them to be docile citizens (or wards) and peaceful farmers.

Kit Carson (no relative of Stokes) was brought out of retirement and delegated to lead the army to round the Navajo up and take them down to Fort Sumner in the plains of eastern New Mexico. With about 750 volunteers, he rode through Navajo territory and achieved conquest with little bloodshed, though his destruction of orchards, gardens, and livestock, (especially in Canyon de Chelly), took away all subsistence in an area where agriculture, and life in general, did not come easily. Some Navajos succeeded in hiding in the northern reaches, around Navajo Mountain on the Utah border, but the majority had nowhere to go and nothing to live on; in 1864, eight thousand or more Navajos surrendered and traveled to Fort Sumner, or Bosque Redondo. Here they lived under the jurisdiction of the army, which gave out rations, blankets, and tools and tried to encourage farming.

The farming was not a success. The Navajo were both herders of sheep and farmers, but the soil at Bosque Redondo was alkaline and dry, and bad weather and infestations of caterpillars destroyed the first crops. The situation was intolerable. The expense to the government was a steady drain, and the attempt to contain the Navajo was abandoned after four years.

In 1868 the Navajo were sent back to their own land, or a portion of it, with a treaty that defined its boundaries, giving them 5,100 square miles of land lying squarely across the Arizona–New Mexico border. Unlike most Indian reservations, it was gradually increased in size, until by 1934 it enclosed 23,500 square miles. White settlers were not much attracted to the area, finding it too dry to farm, too vast and full of canyons to travel, and seemingly without useful resources. Additions in the 1870s and 1880s expanded it in all directions. The twentieth century added more land to the south and filled in corners and edges. In 1882 the Hopi Reservation was created in its center, covering the Hopi Mesas and including a surrounding area to be used jointly by Hopi and Navajo.[5] Ultimately, the Navajo Reservation was a large area, between large rivers but containing none, pinned by mountains at each corner, high, arid, and beautiful.

When the Navajos returned from Bosque Redondo to the small portion of their original homeland that constituted the core of their reservation, there were no towns and no settlements other than the Hopi pueblos and their own hogans abandoned four years before. They were destitute, and the army had to supply them with food, clothes, seed, and tools, which it gave out once a week from Fort Defiance, on the extreme southern boundary of the reservation. Those who lived close by trekked in, and many camped around the fort. Eventually, leaders were allowed to take wagonloads to distribute to outlying tribesmen, but many people took only the first week's provisions and left for distant homes. The treaty specified payment of a certain value to the Navajo. The government decided to pay in sheep, allotting two per person for every man, woman, and child. The sheep arrived in the fall of 1869 after a disastrous late frost and a drought (usual southwestern weather) had destroyed the first crops.

Sheep began again the cycle of Navajo existence. If anything helped them to keep alive in body and spirit, it was the fact that they were living on their own land in their own way, with sheep for the base of their economy and lifestyle as before. Gradually the herds grew larger, and goats, a few cattle, and horses were obtained. Despite the equalizing effects of Bosque Redondo, distinctions of wealth developed, with some families possessing large flocks and most families holding small ones. By the turn of the century there were roughly one million sheep and twenty thousand Navajos. There was also more land in the reservation, although many people lived outside its boundaries.[6]

Navajo sheep, both before and after Bosque Redondo, were of a breed known as churro sheep, a small tough animal that adapted well to Mexico and the Southwest after a long sea voyage with the conquistadors from the equally dry climate of Spain. They were resistant to disease and seemed to suffer less from scabies, a parasite that caused flesh sores, than finer breeds. The meat, according to an early report from Josiah Gregg, a Santa Fe trader and traveler of the 1830s, was delicious. The breed did not produce large quantities of wool, and what it did produce was of poor quality, long, rough, and not as oily as most fleeces, but it was excellent for hand weaving and Navajo women spun and wove it with skill.[7]

Blankets had been woven and traded as well as worn by the Navajo by at least the late seventeenth century, according to Spanish accounts, which by the nineteenth century mention them with admiration. Navajos became expert spinners and weavers of wool, making blankets for use as robes, men's shirts, and women's dresses. Saddle blankets were also woven. Navajos wove not only for their own use but also for exchange, as trade developed with Mexicans, Spanish, and other Indian tribes, and the Spanish describe Navajo blankets as being much sought after in both Mexico and the Southwest. Their colors, said to be tasteful and delicate, were made from vegetal and mineral dyes, as well as the natural shades of the wool, and eventually from dyes such as indigo and perhaps cochineal acquired from the Spanish. Weaving did not die out at Bosque Redondo, though cheap army supply clothing made it less important for personal use, and it is said that the soldiers would request woven blankets from the Navajo, supplying the weaver with yarn to make them and thus introducing commercial yarns to the craft.[8]

Once released, the Navajo went back to making their own clothes and producing blankets for trade. The quality was poorer, but they were still bartered for by Utes and Apaches as well as Anglo cowboys, who liked the thick blankets not only under their saddles but over their bodies on cold nights; the cowboys in fact encouraged a larger size for this purpose.

By the time traders appeared on the reservation, blankets had been made for barter for at least two centuries.[9]

Other items of exchange included silver and turquoise jewelry and all the products of the sheep: wool, meat, hides, and lambs. Navajo wool was shipped to the East mostly for the manufacture of carpets. Originally, the Navajo obtained silver ornaments from Mexico, turquoise jewelry from the Zuni, and beads of turquoise, shell, and coral from other Pueblo groups. Later, and especially after observing the tools of blacksmiths at Fort Sumner, Navajo silversmiths melted down silver dollars and old pieces to make new jewelry, both plain and set with turquoise: bracelets, buckles, rings, necklaces, buttons, concho belts, and hat bands. The silver was worked over piñon charcoal blown with goatskin bellows. Sandstone molds were carved for the pieces, and a variety of tools were used for cutting and decorating the finished designs with a delicate tracery to offset the heavy silver. Jewelry was made by Navajo smiths for Navajo wear. Medicine men took it in payment for ceremonies; both men and women wore it as an ornament and symbol of wealth. By the 1900s, Fred Harvey had begun having Navajo silversmiths make jewelry for the tourists he was successfully luring to the Southwest. In the hard months between fall lambs and spring shearing, jewelry was pawned to traders for cash or, more often, supplies.

The Navajo were no strangers to trade and barter. By the eighteenth century, the Spanish had an extensive trade network between Santa Fe and the rich merchants in Chihuahua. There were also Spanish traders traveling north, south, east, and west, negotiating with the Utes, Paiutes, Comanches, Kiowas, Apaches, and Pueblos, as well as the Navajos, from whom they principally obtained sheep, hides, horses, and blankets. There was also trading between the Navajos and the Pueblos, Utes, and Apaches. Trade with the Jicarilla and White Mountain Apache brought horses and mules, bows and arrows, baskets, mescal, and silver, and trade with the Pueblos was important for food such as corn, flour, breads, melons, and dried fruit. But the Pueblos were felt to be "commercial" by the Navajo: they took what they wanted and drove a hard bargain for it, and this was deeply resented.[10]

Trading with the Utes, their traditional enemies, took a rather different form. It was a dangerous undertaking approached with care and ceremony. A party would set out with their goods on the trip into strange territory, accompanied by a man who knew the correct rituals and songs. Once in contact with their "customers," each individual would select a partner with whom to do business, and this partner would be kept for every subsequent visit, more of a friend than a customer. The Navajo brought blankets, their most important item, and also bartered woven sashes, livestock, piñon nuts, and moccasins in return for horses, buckskin clothing, elk hides and buffalo robes, saddle bags, and tweezers. Besides practical goods, ceremonial items such as special skins, parts of the buffalo, pitch for ceremonial whistles, and baskets were obtained from the Utes, and these were an important part of the trade. Dealings with the Utes were apparently carried on in a ceremonious and elegant atmosphere; they were exercises in courage rather than economic undertakings, challenges by which a man (very rarely a woman) gained prestige, experience and strength by the ceremonies he carried out and the elements of danger he encountered.

Trade with the Anglos was perhaps perceived by the Navajo to be more like that with the Pueblos. At any rate, it was based on the idea of value, which meant, at least to some extent, monetary value. In the early days, however, barter was common and little cash changed hands. Often traders bartered for their own subsistence needs, for meat, melons, and corn.

Indian trade was controlled, at least officially, by regulations drawn up by Congress. Federal legislation first dealt with the cross-cultural situation of Indian trade in 1796, when a bill was passed making traders and trading posts a federal concern. This bill attempted to protect Native Americans from the abuses of fur traders who, in hot competition for skins, exchanged liquor, guns, and worthless baubles—but especially liquor—for pelts. The frontier, (almost by definition), was an area in which regulation was difficult if not impossible. The superintendent of Indian trade, who was supposed to control traders, worked out of Washington, D.C., and was no match for determined entrepreneurs large or small. Considerable legislation followed to try to "Regulate Trade and Intercourse with Indian Tribes." In 1834, Congress, still trying to find a means to control the situation, declared that traders had to obtain both a license from the government and approval from the Indian agent (the local official of the Department of Indian Affairs). Without the license they could be run off a reservation; with the agent's approval would come some local assurance of character.[11]

Before 1864, Anglo-Navajo trade came in the wake of the army to the edge of Navajo territory. It took the form of itinerant peddlers with wagonloads of goods who sold shirts, needles and thread, delicacies, and sundry other items predominantly to the officers and soldiers. Bolder and less scrupulous men ventured farther, selling guns and whiskey to the Navajos, which was illegal but hard to prevent. These were followed by small entrepreneurs who realized that the Navajos were interested in goods and had something—mainly wool, rugs, and jewelry—to barter with. An emendation to the 1834 legislation, passed in 1876, gave the commissioner of Indian Affairs the authority to appoint traders and to draw up rules and regulations on the kind of goods they sold, their quantity, and their prices. These regulations applied only to reservation trade. Off-reservation traders, no matter how close to the boundary they might be, were outside federal jurisdiction.[12]

After the Navajos became familiar with different foods and new tools at Fort Sumner and were supplied with them from Fort Defiance after their release, trade began in earnest. Licensed traders moved onto the reservation (albeit gingerly; only nine on-reservation traders were recorded by the Indian agent in 1890) and around its boundaries, bartering flour, sugar, coffee, and calico for wool, rugs, and sheep.

The first traders sold out of covered wagons and tents. Gradually they set up small stores, which in time became known to both local Navajos and Anglo traders. When one trader moved on, another often took his place. Navajo families were spread out, so proximity to communities was hard to achieve, communities themselves being almost indefinable. There were no roads across slick rock, down dry washes, over sand and sagebrush. It is hard to know by what criteria the first traders chose their locations. Some spots might seem more obvious than others, but at Canyon de Chelly, a busy and prosperous community farming the canyon bottom and herding sheep, trading posts came and went and did not do well for many years. Perseverance was required. Among the elusive Navajo, to whom long journeys were no deterrent, time and custom did much to establish the locations of trading posts.

By the turn of the century, trading posts were becoming stable points on the landscape. The first trading posts on the reservation were in and around Fort Defiance, and they spread out from there. Not all the small stone, wood, or adobe stores that were put up in the 1880s and 1890s survived, but those that did became focal points for more than trade. As the Anglo world interacted more and more with Navajo life, the trading post became the point of contact for jobs, census counts, sheep dips, and mail; with every visit, Navajos learned about the society that slowly surrounded them.[13]

Many of the earliest posts survive, if not on the exact spot or in the same building, then very near or in buildings that evolved from the first construction. A small post in Ganado (then known as Pueblo Colorado) was established in the 1870s and later bought by Lorenzo Hubbell. Thomas

Keam built Keams Canyon Trading Post in 1882 and traded with Navajos, though he was technically on the Hopi Reservation and did business with that tribe as well. In the west, a trading post was first built in 1881 at Red Lake, also called Tonalea, below Black Mesa. Sam Day operated a post at Chinle, near Canyon de Chelly, in 1886. Lukachukai Trading Post, facing the Lukachukai Mountains, was built around 1892. In the New Mexican portion of the reservation, in the yellow landscape between the Chuska Mountains to the west and the sagebrush country of the Chaco Wash to the east, several trading posts were built before the 1900s that still survive: Tohatchi in 1890, Naschitti in 1880, Two Gray Hills in 1897. Crystal Trading Post was also built in 1897, on the other side of the Chuskas west of Washington Pass. Three other posts were built off the reservation in 1880: Fruitland Trading Post and the Hogback Trading Post, near Farmington, and The Gap, in western Arizona (in 1900, the reservation boundaries were extended, and The Gap became a reservation post).

While trading posts were becoming fixed points between 1870 and the early 1900s, traders themselves moved about like will-o'-the-wisps. Some traders became well known: Lorenzo Hubbell of Ganado, Richard Wetherill of Chaco Canyon, his brother John Wetherill of Oljato and later Kayenta, J. B. Moore of Crystal, Sam Day, Thomas Keam, the Foutz family, and later on the Babbitt brothers of Flagstaff—well known, that is, in trader history, either for their influence on weaving (such as Hubbell and Moore), for the large number of trading posts they owned (as the Babbitt brothers and the Foutz families did), or for their interests beyond trading (like the Wetherills' in ruins). Most traders were less than famous, and whether their stay was brief or long, their influence on the trade and their relations with the Navajo went unrecorded. For the most part, early traders were like the churro sheep—hardy, resistant to disease, and quite probably long-haired.

Besides flour, lard, coffee, and calico, a Navajo trader needed a certain amount of courage, for he was not automatically welcomed either by Indians or Indian agents. He had to have a jack-of-all-trades approach to life that would enable him to build a house and cure the sicknesses of his horses, the sheep he might buy, himself, and possibly some of his customers. He needed to be able to hunt his dinner and cook it, or to find someone who would. In addition, he required the ability to learn the Navajo language, or at least some words of it, and to communicate across two cultures to convey, if not the nuances of payment, pawn, credit, and cash, at least their basic tenets. Most of the traders of this period came west as bachelors. As they settled into the life and the landscape, some of them took

17

Navajo wives, which did not always meet the approval of either the Navajo or the Indian Service agents.[14]

The business at the trading posts was generally barter of sheep and wool for groceries and supplies. Cash was scarce, and payment for work done by Navajos around the trading post was in kind, or if in cash, very little. When traders set up stores, they instituted their own metal coinage, known as *seco*, which traders used to pay for wool, and which was only redeemable at the store that issued it. Wage work for Navajos began at the turn of the century, on the railroads, as shepherds or cowboys for white ranchers, and as builders of walls, houses, and roads. There were very few rugs made in this period, and these were in general rough in quality and cheap. A few traders, however—at Crystal, Two Gray Hills, and Ganado, for instance—encouraged the finer weavers in their areas with patterns from old rugs and help with dyes. The reemerging craft of weaving had a definite commercial interest, and one that brought an income to the weaver. Though purists might frown on the alien influence, it did not detract from the beauty or originality of the rugs and did much to bring their earlier high quality back. Rugs, after all, had long been a trade item.

The Navajos studied the trader, his goods, and the new ways he brought with him. The traders studied the Navajo, his sheep and rugs, his possibilities as a customer. By 1910, a little more than a generation had passed since Bosque Redondo, during which time goods had come first through the army, then the Indian Agency, and last by barter at the trading posts. Cash exchange was not an entirely new idea to the Navajo, for they had already encountered it with the Spanish, as some Navajo words revealed: *béeso* for money, *sindáo* for penny or centavo, *yáál* (from *real*) for a quarter. They picked up the new Anglo money system quickly.

The Indian Service agents watched the traders warily, for a number of reasons. In the early days, traders had meant primarily whiskey peddlers and sellers of firearms, and the sale of liquor was still a problem, though many traders did not want the problems of drunkenness and possible hostility if they could avoid it. The Indian agents also saw themselves as protectors of the Navajo, who were presumed to be ignorant of commercial practices and easy to cheat; it had been known to happen. The traders perceived the Navajo, however, as hard to cheat—as canny, clever, and quick to pick up the essentials of fair trade whether in barter or cash. The idea of profit, however, was never quite approved of by the Navajo, and it sat uneasily with the Indian agents as well.

Trading posts multiplied in the first decade of the twentieth century. By 1911, Bisti, Tocito, Sanostee, Newcomb (also known as Nava), Star

Lake, Toadlena, and Tsaya in New Mexico, and Wide Ruins, Chilchin-beto, Kayenta, Shonto, Oljato, Cow Springs, Kaibeto, Cameron, Teec Nos Pos, and Beclabito in Arizona were all in operation.[15] These posts were not much more than cabins: one room for the store, another for living quarters, a storehouse perhaps, or a shed or two, a corral. A spring might be near by, but water was scarce. Time and necessity added out-buildings and extra rooms to the trading post, and trees if they would grow. The buildings were swallowed up by the landscape, by the space and distance, as the building materials blended into the background from which they came.

3

Carson's Trading Post

Now, let us return to Farmington, or rather to the the Carson ranch where Stokes and Jessie continued to live. In 1913, their first child, Mildred, was born, and two years later another daughter, Josephine, followed. By then Stokes was getting restless. At twenty-nine he did not particularly want to remain a farmer. He was energetic, inventive, curious, and he wanted to see more of the world—even if it was only the immediate world of the San Juan Basin. In 1909, two of Jessie's brothers, Bob and Merritt Smith, had built a trading post called Toadlena in the foothills of the Chuska Mountains, southwest of Farmington. They had sold it a few years later and moved on to other trading posts. Perhaps they influenced Stokes; perhaps they gave him some idea of the requirements of trading with the Navajo. Whether or not these were contributing factors, in 1916 Stokes took a job at Star Lake Trading Post with a young trader of German background, Richard Frankel, for a salary of $35 a month plus accommodation and groceries for the whole family.

Stokes, Jessie, and the children drove to Star Lake in two wagons full of household goods. The post was roughly ninety miles south and east of Farmington, one mile southeast of the Continental Divide. Although this area was fifty miles outside the eastern boundary of the Navajo Reservation, many Navajos lived there.

Star Lake was a rather typical trading post. It had been built around the turn of the century by Albert Starr. Starr had sold it in 1913 to George and Albert Blake, who were still its owners along with Richard Frankel, a third partner, when Stokes was hired as manager. There was a little spring nearby but the water was undrinkable and only given to the chickens. Good water was hauled in barrels about nine miles from Ojo Encino to the north, where Bob Smith now had a trading post. Mail was collected from Cabezon, a small settlement and trading post with a post office thirty-five miles to the southeast.

Cabezon is also the name of an eroded volcanic plug, the largest of several in the Rio Puerco valley. The land around Cabezon was an undulating plain where wild grasses grew. Navajos cut it for hay, some of which Stokes would buy from them. To the east lay the Jemez Mountains, pine covered and full of hot springs and, in those days, wild turkeys, which Navajos sometimes hunted and brought down to sell to Stokes. Between the Jemez Mountains and Star lake grew piñon and juniper trees, but closer to Star Lake the landscape was more barren and rocky, with yellow sandstone and yellow grass stretching for miles, though piñon trees still crowned the higher ground. Chacra Mesa lay on the northern horizon. A fine black dust blew in the air and freckled Jessie's kitchen tablecloth; coal lay close to the surface here, and it often caught fire and smoldered under the grass.

Stokes Carson worked at Star Lake for eighteen months, all the while looking for a store of his own to buy. On journeys to Farmington for supplies, in the wagon or on horseback, he cast around for a good location. Cutting across country, he frequently went over the Gallegos Wash, which ran northwest under Huerfano Butte and which, he noticed, usually had water along it. After the long haul for water at Star Lake, this was no small attraction. There were already two stores in the vicinity, one belonging to Shorty Hannan, the other, or rather the foundations thereof, to Nick and George Mayer, who were in the process of putting up a store. Stokes began a discussion with the Mayers on the possibility of a sale, but they turned his tentative offer down; but not for long—clearly Stokes had sniffed dissension or hesitation in the brothers' partnership. Traveling the same route a month or so later (it was the spring of 1918), he found that they had had a falling out and were willing to sell to dissolve a partnership that was no longer harmonious.

The purchase Stokes made that March of 1918 for approximately $400 comprised eighty acres of land on the sloping banks of the Gallegos Wash and the foundations laid by the Mayers. It was eighteen miles from the eastern boundary of the reservation, and about twenty-five southeast of Farmington. The foundations of the trading post were situated on a spot where the banks of the wash were low and a place for crossing seemed natural, though many such places existed here, as on every wash. The land rose slightly to the north, and from the highest ground where the paved road now runs to Farmington there was an unbroken view in every direction. In summer a haze of green cottonwoods marked the San Juan River running to the west, beyond which dry hills rolled into Colorado. To the north lay the snow-covered La Plata Mountains, and on clear days even the Rockies could be seen, very faint on the horizon. Closer at hand was Kutz Canyon, a place of eroding points in dry, faded colors, out of which rose the twin spires called Angel Peaks. To the east, Huerfano Butte sat square and substantial, one of the sacred spots of the Navajo, known to them as Dził Na'oodiłii ("People Move Around the Mountain") referring to myth, or as Yodi Dził ("Soft Goods Mountain"). To the south where the trading post lay was a vast, rolling, sagebrush sea, green and blue-gray, covered with cloud shadows. In this sea hid the small canyons of Gallegos and Blanco and the larger canyon of Chaco through which the Chaco Wash ran past ruins to join the Escavada Wash and head west and north into the San Juan River. On the southwest horizon, the Chuska Mountains were just visible, marking the New Mexico boundary and the rockier, drier country of Arizona beyond.

Stokes returned to Star Lake to inform Frankel of his plans and collect his wife and babies and their possessions. On the Gallegos, the Carsons put up two tents, one for the operation of business and one to live in while they completed the trading post. Stokes built two rooms, one for living quarters and the other for the store, into a shelf of sandstone that formed the base and part of the back wall. Later a small storeroom was added to the other side of the store, also dug into the sandstone, its floor a foot lower so that stepping into it was like going into a cool, dark cave. In front of the trading post, the sandstone sloped unevenly down a few yards to the more level and sandy ground above the wash, a bumpy approach for wagons. The building was long, low, and sturdy; its rough-hewn stone block walls, eighteen inches thick, were carefully squared on the outside corners and rounded with adobe plaster on the inside edges of windows and doors. The plaster was whitewashed. The living quarters adjoining the store, partitioned out of an area thirty-six feet square, consisted of two little bedrooms, a kitchen, and a room for eating and sitting in. The ceilings were low, and though it might have been small for a family of four, it was larger than a hogan.

A door led into the slightly smaller, shelf-lined store. Goods hung from the ceiling: coils of rope, lanterns, tin coffee pots and buckets, bits, and pieces of harnesses. High counters were built on three sides around the front door so that they enclosed a space for people to gather in, buy, sit, and smoke tobacco; this was referred to in all trading posts as the bull pen. The floor behind these counters was raised a few inches above ground level, a psychological vantage point because it made the trader taller than his customers. A wood stove stood in the center of the bull pen, its tin smokepipe running up through the ceiling and several feet above the flat wooden roof.

The windows set into the thick walls in both house and store were not large; they let in only enough of the brilliant dry sunlight to see by without also letting in too much heat in summer or cold in winter. In the back wall of the store a window peered like an eye over the sandstone shelf, almost at ground level. In the opposite wall was the front door, and another lower window facing south across the wash. The wash in those days was narrower than it is today, and water, which appeared in it more frequently, was drawn up into a well. The water was even drinkable, though it tasted a little sulfurous.

There were no trees along the Gallegos, nor on the land within sight, and the wind blew constantly in winter and summer, rattling windows, filling the corners of the house with sand, and strangling the early plants in the small garden behind the house. Later, Stokes planted cottonwood saplings on the south bank, and the trees, growing fast as cottonwoods do, filled out and made a green grove in the gray sand and yellow grass. There were no other buildings in view. Many Navajo families lived in the vicinity, two miles, three miles away, but the hogans were even less visible than the trading posts.

The first goods that the Carsons' store obtained Stokes got on credit from Richard Simpson, a trader who had a post several miles down the Gallegos Wash, close to Farmington.[1] Simpson, an Englishman, had come to America in 1892 at the age of twenty-nine. He had been born in Wiltshire, where he had worked as a bank clerk and cashier. Subsequently, after a brief and unsuccessful career as a London stockbroker, he emigrated to America and came west. It was rumored that he was a remittance man, a man whose family, for reasons best known to themselves, paid him to stay in some distant spot, or just paid him, the distance of the spot being the choice of the young man. He began to raise sheep in the small Mormon town of Kirtland just west of Farmington.

Dick Simpson moved to the Gallegos, where he acquired land and a barn that had once belonged to the Carlisle Cattle Company, a large ranching outfit whose headquarters had been in Chaco Canyon. For a time he ran horses. He built an adobe store, a three-room house for himself and his wife, a wellhouse, and living quarters for his assistants and herders. Later he added a blacksmith shop, a granary, a guest house, and corrals for sheep, to which he had returned after only a brief trial with horses. Simpson dealt in good rugs. His wife was a fine Navajo weaver named Yana-pah.[2] Dick Simpson was a generous, open-handed man, and his first supply of merchandise on credit to Stokes gave the Carson store its start.

The Gallegos was gentler and, for all its sandy vistas, less arid, less desolate than Star Lake. In spring, the banks of the Gallegos were dotted with orange globe mallow, blue delphiniums, and scarlet penstemon. Spring was cold, but summer was hot, and there was no shade to break the glare of sunlight burning off the sandstone. In July, toward the late afternoon, thunderstorms would build up, promising rain. But rain was often more a promise than an event, with so much land to cover, and the storms frequently sprinkled the south bank and left the north bank dry. By evening a few ragged clouds would be catching the sunset, all moisture spent and a clear sky behind them for the next day's heat.

Carson's store was not as isolated as the trading posts thinly scattered along small canyons and washes in Arizona. Farmington was small, but it was close by and had stores, friends, family, and church. The Carsons were not as cut off from their own society as were traders at on-reservation posts like Two Gray Hills or Oljato. The absence of friends who find the same meaning in things and share the same secrets makes life lonely. Navajos who moved away from the reservation to work in cities, as a few did, missed the desert, their sheep, and their families. Trading posts on the reservation were usually solitary spots, and traders were often equally lonely. Stokes, however, was not. Between his family and his customers he had all the company he cared to keep. Jessie felt the isolation more, and when Stokes was away, even the babies could not keep a feeling of desolation from creeping into the house.

The conditions of life for trader and Navajo were similar in those early times, despite the trader's comparative wealth. Though days might pass in which no one came into Carson's trading post, the repeated visits of the local families made them familiar to Stokes and Jessie. Stokes did not learn to speak Navajo fluently—a few words and many gestures sufficed—but he began to learn his neighbors' cares and concerns. Language was a barrier, but it was not an impassable one; it was more often the Navajo who learned to speak English.

The winter of 1918–19 saw a worldwide influenza epidemic that resulted in more deaths than the Great War itself—an epidemic that reached out even to the Southwest, to hogans and homesteads alike.[3] There was little that could be done, and traders, who often helped in sickness if they could, had their own families to worry about. The epidemic reached catastrophic proportions in New Mexico; there were many deaths, many abandoned hogans, and families with no one left to give the dead the accustomed burial rites. A Navajo family living near Carson's store fell victim to the epidemic, and only one member of it, Jim Pierce, survived. He came into the store leaner and sallower, with no brothers left. He told Stokes that he had almost died: "When I got to the other side I saw my brothers. They came to get me. They were all riding horses. But I had no horse, because there was no one left to kill my horse. I couldn't join them without a horse. So I came back." He came back and stayed, and he lived to be an old man. This was one of many small, personal stories that drifted over Stokes' counter and filled in the lives of the people he saw often.

Stokes hauled his provisions to the post by wagon. The major wholesale companies for trading posts were in the towns bordering the reservation: Gallup Mercantile (a subsidiary of the well-known Ilfeld Company of Las Vegas, New Mexico), Gross Kelly Company, and Kirk Brothers in Gallup; the Progressive Mercantile Company in Flagstaff. These same wholesalers bought the traders' wool, which they collected by wagon, usually a four-horse team hitched to a double wagon.

The automobile virtually preceded roads—or at any rate, paved roads—in the Southwest. Wagon trails existed, many of them wide and firm, at least in the dry months, for the use of the freighters that delivered to the supply towns and collected en route the produce of towns like Farmington. A spiderweb of minor trails led from hogan to hogan, from camp to well to canyon—without signposts, crooked, often no more than the faintest of tracks that would fade out of sight without use.

Carson's had easier and closer access to wholesalers than did reservation trading posts, though the San Juan River had to be forded and ferried. Fording was possible at certain points in times of low water—early spring or early on summer mornings before snowmelt water came down from the La Plata Mountains. In winter the river froze and crossing was easier. Farmington finally built a wagon bridge in 1919. The San Juan River was in fact first bridged in 1911, at Shiprock, or what was to become Shiprock. It was then a cool shady spot by the river where the Indian Agency headquarters for the San Juan district, along with a vocational school for the Navajo, had been built. In the wake of government centers came roads, bridges, schools, and offices.

But Shiprock was out of the way for Farmington. The road that Stokes took came across Gallegos Mesa and over the steep bluffs on the south side of the San Juan, a swift descent but a steep haul up. It was the shortest route to town, meeting up with the old wagon road—the Togay Trail—from Fort Wingate and Crownpoint. In 1909, a local trader, W. F. Hunter, had told the Indian agent that if the Agency would rebuild the road, local traders would contribute labor and materials. Traders of those early days, and even later on in the 1930s, built their own roads—clearing, digging, grading, even blasting, as best they could, aided by Navajos whom they hired or who sometimes volunteered their labor.[4]

Navajos frequently requested help from the Carson trading post. Jessie often helped with simple sicknesses, and both Stokes and Jessie wrote letters to or read them from children away at school or sons and brothers away on railroad work. Deaths and burials were surrounded with taboo and danger, and to avoid these, Navajos asked outsiders to bury their dead. Stokes and Jessie, like other traders, buried the old and the young of neighboring Navajo families. Stokes and Jessie were invited to ceremonies at which feasting, exchanges of gifts, serious healing rituals, and dancing took place. There were different kinds of ceremonies, some given often, usually during the summer, some given rarely. Many traders began to encourage families to hold ceremonies near the trading post; it was good for business and it created good feelings.

Navajo religion, like most religion, was visible to outsiders only by its more public rituals and ceremonies. Traders could see the large gatherings, the races, and sometimes the dances, the special costumes, or the sandpaintings and parts of healing rituals. Sometimes customers invited a trader they liked to a ceremony as a guest. Many traders were interested, attended, and were impressed by what they saw. The ceremonies, or Sings, as they are called, also had a social function; they provided opportunities for relatives to see each other, for young men and women to meet. The ceremonies were also important for creating and discharging obligations. Food was prepared to feed whoever might come, gifts were exchanged, and health and the bonds between families and in-laws were strengthened. Since children could not marry into their parents' clans, it was essential to arrange meetings, gatherings at which people could make and renew acquaintances.

Squaw dances and Sings were often held near Carson's post. Camps were set up all around, crowded with wagons and horses and women and children. Square brush-shelters went up, piñon branches tied to a frame of wooden posts at the sides and over the roof, to provide shade. Canvas tents were pitched. All day long, people came in and out of the post for candy, matches, gifts, or soda pop. Coca-Cola was already established, and in remote rural areas sarsaparilla, a sweet, sticky root-beer-like drink poured from a barrel, was still sold. People gathered at the trading post to escape the heat and flies, or they waited on the steps outside. The women sat with long skirts like crumpled flowers, holding babies in cradleboards.

At the end of the day Stokes and Jessie would watch the smoke of the cooking fires drift up into the summer sky, as the dust from horses' hooves and wagon wheels settled over the rabbitbrush. Sheep would have been slaughtered for mutton stew, the hide spread over a nearby branch to dry. Later the dancing would begin, and snatches of the singing that accompanied the dance, a musical chant performed by men, came with the wind that blew constantly around the trading post.

4

Navajo World, Anglo World

The land around Carson's Trading Post, north of the Jemez Mountains and east of Farmington, was old Navajo territory—Dineta—the area of the Southwest in which the Navajo had settled after their gradual separation from the Apaches. It was not part of their reservation lands, and though there were many suggestions from both Navajos and whites that the eastern boundary be extended to include at least a portion of these lands, it was never done. After the exile at Bosque Redondo and the 1868 treaty, many Navajos who had come from that country moved back to the area, which came to be known from the complex pattern of different railroad holdings and executive-order Indian lands, as the Checkerboard region. The army permitted Navajos to live outside the reservation as long as the land was not already settled, providing they abided by the laws of the United States.[1]

The slow movement of settlers and ranchers into the territory began first with Hispano ranchers in the early 1870s; then, a decade or so later, Anglo ranchers followed. Larger and larger numbers of their cattle and sheep, in comparison with Navajo sheep, grazed the land. Waterholes, precious in the dry climate, were often usurped by the herds of the newcomers. In the ensuing tension over land, the Navajos behaved with the utmost constraint. There was no warfare, no raiding; Bosque Redondo had ended that. The headmen kept the peace, making an effort to contain troublemakers, to abide by the treaty. When robbery or even murder occurred, it was frequently of, not by, the Navajos.[2]

The 1880s and 1890s were years of heavy competition for land in the

Checkerboard area. Navajos could homestead, and there was also a movement toward Indian allotments. In this latter system, Indians were given 160 acres, inalienable and tax free for twenty-five years; after this period the allottees could do with the land what they liked, and it was taxed. The Navajo agent of this period, D. M. Riordan, encouraged Navajos to homestead the Checkerboard region, since the reservation was not large enough. Navajo-Anglo disputes over land were frequent and bitter. Though prior occupation gave the Navajo primacy, the new ways of establishing it by paper and writing, laws and "improvements," added difficulties and made the Navajo seem ignorant and easy to ignore.[3] But their determination, their struggle to stay, indicates the opposite. The situation was not helped by alcohol. Both Spanish and Anglo bootleggers sold whiskey to the eastern Navajos (and to each other), and many small traders, also selling liquor, came and went, avoiding arrest (by lawmen) and violence (from their customers).

The land, for the Navajo, was not only a prerequisite to survival, it was also full of sacred places, mountains, springs, and mesas mentioned in their oral histories and legends.[4] Encroachment on what had once been the Navajo homeland by Spanish and Anglo settlers was bound to create stress and hostility, as well as change and even confrontation. The sometimes forceful tactics of ranchers and the lack of respect for Navajos from cowhands and sheepherders strained relations between Anglo and Navajo.

In some respects, Stokes felt, as many traders did, that he represented the Anglo world, or, at least, that he was a symbol of it and an accessible one. The Navajo words for trader are *naalyéhé yá sidáhí* ("he who sits for the sake of the merchandise"). And there were days when Stokes and Jessie felt that they were sitting indeed, not only because they were tied to the store but also because, being between the two cultures, they could be a target for both. Living among the Navajo (unlike the Indian agent), and with some continuity (unlike the ranch hands), the trader was an approachable contact with new ways and a butt for hostile feelings, though these usually came in the form of jokes or comments.

Early traders of the nineteenth century had met with violence on occasion, but traders of the twentieth century, though they kept weapons handy, had less need to use them, at least in seriousness. In the Checkerboard area, however, a few incidents in 1918 seem to have risen from some buried hostility. One incident affected the Carsons in no small measure.

World War I was drawing to a close, though it had only rippled the surface of frontier life in the West. Jessie's brother, Walter Smith, had enlisted. Walter had been working for E. F. Tucker, a trader with a store close to Star Lake, and when Walter left to join the army, another brother, Pat, the second youngest in the family, went to work at Tucker's store in Walter's place. Pat was eighteen years old, and his parents were reluctant to let him go, but he had brothers and a sister at nearby trading posts— Bob and his wife at Ojo Encino, Jessie and Stokes at Carson's, and Merritt at Star Lake, where he had gone when they moved to the new store. It was unlikely that Pat would be left alone.

He left home in January 1918, setting off from Farmington through four inches of snow. The journey took several days. On the second day he got lost and spent all night wandering around in the cold. At Tucker's store he was afraid that he would get lonely, but he nonetheless preferred it to Farmington and hoped for letters and visits, especially from Jessie. Lambing season came and went. On the Fourth of July there was a big celebration, with hundreds of people gathering around Tucker's post; Pat wrote his mother that he had never seen so many Navajos at one time; he guessed there were five hundred. He had received a letter from his brother Walter in Washington, D.C., who was on his way to New York, "seeing the world," wrote Pat wistfully, "I sure wish I was there. I am in notion of going myself. But I think I can serve my country better at home. Anyway I would make a poor target." He was content, the Tuckers were good to him, and though he had not heard recently from Jessie, he was looking forward to visiting Farmington and seeing her, and everybody else, in a week's time.

If Jessie had not written, it was not because she had no affection for her little brother, but no time. The new trading post kept her as busy as Stokes, and she was expecting their third child. One evening in the middle of July she and Stokes were sitting outside the trading post after a long, hot day. It was cooling down. A small dust cloud—a horse and rider— appeared on the far side of the wash, moving fast along the trail. Many riders came and went along this way, but this one rode with an urgency that even Mildred, then five years old, noticed and remembered. Apprehensively, they watched the rider approach and dismount. As they feared, he bore bad news: Pat had been killed, Tucker's store burned down around him. Jessie burst into tears. The death of her brother upset her so much that she never spoke about it, and her younger daughters learned about the tragedy from other sources and only when they were older.

It was a sobering event. On July 18, Pat had been alone; Mr. and Mrs. Tucker had gone to Albuquerque to pick up a new automobile. A Navajo ceremony was being held a few miles from the post. It was said to be an Enemy Way Sing, a healing ceremony that cured the dangers of contact with strange people, and to which all the neighboring communities went for the ritual and for the dancing that followed. Pat was in the trading post, having just closed up, when there was a knock on the door. On answering the knock, Pat found a young man by the name of Luis Chávez who wanted to buy some goods on credit. Pat refused. Chávez knocked him down and with his companion Augustine started a fire with oil and newspapers. The two Navajos then went to the Sing. Later, another Navajo, noticing the smoking trading post, rode off to tell someone of the problem. The group that formed to investigate—Sam Stacher, the superintendent at Crownpoint, Bob Smith, Pat's brother, a couple of other traders, a sheriff—found only a smoking, ruined trading post. By this time it was early morning of the following day. The party went to the Sing in hope of obtaining information. What they obtained were the two Navajos, Luís and Augustine, whom several Navajos identified as the culprits. Luís Chávez confessed. He was given a sentence of twenty-five to thirty-five years in the Santa Fe jail (he died after nine years there). His companion was acquitted.[5]

Not only was Pat a youngster, still in his teens, he was not even the resident trader and had been at the post only six months. Personal animosity could hardly have built up to such murderous proportions in so short a time. A few months after his killing, Ed Doonan, the trader at the post in Chaco Canyon, was shot at through the window of his store as he sat reading by a lamp.[6] He was only injured, but the attempt was serious and might have succeeded had his daughter not kicked over the lamp. It was thought from the footprints that the assailant was Navajo. The shooting by a Navajo of Richard Wetherill, who was trading, excavating ruins, and ranching in Chaco Canyon, had taken place eight years earlier, and though the circumstances were anything but clear (and included a question as to whether or not Wetherill was intended as the target), the act itself indicated the depth of unfriendly feelings.

For Stokes and Jessie, the death of young Pat was a family tragedy and perhaps a reminder of their tenuous position among the Navajo. They tried not to let Pat's death affect them. But in later years, when her daughters and grandchildren were working at trading posts, Jessie insisted that no one be left alone.

If latent hostility was a factor in these killings, it was an indirect factor.[7] Ranchers were more culpable of land encroachment than traders, but the trader was an easier target. Furthermore, he was a constant figure, a continual reminder of Anglo presence. Like most traders, Stokes was a part of the Navajo community. He lived in it, and he was called on in a number of situations because as a non-Navajo he was unaffected by the taboo and restrictions of the community. He had access to a wealth of possessions and information. He was useful in the disposition of the dead, his goods were necessary, and his trading post was a meeting place, post office, employment center, and bank. But as long as an uneven distribution of power and goods existed between Navajo and Anglo, the possibility of hostility also existed and the trader lay very close at hand for its expression.

However vulnerable traders were to occasional acts of hostility, those who held their ground earned a certain tolerance, and occasionally respect, from the local Navajos. Psychological pressures carried a considerable weight, and the Navajo used the subtler means of jokes, remarks, and persistence to make a point. The trader-Navajo relationship was an interesting one, uneven, occasionally unfriendly, more often mutually dependent. Hostility, recognized or unconscious, was to some extent an ingredient of the situation, perhaps of any cross-cultural situation. Violence, however, was less common.

In 1920, another incident took place that seemed to indicate something of the depth of feeling of the Navajo toward the changes in their lives. A Singer was struck by lightning and had a vision that a great flood would destroy everything and sweep the Anglos away, but that Navajos, knowing about it in advance, would be saved if they went to high ground. The flood was predicted for a certain day in July, and the word spread swiftly. Just before the Fourth of July, Navajo families loaded wagons and pack animals, destroyed the crops, bundled up their small children, and set off in a strange and anxious exodus for the mountains, the Jemez or Mount Taylor. No reassurance from anyone, trader or Indian agent, removed the fear—or perhaps the hope. Even wagons were abandoned in haste, chained to trees to prevent them from floating away in the flood. There followed a quiet, empty week; no laborers on construction work, no customers in the posts, no flood. Slowly the Navajos returned and without comment took up hoe and continued the daily round, burying whatever embarrassment or disappointment they might feel.[8]

Carson's Trading Post (taken about 1932)

Pat Smith

Jo, Mildred, Chin, Marie (note doll in cradleboard) circa 1922

Carson Family at Red Rock, 1926
Standing: Marie, Jo, Mildred
Sitting: Chin, Stokes, Jessie

Inside Carson's Trading Post

The road outside Carson's Trading Post

A local weaver

White Cow Begay and family bringing rugs to trade

Gathering to watch the races: Stokes, hatless, in the center, Jessie, in white, on the left

The races

Part II

1919–1928

5

The Goods

Carson's Trading Post went into operation with a tiny inventory consisting of flour, baking powder, lard, sugar, coffee, tobacco, calico, needles and thread, a few tools, and a few patent medicines. Early trading posts of the late 1800s had begun with the same goods, primarily basic necessities to which were added more items by entrepreneurial traders and occasionally by requests from Navajo customers. Stokes quickly added to the list of goods. Candy and soda pop—in early times a sweet syrup not unlike sarsaparilla—became and remained popular. Canned goods such as tomatoes, peaches, milk, and corned beef were essential. Stokes sold salt, crackers, jam, peanut butter (though the latter, introduced in the late 1920s, was not always liked), bacon and salt beef, and fresh fruit when it was in season. Hay, twine, shears, and rope were sold to the sheepmen. Vicks Vaporub and Mentholatum (another chest rub for coughs) were especially popular, for colds and respiratory ailments were common. Stokes had household goods such as basins, tin coffee pots, cups, sewing needles, and lanterns. Saddles and harness parts could be ordered if needed, for although Navajos generally made their own, the well-to-do (some Navajo families ran big sheep herds around Carson's) occasionally bought them.

Sometimes a wagon would be ordered. Most Navajo families possessed one or had relatives who did. Studebaker (the same company that later manufactured automobiles) made wagons. Stokes ordered one and had it on show outside the store, a handsome vehicle. The body was a box with low sides about six or seven feet long and four wide, with a hinged tailgate held in place with iron pins. The high rear wheels had fourteen spokes, the smaller front wheels twelve. There was a seat before the shafts, with a back on which the name STUDEBAKER was painted in large letters. Wagons usually had no canopy or a frame for one, but many Navajos made their own adjustments for protection from the sun or snow. A wagon was large enough to transport firewood, children and adults, lambs and sheep, and it was indispensable for driving long distances with goods and groceries.

Hardware was, of course, a crucial item at Carson's, consisting of the kind of factory-made goods that Navajo technology either did not produce or produced only with great effort. Knives and shears, metal axes, stoves, cast-iron pans, and other metal household goods became indispensable. Stokes carried other goods from industrial America: combs, safety pins (these were used as decoration on women's blouses when they could not afford the more traditional rows of silver coins), kerosene, oil, lanterns.

Carson's stocked fabric, a necessity at every trading post: calico, sateen, and velvet for women's skirts and blouses, which were sewn by hand or on treadle sewing machines given out by the Indian Agency. The men had dressed in loose cotton pants and blouse, Mexican style, often white and often, at Bosque Redondo, made out of flour sacks (for want of better material). In the 1920s, they began to wear Levis and shirts. Plaid flannel was stocked at Carson's to sew into men's shirts, but men took far more readily than the women to ready-made clothes. Headgear for men had been red bandanas tied over the forehead; now hats began to be popular, especially when a band of silver conchos was added for elegance. The high-crowned black felt hat with wide brim was a popular style at a certain period, and it remained popular with the Navajo and became distinctive to them. It is still worn, though more rarely. In Stokes's community, the favorite hat was the classic silver gray cowboy hat.[1]

Shoes were also sold. Navajo footgear was a moccasin with red suede uppers that wrapped the calf almost to the knee and a sole of thicker and sturdier hide. By the 1930s (earlier in many places), men began to wear plain lace-up shoes, or cowboy boots; women continued to wear moccasins, but they, too, eventually bought lace-up shoes.

Later, when more children went to school, Stokes carried ready-made clothes for children: shirts, sweaters, skirts, jackets, denims, and pants. The BIA schools insisted that children wear Anglo-American clothes, even military uniforms, rather than traditional dress. When students returned to the reservation, they often faced the problem, and the mean-

44

ing, of choice of dress. In traditional communities they frequently returned to traditional clothes; in other places they remained in "modern garments."

Not only the traders' goods but also their containers were useful. The Carsons and their customers alike coveted the wooden crates in which Arbuckles sold coffee (it was universally sold at trading posts; perhaps its popularity stemmed from the usefulness of these crates in construction). K & C Baking Powder also came in wooden boxes. Carson's was furnished with these boxes, as seats, storage chests, and dressing tables (decorated with calico curtains they made fine dressing tables). They were useful for chicken coops, lean-tos, and fences. In hogans they were used for furniture. The large cans in which lard came were turned into pails, and one hogan of the 1930s boasted a stovepipe made of stacked lard tins.[2] Flour sacks became curtains, door hangings, dishcloths, and occasionally clothes.

The trading post was accurately named. The operation was based on an exchange of commodities, on barter. In exchange for groceries, hardware, clothes, and other products, Stokes took wool, sheep, jewelry, baskets, pottery, rugs, and any items that the Navajo thought and the trader agreed would constitute an article of value. Labor, too, was a commodity. Odd jobs came through the trading post: construction, shearing, herding, hauling supplies, loading wool, even babysitting and housework. Sometimes Navajos were paid in cash, often in exchange for groceries. Stokes and other traders had to find or create markets for the crafts.

In the early days, the wholesale company that Stokes bought from took all the products of trade in payment of his bill. The wholesalers played no small part in the development of steady trade with the Navajo. They not only supplied most of the goods that the traders sold (as well as the credit that the traders, like the Navajo, required), they also provided a market for the wool based on their contacts with and knowledge of the manufacturers in the Midwest and the East, where the mills and the money were. Though their main interests were wool and livestock, they took rugs and silver as well; they too had to find an outlet for them. If the proceeds of these sales more than covered a trader's bill, the surplus was his profit and was usually credited against the next quarter's debt. If they did not, the trader owed the company the difference.

The value of goods was to a certain extent based on their cash value. Certain things such as sheep and wool, fluctuated in value, reflecting the economy of the outside world (often very distant worlds beyond the confines of the United States). Wool rose in price following the outbreak of World War I with the need for large numbers of thick woolen army greatcoats for U.S. soldiers in Europe.[3] In the case of crafts, demand depended on personal taste, knowledge or appreciation of handiwork and design, and the changeable, elusive criteria of fashion and luxury. Some Navajo saddle blankets were utilitarian, but many blankets and large beautiful rugs could be considered luxuries.

Stoke's overhead expenses were low. He had bought the land on which the store stood, so he paid only taxes. Reservation traders could not own their land, but they paid no rent and no taxes. Instead, they had to put up money (in those days $5,000) for a bond and a license from the Indian Agency. There was no electricity, hence no bills, though by the 1940s traders began installing their own generators. Telephone lines were equally rare. Carson's had a phone in the 1920s because Dick Simpson, a few miles up the Gallegos, brought the line out to his store from Farmington. Stokes extended the line down the Gallegos to his own store, and in return for maintenance he had virtually free service. Telephone lines for reservation posts came thirty or more years later and worked sporadically at best. Plumbing was a luxury in the 1940s; before that it was nonexistent. The amenities usually consisted of an outhouse and a tub. Professional maintenance was not available, and what skill or ingenuity on the part of the trader or the Navajo could not fix was left to moulder in the dry sand. The largest expense for a trader of the 1920s was perhaps an automobile.

Supplied with both goods and customers, Stokes still had the problem of timing. Wool came in spring, lambs in fall. This was the seasonal cycle in the larger markets, and the Navajo, encouraged by traders, began to adopt it into their routine. At these times, major shopping expeditions took place at Carson's. Families would arrive by wagon and on horseback, with one fleece or many, two sheep or twenty, to sell for groceries and dry goods. Supplies, tools, and clothes were purchased for the next six months—a careful, three- or four-day-long process, (especially in remote areas of the reservation where travel was more difficult than in the open sagebrush-covered land around the Gallegos). Sacks of flour and sugar were bought, boxes of coffee, cans of baking powder and lard, yards of cloth, tin dishes, coffee pots, perhaps tackle or parts for the wagon, Pendleton robes, and matches. Customers needed goods between these times too, however, and credit began to appear as a means to cover the lean months, usually secured by an item of value, a concho belt or a turquoise necklace. Bills were paid in spring and fall. Often, as wage labor began slowly but increasingly to provide a small portion of Navajo subsistence, payments were made between seasons.

Long before the traders gave unsecured credit, there was pawn. Navajos would bring in a piece of jewelry, a gun, a saddle, even livestock, and leave it with the trader as security for the bill. When wool or sheep were later brought in, the bill was settled according to the value of the commodities and the pawn was returned. Often an item was left in exchange for a cash loan, with an agreement to repay the loan with interest by a certain date. As is typical of pawn, the amount loaned against it did not reflect its market value. Pawning went on daily. The slower trade of the earlier posts would always include exchanges of small items—bracelets, beads, a hatband, sometimes even a cow—the value of which would be entered in a ledger with the details of the transaction, the date, the pawner's name, and the amount loaned. When the piece was redeemed, the date was entered and the entry crossed out. Paperwork rarely changed hands, but *naaltsoos* ("paper") was of little interest to the Navajos, most of whom at that time had not been taught to read and whose children (who later would read and translate for their elders) were still small and still learning.

Pawn was an idea that caught hold, but it also caused problems from its advent.[4] The Indian agent of 1887 saw it as a cause of disputes and persuaded the traders to stop, but they did so for only a few months. The fact that a fine piece was valued at less than its worth gave the owner a fair opportunity to redeem it (not easy in days when wage work was scarce and pay low). It also gave a trader who was dishonest, broke, or both an opportunity to sell it at considerable gain.

The Indian Agency, which regulated trading post business, prohibited the sale of pawn before six months. Stokes—in fact most traders—kept pawn at least that long, and normally longer. It was not unusual for a piece to be put in pawn for safekeeping. Sometimes jewelry was a movable good, perpetually pawned and redeemed, a savings account, and Stokes might be asked to lend a good piece back to its owner for a big ceremony.

Many things besides jewelry were pawned: saddles, rifles, rugs, Pendleton blankets, and *jish*, or sacred medicine bundles, though the latter was less common and done not for a loan but for safekeeping.[5] No trader would sell a medicine bundle if it was not reclaimed. His reputation in the community was too valuable, and had he not been trusted he would never have been asked to keep the *jish*. Many traders were detached and businesslike in their dispatch of dead pawn, often to the distress of customers whose notion of time may have been less rigid. Many others were lenient, careful, and generous; there were many, like Stokes, who would loan out a pawn piece to its owner for a dance, a sing, or a wedding.

Indian agents, trying to ensure fair dealings between trader and Navajo,

47

looked on pawn with a jaundiced eye. Pawn often got lost; record keeping in those days was minimal, though most traders kept a ledger that separately recorded purchases, sheep sales, and pawn from different individuals. Lost items strained relations between trader and Navajo and also between agent and trader, where trust was often at a minimum. Interest on pawn was high. Sam Day, a well-known second-generation trader in the Chinle area, kept records on pawn, pawner, and charges, which in 1914 were one dollar on ten per month—120 percent annual interest. This was, and in Arizona pawnshops still is, legal, though not all traders charged as much.

The system of credit made business possible, at Carson's as at other trading posts. There was no cash. In 1918, trade was based on the value of a family's sheep, and the credit they might be given against this value (seen on the hoof) was secured by a pawn piece. Stokes was cautious about credit. He never liked to extend too much, and when refusing requests for credit and loans alike he would say that he was too poor—"*baa hojooba'i*," as he said it in Navajo. From which came his nickname, Hastiin Baa Hojooba'i ("Old Poor Man"). No doubt there was humor in the nickname, for to the Navajo the trader seemed rich, surrounded by hardware, food, and clothes.

A good trader walked a fine line between extravagance and thrift, between offering those goods his customers could not afford and those they might need. The line also lay between old ways and new. A trader might introduce items, but success depended on his talent for predicting what might be acceptable in the community and what would never sell. He also had to determine the wealth of his customers. To stock a small store in a poor community full of goods the people could not afford or would not use was of no benefit, least of all to the trader, who was, when all was said and done, trying to make his living.

Credit seems to have begun around the early 1920s in the Checkerboard area as a means of attracting customers in response to competition. It was looked on with disapprobation by the Indian agents as a means of holding the Navajo in debt, but in general they felt that the competition kept the prices low. Credit meant debt collection, and many traders did not hesitate to bully, or even to confiscate livestock, to obtain payment of a long overdue bill. In the collection of debts, problems arose.[6] Impatience, contempt for the Navajo, and eagerness to claim their belongings and to thwart the Navajos' attempts to survive characterized the settlers in the region.

The Indian agents wanted to enable the Navajo to get jobs—in effect to enter the cash economy—but they also wanted them to maintain some of the traditional virtues and habits, which included a frugal way of life. Credit, they felt, could tempt Navajos to buy more than they needed. Cash loans, which the traders gave, were something else toward which the Indian agents had an ambivalent, if not disapproving, attitude. In many cases, cash loans made it possible to purchase such items as fine leather boots, fancy saddles, and liquor, which the agents considered unnecessary luxuries. "Prosperity," as Indian agent Stacher put it in his annual report for 1926, "is the cause for more drunkenness."[7] There was a concern on the part of the Indian agents for the goods the Navajo purchased, for the way they spent their money—in short, for their consumption habits. Traders were looked at with a wary eye by the government officials, who were, or felt they were, guardians of the Navajo entry into the Anglo world. In part, this entry was made or signaled by the use and knowledge of goods, and thus the trader stood, at least symbolically, at a crucial doorway, one that gave him a great deal of power and influence.

It is partly by virtue of goods that different groups recognize each other, or fail to recognize each other. More than that, it is by goods that groups place each other in context—as friend or enemy. Stokes could estimate the relative wealth, the status, the attitude toward tradition or modernity, of any stranger who came to the store. He knew it partly from behavior, partly by the visitor's possessions: clothes, shoes, horse or wagon (or none), jewelry or lack of it. Undoubtedly the Navajo made similar assessments of the white people they met. Their exposure to the trading post goods, as well as experience in the Anglo world, gave them information about Anglo behavior and possessions. No doubt the Navajo compared trading posts, as well as individuals, and continually adjusted their view. What they perceived, or rather their interpretation of what they preceived, goes unrecorded.

The Navajo could acquire, through the trading post, the means to enter the Anglo world when they chose—or, more realistically, when they had no choice. In reality, they had little choice. The Anglo world did not intrude into every aspect of Navajo life, at least in the 1920s and particularly on the reservation, but it was inescapably dominant. Anglo dominance affected first where Navajos lived, and second the way they made their living, how they sheared their sheep, when they traded them, what they ate, and, as wage labor increased, when they held their ceremonies. The struggle to deal with these facts was one that concerned the Navajo deeply, entered into their politics and activities, even created divisions within their leadership. But deciphering the white men's goods was the beginning of power.

The trading post lay on a boundary between tradition and novelty, and the trader could and did cater to both. The Indian agents discouraged ceremonies. but Stokes make certain that he had soda pop and candy, tobacco, and Pendleton shawls on hand for them. Sixty years later posts stocked, among the car parts and cornflakes, "sing cloth"—lengths of fabric, usually cotton, in different patterns and colors, to be bought and given as gifts at sings. Each community, each trading post, had different tastes and requirements, different attitudes, different kinds of feelings toward the old or the new. The good trader, like any storekeeper in any community, learned them.

Life changed swiftly enough that Stokes was constantly bridging a gap between an older life, a frontier life of which he was in a way a remnant, and a modern life of speed and machines. He did not by any means have an aversion to new goods, especially if they made life easier and more comfortable; it was merely that he did not take them for granted. Moreover, he knew that the vagaries of nature could interrupt the most efficient machine: storms blew down telephone and power lines; rain and mud found a way through most roofs and doors and deterred the most landworthy automobiles. Anything that ran by itself could break down, and humans had to devise a way around or through the obstacles that nature provided. Stokes saw no reason why something that made his own life easier might not make it easier for the Navajo also, and in this way he was a harbinger of change. As a trader, Stokes was not only a bridge between Anglo and Navajo, he was also a bridge between ancient and modern, sustaining the old at the same time that he introduced the new.

6

Sheep:
The Backbone of Trade

Carson, like all traders, was involved with sheep. Their wool was a link between the Navajo and broader economic and social factors. The fleeces, gathered up from grazing lands under mesas and buttes, in canyons, down washes, along the cart tracks and arroyo bottoms, were taken east. Boston— the New England mills—took the wool from Wyoming, Ohio, Texas, and the Navajo sheep and sorted, cleaned, and spun it for the weaving of cloth for hats, coats, carpets, padding, and army uniforms. (Rayon, the first synthetic, first appeared in the 1920s.) All the wool that could be used *was* used, and much of it came from Australia, Britain, Argentina, and Russia.[1]

Sheep were essential to the Navajo, and, as much as anything else, ensured their survival. Sheep were there before the disruption of Bosque Redondo, and after; sheep provided food and wool and, as the Anglo world infiltrated both the land and Navajo life, they were a commodity that worked into the economy of this encroaching world. The staple of the trading post was sheep, either as lambs or wool, and the changes that came to the tribe—education, cash, machinery, paid jobs, politics, oil— did not eradicate their importance. Though the young grew up and went into politics or teaching, they had the touchstone of a familiar and constant life. There was always, somewhere in the family, a sheep herd grazing on the desert grass, tended by mongrels, small children, aunts. Then there was weaving, for which the sheep provided wool, to be cleaned, carded, dyed, spun, and woven into the blankets that had been items of beauty and trade for at least two hundred years.

Sheep fitted into the economy of the United States beyond the reservation, fitted so well that from the early years of the twentieth century the Indian agents and some traders began to bring in—and wealthier Navajos began to buy—rams of different breeds in order to produce fatter, meatier, finer-fleeced animals that could be sold for better prices in a market hungry for wool and meat. The United States was no small producer of sheep; it was one of the major sheep-raising countries, after Russia and Australia. But unlike them, it exported very little, consuming most of what it produced and importing on top of that a considerable amount.

Originally sheep were raised in the eastern states, and small mills, following on the heels of home industry, were mainly built in New England. As the price of land grew and space shrank, sheep moved slowly west, principally into Ohio, and then, with competition from industry and more profitable agricultural products, to the Southwest, the Rocky Mountain states, the Northwest, and California. By the late nineteenth century, industry of all kinds, including the manufacture of woolen goods, was becoming large scale. With this growth in the industry came a concomitant expansion in the buying of wool, and since the sheep were farther west than the mills, this gave smaller enterprises in the West an opportunity to sell wool to the East while also buying commodities there to sell in the West.

New Mexico had a long history of sheep raising. Sheep came with the Spanish. They first appeared in 1540 with Coronado but did not survive, and it was Oñate who brought the ancestors of Navajo sheep with him on his march north in 1598. It is said that he had 3,000 head of sheep of the Spanish breed known as the churro. This small, hardy, coarse-fleeced animal was used to foraging for itself in terrain not unlike the American Southwest; southern Spain was rocky, sparsely vegetated, and arid. The churros thrived in New Mexico.[2] The Navajos acquired sheep from the Pueblos, and not infrequently by raids on the Spanish. By the time the Navajos were taken to Bosque Redondo they had large herds of sheep. When they were released, they returned to sheepherding and a way of life that in many respects revolved around their flocks, moving them with the seasons, tending them day and night, shearing and slaughtering them. The sheep given out by the Indian Agency fifteen months after the signing of the treaty with the Navajos to replace those that had been destroyed were most probably churros from New Mexico.[3]

Breeding new strains became a practical interest to the Indian agents: both Shelton, at Shiprock, and Stacher, at Crownpoint, brought in rams to experiment with. A churro sheep usually produced about two pounds of wool,[4] in contrast to sheep bred for their wool, which produced anywhere from eight to twenty-five pounds. The breeds of sheep, though they may look alike to the uninitiated, are various. Certain breeds had fine fleeces, like the merino sheep that were popular with white ranchers. Others were bred for meat. Both virtues could be combined, but the animal had to be tough enough to survive the conditions of the land and the manner of herding. No purebred animal, dependent on man and feed barns, would survive on the reservation. Shelton had a small herd of lincolns, an English breed known for heavy fleeces but not for mutton. Lincolns are coarse and ungainly, but the wool, dangling in loose, curly locks from backbone to ankle, is twelve inches long, white, lustrous, and weighs about fifteen pounds a fleece. However, they did not do well on the range and were poor rustlers—that is, they did not manage to search out grazing by themselves. Navajos did not like them at all, with justification, for one hundred rams of the experimental herd died, and the lambs were weak and did not always survive. Shelton tried a number of breeds: cheviots, hardy English sheep with thick, light fleeces between six and eight pounds in weight, and good to eat; shropshires, also English, woolly from hock to nose (most sheep have bare muzzles or bare faces), short fine wool weighing eight to ten pounds, and tasty mutton; the American tunis (obtained by the U.S. consul from the Bay of Tunis in 1799 and shipped home to Philadelphia), a long coarse-wooled sheep, often gray as well as white, a good meat breed, and a hardy animal.[5]

The breed the Navajo Service Agency decided was the best animal for the terrain (the first herds were tried by them in 1920) was the rambouillet. This sheep had an interesting history. It was a merino, and merinos were a Spanish breed so highly prized for their fine fleece that the Spanish Crown would let no merino leave Spain without royal permission. They were given as gifts between monarchs, however, and Louis XVI of France received a selection of the finest sheep from several royal herds. Each sheep was the pick of a certain flock, but together they were a motley group. They were kept on the king's estate at Rambouillet, and the sheep that descended from this flock, known by the name of the estate, were a fine combination of meat and wool. They were large, broad-backed, and robust, with a curly fleece and characteristic folds at the neck. The mutton was excellent and the fleece, though not as fine as that of the merino breed from which it had originated, was still good and weighed between ten and twenty-five pounds (ewes, being smaller, produced less than rams). This breed was imported into the United States in the nineteenth century, and though it was not popular at first—the true merino having won the hearts of sheep raisers—by the 1890s, following a depression in the wool market, the rambouillet was a favorite.

Stokes Carson became involved in the virtues of different breeds, the results of crossbreeding, and the adaptation of the new sheep both for his own herd and for the Navajos; it was, after all, the interesting part of sheep raising. He too liked the rambouillet, though after some years of experience he came to the opinion that no one strain should be bred constantly into the herds. He thought that this would only bring out the problems of adaptation any pure breed might have. Though by now the original churro was a faint genetic shadow in the flock, the sheep that survived and multiplied obviously were resilient animals that could stand the heat, the cold, the sparse forage and could produce wool and meat that brought a decent return. Stokes liked to bring in rams of a different breed each year: hampshires, lincolns, and corriedales as well as rambouillets. Hampshires were an English sheep that became popular in America for crossbreeding, especially in the West. They were large, low-slung animals with square rumps and, often, black faces, and their wool was thick and short and weighed about eight pounds a fleece. Hampshires were said to be hardy, they were prolific breeders, and their lambs matured quickly and sold well. The corriedale was developed in New Zealand for mutton. They were large, with medium-quality fleeces of about ten pounds. The lincoln was the sheep that did so poorly in Shelton's herd, but Stokes had better luck crossbreeding it.

In practical terms, in the eastern reservation and Checkerboard regions, the breeding of new strains of sheep resulted in heavier lambs in the Navajo herds, bringing in around $6.00 a head in 1926—almost double the price of a lamb a few years earlier—and this reflected an increase in weight rather than higher prices. The hybrid sheep not only produced more wool, but also better-quality wool for which traders paid more. In fact, traders began to offer two prices for wool, a high price (around 35¢ per pound) for "improved" wool, a lower one (around 25¢) for low-grade wool. Clearly, the new attitude toward breeding had successful results in economic terms.[6]

Only a few negative comments were raised about breeding plans. One complaint was that the program for breeding was anything but unified; every change in Indian Agency appointments brought a new approach to the project, and the independent activity of traders was not integrated with that of the government at all.[7] This was a common observation and one frequently made by the Agency personnel with regard to any dealings between traders and Navajo. From the agents' point of view, wherever the government might be trying to modernize the Navajo, the trader encouraged traditional ways (as with ceremonies), and wherever the government might uphold the old ways, the trader brought in new ones, such as cash. A perpetual minor tension existed between the broad perspective of the Indian Service and the practical knowledge of the trader, between organization of things from the center and the direction of them by the individual at the edge. Neither was right or wrong, and perhaps the tension was a creative one, with each side offsetting the problems of any single-minded approach.

Another comment came from a man interested in Navajo weaving, Charles Amsden, whose *Navajo Weaving* (1934) remains one of the best-informed historical and technical accounts of the subject. Amsden grew up in the Southwest (his aunt, Mrs. Sammons, lived in Farmington), and he knew his subject with some intimacy. He observed that the rambouillet crossbreeds, though fine for the market, did not suit Navajo weaving practices well, because "the wool is short, fine, and closely curled, forming tight little knots that the Navajo woman with her simple cards and spindle cannot straighten out; it is excessively greasy too, and almost beyond cleaning by hand washing alone."[8] Amsden feared that the art of weaving would suffer from the change in wool the new sheep brought about; however, the art was a resilient one. Amsden wrote in 1934. Fifty years later, Navajos were making rugs of every variety: thick saddle blankets and fine tapestries, tightly woven large rugs like those from Ganado and the exceptional ones from Two Gray Hills, rugs of extraordinary colors produced from vegetable dyes from Crystal and Wide Ruins, rugs with strange, old, designs and brilliant new ones. Whatever problems the wool presented had been worked out. In part this was due to an experimental breeding program set up at Fort Wingate that continued the breeding of the old Navajo strain for the wool that was then supplied to the weavers.[9]

Navajos living on the Gallegos and around Carson's ran sizable herds. Many were members of the newly created Stockmen's Protective Organization and bred their lambs with care. A few were rich, which meant in Navajo terms rich in sheep. Large herds gave one considerable prestige; they were to the Navajo what money in the bank was for the Anglo. Consequently, sheep were sold to pay debts and buy goods, not to bring in a large, unspent amount of money. Banks were still new, both to the territory and to the Navajo. Possessions do not multiply; sheep do. As a Navajo called Fred Nelson put it, "For the white people the good old dollar is where they get their substance of life, and the Navajos get their substance of life from the goats and the sheep,"[10] and though he said it in 1934, it was no less, probably more, true of earlier times.

7

The Annual Cycle

In the late 1920s, Stokes began to acquire his own herd of sheep. As an off-reservation trader, he had the ability to do this, and herein lay a major difference between on- and off-reservation traders. Reservation land was not privately owned by Navajos, but Navajo families had use rights for grazing and farming to which the Anglo-American was not entitled. In the Checkerboard region, as in any off-reservation area, anyone could own or rent land, or could run herds on public-domain land. For traders this meant that the tenuous business of trading could have other economic supports, in ranching or land ownership. Stokes had both. His sheep, and later on his land in Colorado, as well as the acres he owned around the store, gave his trading activities a firm economic underpinning. On-reservation traders lacked such security. They owned neither land nor trading post, and as trading became institutionalized, there was little returnable investment they could make on the post.

Sheep came to Stokes from the sale of ewes by his customers in between the regular buying times in October. This was disapproved of by the Indian agents, who were trying to encourage Navajos to build and improve their herds, an approach they were to change radically during the stock-reduction program of the mid-1930s. Stokes, being an off-reservation trader and therefore technically outside the jurisdiction of the Agency, could buy, and Navajos could sell, ewes without any problem. His herd began with such transactions.

Already familiar with the seasonal cycle of sheep, Stokes acquired his own sheep and continued the annual routine. He built a dipping vat and

57

shearing pens. Navajos, men and women, were hired to dip and shear both Stokes's sheep and those of other local ranchers. In 1929, the *Farmington Times Hustler* reported that 11,000 sheep had been sheared at Carson's; the ranchers paid 9¢ a sheep, and a good shearer could clip fifty sheep a day.[1]

Stokes also hired Navajo herders, and he grazed the herd on the acreage he homesteaded. Shearing occurred in the spring, toward the beginning of April, and the sheep were dipped after they were shorn. In May, like other white ranchers, Stokes moved the sheep to summer grazing in the mountain meadows in Colorado, where the land was in the public domain. In October the herd returned to New Mexico for the winter. Winter camps, too, were moved from place to place, to benefit from water, fresh forage, and sheltered spots in stormy months.

The dipping of Navajo herds began in 1895, when scabies was first noticed on Navajo sheep and reported to the Indian agent at Fort Defiance, who acted immediately to eradicate the disease.[2] Scabies are caused by a mite barely visible to the eye which feeds on the sheep and causes inflammation and an exudation that dries into a scaley crust, beneath which the mites multiply rapidly. Scabies is infectious, and it spread fast, not only over the sheep's body but to other animals in the area. The sheep, uncomfortable and itchy, rubbed against fences and trees until they were bald and every post was infested. There were other parasites, too: ticks and lice, which also itched and spoiled the wool and impeded the growth of lambs. The solution in which the sheep were dipped was a combination of lime and sulfur boiled in water for two hours to produce concentrated calcium sulfide; more water was then added and the whole quantity reheated. A fireplace was required that was capable of heating large quantities of liquid.[3]

In the early 1900s, the white stockmen raised a considerable commotion over scabies. Shelton, the Indian agent at Shiprock, did what he could to dip the many Navajo sheep located off reservation in the region where Navajo and Anglo ranchers competed for land. He used federal monies that were intended for reservation dipping vats. With this restriction on his funds, he was only able to set up one vat in the eastern section, and the ranchers clamored for the return of Navajo sheep to the reservation. However, Navajo sheep—hardy little rustlers even if they were scrawny and rough fleeced—had a natural resistance to scabies. Shelton, overseeing the dipping of the herds, noticed that the scabs on Navajo sheep were dry—in other words, dead and not infectious.[4] The ranchers were simply eager to find a reason to agitate for the removal of Navajos from land that they themselves wished to claim.

Dipping was not immediately popular with the Navajo, but they accepted it with a certain resignation after prompting by the Indian agents. This attitude eventually grew more positive, for besides being beneficial to the sheep the dippings afforded an occasion to get together. The annual dippings at the Carson vat of his own and other local stockmen's herds were social if exhausting events. Fences almost as high as a man's shoulder guided the sheep to the dipping trough. Young boys watched intently, helping to push the sheep toward the vat. Children played on the sand behind their mothers. Jessie came to take photographs; the girls in their cotton dresses came to watch. Stokes, a pipe between his teeth, stood on the edge of the vat directing the woolly, bleating traffic. Navajo men and women hired for the dipping (care of the sheep was traditionally women's work), stood on either side of the vat and, with long cotton-wood poles forked at one end, poled the terrified sheep along the trough and under the water, the fork against their necks. It was necessary to immerse the sheep as completely as possible without drowning them or getting their eyes and noses full of the solution in which they swam. Sheep are recalcitrant animals and balk at shadows, gateways, and all manner of objects. The job of dipping required strong shoulders and tireless arms and backs. The young boys drove the sheep between the fences, hissing and waving at them. The women, with necklaces and skirts swinging, and the men too, their high-crowned hats jammed firmly over their hairknots, bent and pushed their poles.

Later, while the sheep dried out, skittering about and bleating nervously, the women made fry bread, a large thin pancake of flour and baking powder plunged into hot oil so that it expanded like a balloon, crispy on the outside and soft inside, greasy and delicious. The camps were full of talk and soft laughter, falling silent with dusk, a few wild youths perhaps disappearing at a fast canter, shorn sheep moving around, the smoke of dead fires a flavor in the air. Inside Carson's, Jessie cleaned the last of the dishes, Stokes sat, smoking his pipe, working on the accounts, and the girls talked and yawned. By dark all the world was asleep; by dawn it would be up again, ready and bustling.

Shearing took place in late March or early April at Carson's. The moment of shearing was decided by the weather, which then as now, had to be just warm enough that the shorn sheep would not catch cold. The weather also determined, to a certain extent, the condition and the weight of the fleece. The beginning of warmer temperatures makes oil rise up into the wool, so that it is heavier and in better condition, although scouring or cleaning will remove the lanolin and shrink the wool. Too much warm weather, however, causes the sheep to shed, losing their thick winter fleece. Spring grass affects the sheep's digestive track; the wool on the hindquarters can become covered with dung and must be clipped off the fleece. Timing was important.

April on the Gallegos was still cold and windy, but bright sunshine took the edge off the chill. Navajos rode to Carson's to be hired to shear Stokes's sheep, and the sheep of other ranchers, in the corrals behind the trading post. Each pen would have half a dozen shearers, men and women, each working on a sheep, with a few people resting nearby from their last shearing and lending a hand to hold down an animal or sweep up shreds and scraps to keep clean the ground on which both sheep and fleeces lay.

Stokes sold modern hand shears in the store. In earlier times, Navajos had used sharpened knives obtained in trade, or any sharp piece of metal, such as the lid of a tin can, that would hack the fleece from the body. In the late nineteenth century, the Navajos began to obtain shears—two metal blades, triangular in shape, fused onto a continuous piece of curved metal that formed a kind of spring or hinge.[5] By the twentieth century, most traders stocked modern shears, sometimes introducing the tool to a community that had not been able to obtain it.

Stokes encouraged the shearers to cut in one continuous clip so that the resulting fleece adhered fiber to fiber. This technique helps to keep the fleece the same length, avoiding short clumps of wool that cannot be spun as strongly or together with the longer fibers. The weaving mills discard these short pieces, *noils*, as they are called, to be used to make felt or padding or any cheap material that does not need long threads. The shearer had to cut close to the body, but not close enough to cut the skin or to leave the animal so bald that it could not keep warm.

One by one each sheep was driven or pulled by a hind leg into the shearing pen, tied at the ankles, and grounded. An experienced shearer could handle a sheep without assistance. The shearer, with bent knees, or in the case of women, with a leg folded under them hidden in their full skirt, clipped with one hand while the other pushed back the fleece and held down the sheep. Sometimes it was necessary to hold a wriggling sheep firmly, and the shearer had to clip almost by feel, the hand that held the clippers out of sight beneath a creamy wave of wool. Each fleece was tied separately with hard twine that was glazed to prevent its fibers from getting mixed into the wool, an occurrence to which mills strongly objected since the twine was impossible to remove and created an ugly flaw of coarse sisal in a finely spun thread. Stokes sold glazed twine for the purpose. (In recent years fleeces have sometimes been tied with plastic, almost a worse sin than loose twine. Fleeces are thrown, still tied, into the scouring vats and the plastic is shredded into a million insoluble pieces, melting in the drying process and becoming inextricably bonded to the wool.)

Shearing was backbreaking work. The shearer had to bend to seize an unwilling and muscular sheep—several pounds of worried meat and wool with sharp small hooves—haul it to a shearing spot in another pen, roll it over, with a twist, to the ground, and then, as swiftly as possible, kneeling for closer contact and control or standing straightlegged and bent from the waist, cut through the animal's curls on the body, head, and as much of the legs and rump as might have clean wool. Stokes would stand on the walkway, watching and smiling, jumping down into the pens to check the sheep or the fleeces. The April wind blew dust and shreds of wool into the eyes and nose, into the mouth and collars of shirts and blouses, and the smell of lanolin hung in the nostrils.

A wool sack is six feet long and three feet wide, a huge burlap bag that, when filled, weighs around two hundred pounds. It hung from a frame that, looped around the mouth, kept it open for stuffing; the frame was attached to a plank walkway running along one side of the corrals. When the burlap sack was partially filled, a man would get into it and pack the wool firmly down with his feet.

Black and brown fleeces, bought from the Navajos, would be put in separate sacks. Dark wool could not be dyed and the mills paid less for it. They also paid less for bags that on inspection proved to contain mixed dark and white wool. Stokes's sheep were white, but the Navajos used the dark wools for weaving, and their flocks of sheep and goats contained many with rich brown or black fleeces. Traders kept back a little wool, often the dark wools, to sell to weavers who ran short over the summer. The filled sacks would be sewn up and rolled aside into a great pyramid of bulging burlap. Wool will keep, though not indefinitely. In the damp it molds, and grubs and moths will discover it eventually. However, with the dry air of this country it was safe for months.

Stokes's wool, both from his own sheep and that which he bought from the Navajos, was sold to an Albuquerque wool dealer whose freighters picked it up from the trading post. The early freighters hauled by wagon, often with a second wagon bed hitched behind. By the end of the 1930s, they were hauling by freight trucks, ancestors of the lordly semis that come down today to those trading posts that still deal in wool.

Lambing was supposed to occur in early spring, but in long, drawn-out winters lambs and snowstorms often arrived together. Newborn lambs had to be watched for, and if the weather was especially cold, the newborn was weak, or the mother refused to suckle, which happened occasionally, the herder took the creature into camp to be kept warm and fed by bottle. The larger the herd, the more chance there was of loss, and consequently the harder everyone worked. Navajos were encouraged to separate rams from ewes and to mix them for breeding in order to ensure that lambs were born in the spring and all together. This made it easier to care for lambs, and the suckling ewes had moisture and new grass. Small Navajo children were often expected to help care for new lambs, so they learned the rudiments of herding early. By fall, the lambs were ready for market and were sold to the traders, who then trailed all the lambs they had bought up to the nearest railway stock depot.

Stokes's first sheep were those sold to him by Navajos after the major fall purchase, but the major portion of his herd came from a friend and neighbor, a man named Brown whose land adjoined Stokes's and who sold his sheep partly to retire and partly because of the Great Depression. The annual trek to the mountain pastures around Durango, some fifty miles from Carson's, took place in May. Navajos from around Carson's were hired as herders, and together with Stokes they rode north with the herd and a pack train of burros carrying supplies. The sheep traversed the country slowly on trails and roads (easier to do before the roads were improved and traffic became heavier), kept together by dogs and riders. Other ranchers from New Mexico also took sheep up to the mountains, and their arrival there would be an item of news for the Farmington inhabitants. The *Farmington Republican* for June 3, 1927, reported with enthusiasm the arrival "of 200,000 sheep in the mountain ranges. Tracy Hubbard of Aztec was the first to arrive."

Once in the mountains, the herders set up camp, pitching canvas tents with portable stoves (these, too, packed on the backs of burros) the tin chimneys of which poked up strangely from the canvas roofs. The camps looked very much the same as sheep camps look still (and in the same locations), though without the sheets of black plastic that sheepherders now put on the tent roof to help keep out the rain. The sheep needed constant protection from coyotes and bears, and the herd would be moved during the summer to supply them with fresh grass.

Stokes went to the mountains frequently throughout the summer, bringing up supplies for the Navajo herders, sometimes returning with herders who wanted to visit home. The sheep remained in the mountains until the beginning of October, when they were trailed back to Carson's. The hired Navajos would spend all summer in the high pastures with the herd, watching the thunderclouds pile up over the peaks and listening to the nightly chant of coyotes. Occasionally they would slaughter a sheep for a good mutton stew or roast, but their daily fare was usually beans, corned beef, and coffee.

While Stokes took his sheep to the mountains, the Navajo herds stayed on the New Mexico rangeland, or on the reservation, but they, too, were moved to fresh pastures in the summer. During the summer months, Navajo families left their winter homes and moved with the flocks to graze near water and if possible the shade offered by scrubby piñon; at such places they set up temporary summer camps. Water was a rare commodity, especially in the 1920s before deep wells were drilled for stock tanks. The range around the Gallegos and to the east and west was richer than the Arizona portion of the reservation, but water for the sheep often had to be brought in by wagon in huge barrels. Around Carson's there were four or five Navajo families with herds numbering anywhere from one to three thousand head. In fall, the family and their herd returned to their permanent winter homes, and the sheep were kept in corrals at night to protect them from fierce winter storms and hungry coyotes.

Stokes rented land for his sheep from Navajos, both those whom he and Indian agents had encouraged to homestead and those who had allotments. Sometimes the Navajo landowners would grumble to him that they were not sure that owning land had any point except to rent to his sheep.[6] Sheep took up a great deal of Stokes's time, and much of the business of the trading post was left in Jessie's hands. Stokes was also involved in the Wool Growers' Association; he attended their meetings and banquets and discussed the serious matters of sheep with other stockmen. Later, in 1940, he was elected to serve on the advisory board of the San Juan Wool Growers' Assocation. Sheep were his concern, the major interest of this period of his life. More photographs of sheep fill the pages of Jessie's album at the end of the 1930s than do photographs of the family. There are many pictures of the sturdy pens of Stokes's corral full of fat lambs—long shadows over the Gallegos range as evening light reflects on the herd of sheep with long curly fleeces; of shearers at work, faces hidden beneath high-crowned black hats, while Stokes watches from his seat on a fence post, tugging at the brim of his weather-beaten hat. Sheep filled the horizon of Stokes's world, very much as it did that of the Navajo.

8

The Carson Daughters

Stokes still traveled by wagon for the first few years at Carson's, and he built a stable for the horses behind the store. The half-wild Navajo ponies were never easy to catch when they were set out to graze, even with rawhide hobbles on their ankles. Runaway ponies were to a wagon journey that took two or three days what a flat tire was later to the automobile traveling the same roads. Hours were spent tracking recalcitrant horses over the mostly unfenced land.

The stable was not just winter shelter for the horses; it also kept them close and accessible for the emergencies that, with small children, one had to be prepared to meet. Farmington was a three- or four-hour wagon trip, on the average, and Stokes kept a light buggy for faster travel. One bitter-cold winter, daughter Jo became ill, more ill than Jessie's common-sense care and remedies could cure. The horses, full of energy, were brought out of the stable and harnessed to the buggy. Jessie heated rocks to put on the floor to keep them all warm and bundled Jo in blankets, and they raced off. The ground was hard, and the horses were fresh and frisky after being stabled, so they flew over the frozen sand. Within an hour they were in Farmington. Jo recovered, but the stable kept the horses close and the mind at ease for other emergencies.

Another daughter, Marie, had been born in November 1918, the first fall the Carsons spent at the newly built trading post. Jessie went to Farmington to stay with her parents for the baby's arrival. In 1921, a fourth daughter, their last child, was born. Mildred was now eight, Jo six, and Marie two and a half. The baby was named Virginia Lee, shortened to

Chin when Lester Setzer, visiting from Dick Simpson's store where he worked, asked her name and, not quite hearing it, remarked, "Chinle? How unusual." (Chinle was the name of a small settlement at the mouth of Canyon de Chelly.)

1921 was also the year Stokes bought his first automobile, a Dodge touring car, to travel a little faster, if no less bumpily, between the Gallegos and Farmington. Roads in 1921 were dirt or "improved" (meaning graveled). After the fierce rainstorms of July and August, or the melting snows of March, they were deep and glutinous mud. But Stokes, in his tin-can automobile, drove with impunity over rock and through sand and mud. Later, much later, about 1928, he bought a truck, not handsome but functional, consisting of a cab attached to a wooden flatbed without sides. He used it to take the wool clip to town, among other things—the two-hundred-pound sacks loaded crosswise, four deep and five high, roped down but with the top of the pyramid higher than the roof of the cab.

The truck was often driven by Alfred Eaton, a Navajo who had worked at the Hogback mission while Jessie was there and then had come down to work for the Carsons at the trading post. "That truck will never turn over," he would say, "It's got too many wheels." But it was a reckless boast in the face of the roads, and despite its six wheels the truck did roll one snowy spring, and Stokes and a couple of strong young men had to go up and help Alfred turn it right side up again.

The automobile was useful for travel, for bringing in small quantities of supplies, and for taking Jessie and the children to Farmington for visits to family, dentist, or doctor. Once, as Stokes was driving Mildred and Jo up to town, he saw a coyote lying at the side of the road. He brought the car to a halt, got out, and turned the animal over with his boot. It was quite dead. He knelt down, pulled out his knife, and skinned it quickly while the girls watched. Then he threw the skin into the car, hustled his daughters back inside, and drove off with a roar and spurt of sand. There was a bounty on coyote skins in those days, to keep down the attacks on sheep.

By 1924 Mildred was eleven, Jo nine, Marie six, and Chin three. Jessie and Stokes were busy. Stokes was often out, and Jessie would work in the store as well as keeping the family fed and clean. Laundry was no light task in those days. A fire had to be lit to heat tubs of water, which itself had to be brought from the well. The older girls were often called in to help. Stokes built Jessie a bench with a tub at either end and a wringer in the middle. Into the tubs and through the wringer went sheets and shirts, pillowcases and pinafores, underclothes, oily dungarees, four sets of small stockings, four sets of cotton dresses. Often Jessie would wash late at night.

Only the drying of clothes was relatively simple and quick. A few years later, in the 1930s, Jessie began to keep a journal in which she entered, with a certain succinct monotony or perhaps dread, "Jo and I did a laundry"—a fact, along with the weather and the breaking down of automobiles, less interesting than visitors but of enough weight or constancy to be recorded.

The girls ran about in the sand in lace-up shoes (Mil and Jo had by now graduated to darker stockings), playing with prairie dogs, kittens, or puppies. The Gallegos Wash was a wonderful playground. When summer storms came, the girls would wait for the rush of sandy water, rolling and roaring. They would race ahead of it, until it forced them, breathless and pink, up onto the banks with muddy shoes and stockings. They had lessons with Miss Wilcox, the missionary. They rode and they read books. Stokes, always the first to get new machines, bought a radio as soon as it was possible to get one, and then they listened to radio plays.

There were picnics in the summer in the Bisti Badlands, or among the ruins of Chaco Canyon, or at the "lake"—a pond in the wash that Stokes had dug as a reservoir—with their parents, Miss Wilcox, Mr. Brown, a neighbor who ran sheep on land bordering Carson land, and other friends and relatives. Jessie's brothers Bob, Merritt, and Walter Smith were all traders, and Bob was now at Star Lake. In the winter, Stokes's pond froze up, and the girls skated on it, in coats and skirts (except for Chin, who was always in dungarees), bent double at the waist. Precariously balanced on unaccustomed ankles, they went round the piece of ice that lay so magically between the sand banks. The winters were not mild, and one especially bitter winter the cold was so fierce, so dry, that wagons creaking and crackling in the icy stillness could be heard from several miles away as they approached the store. But standing water deep and wide enough to freeze to solid, skateworthy surface, was rare.

Miss Wilcox, the Episcopalian missionary, spent a good deal of time with the Carsons. (Much later, in 1930, Stokes donated about half an acre to the Episcopal mission to build a small church on, and Miss Wilcox presided over it.) She was a woman with a gentle face and smile, and eyes that squinted in the sharp sunlight of the Southwest. The Navajos seemed to like Miss Wilcox. However indifferent they might have been to her creed, they enjoyed her hospitality, her Christmas parties, even her presence. Navajos often seemed shy, especially young matrons, young men, and adolescents. In part such reserve was considered by the Navajos to be polite, decorous behavior; in part it was a normal reticence in new situations. Navajos also possessed a healthy curiosity, and they did not avoid

Chapter 8

Miss Wilcox or her missionary activities. Eventually, she, too, became part of the community.

Early one windy morning, in March of about 1925, a Francisco Nephi came up to the house (it was before opening time, though little attention was paid, then as now, to times of opening and closing). Stokes let him into the kitchen, He had just put juniper wood into the stove and was boiling a pot of coffee. Nephi talked while Stokes poured coffee. Mildred, hearing voices, came in too, noticed the serious faces of the adults, and wanted to know what the matter was. Stokes told her that Agnes Nephi, Francisco's daughter, had contracted tuberculosis and been sent home from the boarding school. She was very low, and Francisco wanted Jessie and Miss Wilcox to come over to the camp. Breakfast was hurried and grave. Jessie left Stokes in charge of the children, and she, Miss Wilcox, and Francisco set out for the Nephi camp two miles away. When they got there, it was clear that Agnes was dying, and she was for the most part unconscious. At midday Mildred saw her mother coming down the road. Agnes, in a lucid moment, had talked a little. Miss Wilcox thought she had said "I'm not afraid to die," but Jessie had heard "I'd like some apple pie," and characteristically, glad of something she could do to help, she had returned to bake one. She took it to the camp, but Agnes could eat little. By late afternoon Jessie was once more back at the trading post, to ask Stokes to make a coffin. Mildred watched them build it in the workshop, nailing boards together, lining it with muslin from the store. When the coffin was finished, Jessie returned to the Nephi camp for the last time; Agnes died around sunset. One of Agnes's nephews rode over to tell Stokes, who locked up the store, left Mildred in charge of her sisters, and drove over with the coffin. The hogan had been emptied of belongings before being burned, or perhaps left with the north wall pulled down, the sign of a hogan contaminated with death. Stokes, accompanied by Miss Wilcox—no one likes to be alone with the dead—drove the bumpy thirty miles to the San Juan mission near Farmington, where there was an Indian graveyard. Jessie returned to her daughters.

A week later Stokes went away on business, an overnight trip. Jessie asked an aunt of Agnes Nephi, Mrs. Miller, to come and stay with her to help with the children while she minded the store. Stokes had already left when Mrs. Miller came down to the trading post. She arrived in a state of excitement and told Jessie that wolves had come down to the Nephi camp, prowling around the remains of the hogan in which Agnes had died, looking for the body. None of the men had been at the camp, and the women had been terrified, lying awake all night listening to the

68

dogs fighting off the two wolves. The camp had been in an uproar, though the sheep, penned in a corral nearby, were unharmed.

There are no wolves in the desert, said Stokes when he returned the next day and was told the story by his wife and Agnes's aunt, an anxious chorus. These were not ordinary wolves, however. Agnes's aunt showed Stokes wolf tracks in the sandy ground. Stokes did not believe her, but he said nothing and looked at the tracks. He learned later that grave robbers dressed as wolves were rumored to visit Navajo camps after a death, especially in a family known to be wealthy in sheep, horses, or jewelry. But the tracks left a feeling of fear and tension, and no one in the community knew whether the wolves at the Nephi camp had been men or spirits.

Fear of witches was serious. In contrast to the medicine men, who healed and balanced, there was a darker side to Navajo society. Witches were believed to exist (known also as skin walkers, or *ma'iitso*, "wolves") who possessed the power to harm, power that used bones, nail pairings, or hair clippings of the victim for spells. This malignant power was unconfirmed, half-buried, and not even family members were clear of suspicion. Rumors were persistent and obsessive, and they had the effect of encouraging conformity to approved behavior, especially in a community where every man and woman was his or her own authority.[1]

In about 1926, Stokes became a partner at a post called Red Rock. He and his family moved there, leaving Jessie's brother, Walter Smith, and his wife, Winnie, as managers at Carson's. Red Rock Trading Post was on the reservation, about twenty-five miles southwest of Shiprock. It was close to the Chuska Mountains, and the family would picnic and explore there on weekends. Red Rock was a beautiful place, surrounded by dramatic buttes and rock formations, and the store had good customers and served a reasonably large community in the mountains and foothills. A string of trading posts ran south from Shiprock for about seventy miles along the edges of the Chuskas: Sanostee, Toadlena, Two Gray Hills, Newcomb (known earlier as Nava), Sheep Springs, Naschitti (known also as Drolet's), Tohatchi, and Mexican Springs. The area was a good one for sheep, which grazed in the Chuskas in summer, and the influence of George Bloomfield, the trader at Toadlena, and Ed Davies, at Two Gray Hills, was making it a good one for rugs.

However, Stokes did not get on well with his partner, who he thought was tightfisted, almost mean. Stokes was disappointed, because he had liked the place and thought it could have been a fine post, a good business, if he and his partner had seen eye to eye on the manner in which they should run the store. Carson was a generous man with a good head for business, and he felt that one did not make money by pinching corners—in trading with the Navajos or in any other kind of business. Though it was a good store, they stayed there only eighteen months, returning in 1928 to Carson's.

When the family had settled down again on the Gallegos, it was time to consider schooling for the girls. First Miss Wilcox had taught them, and at Red Rock a Miss Virginia Wade stayed with the family in order to give them lessons. By now, however, the older girls needed to attend high school. For the Carsons, being off the reservation and close to Farmington, where members of the family lived with whom the children could stay, the problem of schooling was solved more easily than for reservation trader families.

Education presented difficulties to both traders and Navajos. School was a problem for the children of reservation traders as it was for anyone in solitary areas, especially in those roadless days when the automobile was still a luxury and the schoolbus nonexistent. Schools on the reservation, what few there were in 1927, were BIA schools or mission schools, primarily for Indian children. Some trader families separated for the sake of their offspring's education. The trader's wife and children moved to the nearest off-reservation settlement with a public school, while the trader remained at the store, often hiring another person to help out if he had not already done so. Other families left the reservation entirely for Flagstaff, Holbrook, Gallup, Albuquerque, Farmington, even Tucson or Phoenix. These were small but growing towns where, if he were lucky, a trader could find a job and settle down on a tree-lined street with stores and gas pumps as well as schools within easier reach.

Schooling was no less a problem for the Navajos. According to provisions of the treaty of 1868, "The United States agrees that, for every 30 children between said ages [6 and 16] who can be induced or compelled to attend school, a house shall be provided and a teacher competent to teach the elementary branches of an English education shall be furnished." The first attempt was made at Fort Defiance in 1869, but very few children attended. Boarding schools at Keams Canyon and Tohatchi were built by the government in the 1880s and 1890s. The Methodist missions provided one of the earliest schools for Navajos in the Farmington area, and two more schools were built by the BIA at about the same time, at Shiprock in 1903 and Crownpoint in 1910.[2]

A few Navajos found education useful later on, though they might not enjoy the manner in which it came. These few, of which J. C. Morgan, a

Navajo leader in the 1930s, was an example, saw education as a means of survival and success. But Navajo parents wanted some of their children to be versed in the old ways, untouched and unharmed by Anglo education. The traditional ways of life were particularly well adapted to the land and conditions, and so they persisted. The Navajo maintained to a very large extent their particular identity and their traditions. Small children were often shepherds, and families did not surrender all their offspring to schools willingly. But ways of life were changing rapidly, and if the skills the children learned at BIA schools did not fit them for traditional life on the reservation, neither did the skills learned among the sheep and cornfields help them in the world off the reservation. Increasingly, Navajos moved into a world in which they needed to know about politics, business, laws, and later, oil leases and water rights.

In the 1920s, Navajos could still remain aloof from any interaction with the Anglo world, but such isolation was becoming rare. Too much was needed, in goods and services, from the outer society. The trading post was one of the meeting points of the two cultures, often the first contact, a source of information as well as goods.

The four Carson daughters attended school in Farmington, at first living with their maternal grandparents during the week and returning home on Friday for the weekend. Eventually Stokes bought a house in town, where the girls lived by themselves, with Mildred in charge but with grandparents and aunts and uncles to help. They were all homesick, especially Jo. The Gallegos was home; despite family ties in Farmington, it was another world. They all had difficulty in school making friends at first, for though Farmington was a small town full of hardworking country people, it was still far removed from the life of a trading post. What would one talk about, after all, with the other children? Chin, who had an earlier recess than her older sisters, would wait by the school door, shy, uncomfortable, and out of place, until they came out. They longed for Fridays, when Stokes would drive them over familiar obstacles of sand or mud, a two-hour journey back to the familiar sights and sounds of Carson's. The sisters were each other's own and often only friends, and they remained so through school, college, marriage, and moves to distant posts.

Nepi Bedoni, a customer, and sheep

Jo Chili, a customer, and goats

Sheep and shepherds

Dipping the sheep at Carson's

Shearing the sheep at Carson's (Stokes is sitting on the fence)

Shearers at work

Shearing the last few sheep
Hauling the wool, old style

Part III

1929–1948

9

Oil, Sheep, and Politics

The discovery of oil had preceded the Great Depression by several years. In 1921 gas was discovered in Utah and the U.S. Geological Survey, as well as individual prospectors, began a survey of the San Juan Basin for the possibility of oil. Though Navajos were, on the whole, opposed to prospectors wandering over their land, the Metalliferous Minerals Leasing Act of 1918 had declared prospecting treaty lands to be legal. The hunt for oil was on.

The discovery of oil affected both the reservation and the Checkerboard area. In fact, oil had an effect on Navajo political organization even before it was discovered. Though the Geological Survey had been pessimistic about its existence in the area, the oil companies were not (gas had been discovered in southern Utah in 1921), and early in 1921 they requested a meeting with a Navajo council for the purpose of negotiating a mineral lease. The Shiprock superintendent, E. W. Estep, had advised the commissioner of Indian Affairs that there was no organized Navajo council, at any rate in his area, but the treaty of 1868 said clearly: "no . . . cession of any portion or part of the Reservation . . . shall be of any validity or force against said Indians unless agreed to and executed by at least three-fourths of all adult male Indians occupying or interested in the same."[1]

The Navajo tribal council was born out of an odd combination of circumstances that were not yet concrete events. The hope for discovery of oil on the part of the oil companies, their need for a formal lease in order to reap (and restrict) the benefits of the bounty that might pour forth, the consequent desire for a legally constituted body with whom to negoti-

81

ate such a contract, and last but not least (especially in view of the slights to many such contracts with Native Americans) the recognition of the terms of the treaty of 1868 between the United States and the Navajo resulted in a more or less formal council. This council was called on May 7, 1921, to be attended by all adult members of the tribe living around Shiprock, where the lease was sought. The assembly that gathered voted against granting a lease. Another meeting was called on August 13, and this time the Midwest Refining Company was granted a lease to drill on 4,800 acres—the Hogback lease, as it was called. The Navajos had decided to see if there was oil on their lands, and Midwest was to be the test case.

Other oil companies immediately began to push for another formal meeting so that they too could obtain leases, and a tribal council meeting was called for September 23, 1922. Oil was discovered by Midwest a few days later. The general reaction in this northeast corner of the reservation was feverish, at least among the Anglos, and Farmington had its first taste (but by no means its last) of what it was like to be an oil-boom town, an attraction for speculators, real estate men, whiskey peddlers, and various questionable characters, along with the drillers, drivers, and foremen. It was also the beginning of the political organization of the tribe. Not only did the discovery of oil create the need for a council, but it put a focus on the tribe as a whole unit rather than on local fragments of it.

The depression that began in 1929 affected the San Juan Basin less seriously than it did other regions in the United States. Many of the inhabitants were still partly self-sufficient, living off land that was arid and difficult at the best of times. The Navajo were only loosely tied to a cash economy, and they continued as they had for so long—poor, tenacious, and dependent on sheep. In 1930, the price of lambs fell from 10 to 4¢ a pound, the price of wool from 25 to 17¢ a pound. Often prices decreased after traders bought wool and before they sold it. The Navajo fell back a little more on barter between themselves. Cash wages provided, in 1930, about a third of their subsistence. With the falling value of their sheep, more went to wage labor to obtain the trading post goods they needed. The Navajo had acquired a reputation for hard work, and there were at least some jobs available on the roads, in lumber camps and sawmills, and with the railroads; this work of course, meant leaving home.[2]

During the depression, Stokes hired a young white man from Farmington just out of school to work at Carson's. His name was Walter Scribner, but he was called Uncle Freddie by the Carsons to distinguish him from Walter Smith, Jessie's brother, who often worked for Stokes. He was Jo's age, but those were formal days. The term "uncle" denoted closeness and familiarity, the alternative "mister" would have been a little *too* formal. Freddie became a member of the family immediately. He thought Jessie was wonderful, and he was shy, hardworking, quick. By the time he was in his mid-twenties, he had worked at many of the trading posts on the northern part of the reservation and spoke good Navajo, but when he began work at Carson's he was a green youngster—"just a city kid," Stokes used to say to tease him.

Jessie took photographs of Freddie dressed up in fancy cowboy gear— chaps, boots, and spurs. He was tall and skinny and the gun belt and holsters hung so large at his hips that he looked a little like a pack mule. Though he was shy, he was also adventuresome, and he got on well with everyone, especially Navajos. When he began to pick up a few words of Navajo, Stokes, pleased and amused, would point anyone who spoke no English in Freddie's direction. Freddie would strain to hear the words. Navajos speak softly and the language is full of consonants not used in English, combinations of nasal vowels, of falling or rising tones that distinguish meanings in otherwise identical words, of breathy *l*'s and glottal stops. As a result, Freddie got the nickname Jaa Nilts'ili ("Ears as Hard as Crystal"). Navajo nicknames are full of subtleties and metaphors, never exactly explained to the bearer. Freddie assumed it was his difficulty with the language that earned him this name, but he was not told its meaning.

Far more severe than the depression was the weather. Storms in November 1931 brought sixteen inches of snow to Crownpoint, some twenty miles south of Carson's. The winter never let up. Snow and more snow fell, covering the land, burying sagebrush and sheep, and stranding Navajo piñon pickers in the mountains. Snowplows cleared the dirt roads, but the snow drifted back behind them. Feed had to be brought to the sheep, and as people ran out of money the government supplied oil cake and hay to the Navajo herds. Stacher, Indian agent at Crownpoint, was indefatigable that winter, driving out with relief supplies for stranded families and feed for the animals, sometimes spending the night in a cold automobile on some snowbound dirt track.[3] Carson's, too, lay under thick snow. Stokes and two or three Navajos cleared the road and the sandstone slope in front of the door. One enterprising Navajo put runners on a wagon bed to haul goods and hay over the snow. Jessie, delighted, photographed his invention.

The toll in sheep was high. December, January, and February came and went, and the sheep, cows, and horses of both Anglo and Navajo had been decimated. The estimated losses ranged from 10 to 20 percent, depending on the area. At Kimbeto, 25 miles east of Carson's, an estimated 50 percent of Navajo herds had been lost.

A newspaper commented that the losses were a blessing in disguise, since the range was seriously over grazed and such a natural cutting back of flocks would help it recover, especially with the moisture which winter snow provided. The comment was a harsh one but not untrue. Overgrazing was a problem which had existed for several years. The Indian agents had noticed it, the superintendent of Chaco Canyon, Hearst Julian, had noticed it, the government stockmen hired to inspect sheep and mediate problems had noticed it. The herds, large and small, which were so basic to Navajo economy and which had been increasing with the number of Navajos (the Navajo population now numbered about 39,000, and that of sheep over 2 million), had eaten the land bare.[4] Once vegetation is stripped off the arid land, the soil, loose, sandy, and without cover to protect it or roots to hold it, washes away in the rain and blows into fine dust in the wind. Even raindrops bursting onto bare dirt scatter the particles farther and farther. Cracks widen in the ground, encouraged by whatever moisture runs down their easy path. Sandy banks of washes, undercut by spring thaws, collapse and widen. Gallegos Wash is now many feet broader than it was in 1925. Head-cutting—the enlargement of a small gully, a tiny channel, into an arroyo several feet deep—spreads visibly. In the dry climate, growth of new vegetation to fill the cracks and hold the soil proceeds slowly, and it was getting no encouragement from the sheep. Though the reservation was large, it had not, like the tribe, grown larger. What the Navajos needed was more land, but this was a solution unlikely to occur.

On the national stage, Franklin Delano Roosevelt was elected in 1932, and he burst into action with new programs for resolving the economic crisis. The New Deal created, as much as anything, new attitudes and optimism, perhaps as large an ingredient to recovery as the flow of money that it was hoped would restore economic stability and the high standard of living—for everyone—for which America was so envied and admired in other countries. The vision of poverty, the kind of poverty that the individual felt powerless to overcome, stemming as it did from economic forces and interdependencies that few people could grasp had struck America hard. The country had grown up with the belief that everyone could, by their own toil, be well fed and comfortable, could escape the rigid structure of wealth of the hierarchical societies of the Old World. The ideal that each individual was free to climb to whatever peak he or she chose, in government or business, of wealth, power, or intellect, was crucial to America. The depression seemed to distort this vision of hard work, freedom, and success.

For the Navajo, the New Deal brought work programs, stock reduction, and a new commissioner of Indian Affairs, John Collier. Collier was a man with a considerable knowledge of Indians and a vision for the development of Indian self-sufficiency and self-government that saw Indians maintaining traditional ways while moving into the modern world of politics and finance. He was later remembered on the reservation only as the man who brought about the stock-reduction program that cut the Navajo herds almost in half in order to restore the grazing lands. His name, a curse word among older Navajo, came to conjure up the bitterest of feelings.

The government solution to the overgrazing problem on the reservation (and there was no question that it was heavily overgrazed) was a plan for a concentrated reduction of livestock to be achieved within the four years of Roosevelt's term of office.[5] The problem was seen to be critical, and the program had to be implemented swiftly because Roosevelt's future reelection was uncertain. Reduction of sheep, goats, cows, and horses would cut back on the mouths browsing on the sparse vegetation. Herds would be maintained at the carrying capacity of the range, so there would be better grazing and the remaining livestock would be fatter, healthier, and better for market. There were calculated from dipping records to be 1,152,000 sheep and goats on the reservation in 1933; the carrying capacity of the range was estimated at 600,000 sheep (a cow or a horse was considered the equivalent of five sheep). The government decided that 100,000 sheep, or their equivalent, had to go. The excess animals were to be bought by the government and shipped to meat-packing companies; the canned meat would then be used for the Navajo.

In 1933 the plans were presented to the tribal council and later on to the chapters, the local groups. They met with no immediate opposition. They were eventually approved by the council, including J. C. Morgan, a tribal councilman since 1923 and an influential and outspoken leader.[6] But Navajo opposition to stock reduction grew with the implementation of the plan. The Navajo resented the forceful, authoritarian tactics that came to be used, and the threats, which were not always mere implications: your sheep or jail. Their bitterness at the situation came also from a deeper source, a difference in vision. The rationality of the reduction plan never took into account the place of sheep in Navajo life. To have few sheep, to *plan* to reduce herds rather than to increase them, was symbolic of lazi-

85

ness, of imminent starvation, of a change in Navajo character. It went against nature. Reduction flouted the concern for hard work, thrift, and the increase of wealth that sheep symbolized. It took away the central Navajo routines. Often the reduction of a small herd left so few sheep that subsistence was impossible.

As the government began the program, buying up stock from every region, as its stockmen brought in figures, calculated more figures, and told Clah Chischilligay to bring in 5 of his 50 ewes, or Old Lady Pete to bring in 250 of her 1,000, rumors followed of wanton slaughter of sheep too numerous to ship east. Navajos still living have memories of such slaughters, of the running blood of their sheep and goats, of places where the bones still lie untouched. These memories reflect the emotional impact of the reduction.[7] Because it left nothing for the Navajo future, the stock reduction was worse than the sojourn at Bosque Redondo. The Anglo world wanted the last Navajo crumb: the sheep.

Without sheep, the Navajo, not being fully involved in wage labor or indeed any other economy, had no livelihood. The New Deal proposed a cut in livestock to save the land and provide better grazing for the future, better animals for their markets, and higher prices. Its designers failed to realize that something was needed to take the place of the immediately lost income—and lost occupation—something longer-lasting than CCC work and broader in scope than the few jobs that the Indian Agencies or the trading posts provided. Emotions arose from the demand to cut out what the Navajo perceived as essential factor of their life and livelihood.

In the first years of the program, the market for sales of lambs and wool was bad, and the Navajo saw the government as an alternate purchaser. However, by 1934 the work programs, especially the CCC, had brought jobs and money to the Navajo, so there was no compelling reason to sell the number of livestock the plan required. Furthermore, in resisting sales they had the sympathy of traders, who understood more clearly than the government the desire of the Navajo to maintain their herds.

The Checkerboard area was not in exactly the same situation as the reservation. Some of the land east of the Chuska Mountains was only moderately overgrazed. Many of the sheep, especially the larger herds, belonged to Anglo ranchers, who took them to the Colorado mountains for the spring and summer. Moreover, since the area was technically outside the reservation, it was questionable whether the Navajos there were subject to the reduction plan; white ranchers were not expected to reduce their herds. Nevertheless, government agents attended local sheep dips to count Navajo sheep and encourage "volunteer" sale of livestock. There was a plan to extend the reservation to the east, giving Navajos more land and bringing them formally under the stock-reduction program; it was fought energetically by the Anglo ranchers and settlers and was eventually buried by the activity of Senator Dennis Chavez, who was strongly supported by Tribal Councilman Morgan.

In the case of stock reduction, traders usually took the side of the Navajo out of sympathy and practicality. They realized that jobs were often temporary and never very lucrative. Wage work was not yet smoothly dovetailed into the Navajo lifestyle. The clockwork routine of Anglo labor took little account of Navajo family concerns, of ceremonies, or of distances; traders had become accustomed to the disappearance for a day or two of Navajos who worked for them. Sheep paid the bills, and a Navajo without sheep was a person without a bank account. Jim Counselor, trader at Counselor's, fifty miles east of Carson's, was active in his involvement on behalf of the Navajo, advising them against complying with the reduction demands and writing letters for the community around Counselor's trading post.[8] Despite all obstacles, reduction of stock continued, and by 1934 the growing sentiment against it began to make itself heard at the level of chapters.

The organization of chapters marked the beginning of community involvement in the political development of the tribe and in the running of local affairs. This system of community organizations had been set up in 1927 by John Hunter, superintendent of the Leupp Agency of the Navajo Service. The publication in 1928 of the Meriam report on Indian administration, which came out strongly in favor of community input and participation, did much to encourage Navajo chapter organizations. Chapters provided the mechanism by which each community voiced its opinions, settled local matters, and eventually voted for members of the tribal council. Chapter meetings consisting of local leaders and families were held more or less monthly, usually at trading posts, which provided the closest thing to a communal public building for the scattered camps. Later, chapter houses were built, frequently situated near a trading post.[9]

In 1931, Stokes donated a couple of acres behind the store to the local chapter, the Huerfano Chapter, and the community began to put up a meeting house, a small stone building with a gabled roof. It was completed in 1932, and the dedication, which took place in June, was a local event. The day was clear and hot, with white clouds calmly drifting over the little crowd, catching the colors of ochre sand. Trestle tables were set up outside the new chapter house, and pits were dug and filled with piñon nuts and juniper branches for roasting mutton. The tables were piled with loaves of bread, plates, cups, pies, pots of coffee, and watermelons. Agent Shelton came, and J. C. Morgan, who was not only a councilman but also a Crownpoint man. People gathered from all around to listen to the speeches, look at the new building inside and out, and feast and visit. The Carson daughters, teenagers in cotton dresses (except for Chin, who was eleven and continued to prefer dungarees), stood in a knot at the back of the gathering, listening politely to the speeches. The smoke rose up from the barbeque pits and hung in the air, rich with roasting mutton. The new chapter house was a sign of the Navajo's political voice, and the dedication was a moment of pride and good faith—before the confrontation over livestock reduction made people realize that the voice fell on deaf ears.

Demands by government range riders that local Navajos obtain grazing permits and reduce herds also fell on deaf ears. Immense reluctance, distance, and a disregard for pieces of paper led to noncompliance, a passive resistance to the government's program. The government began to apply pressure. Police began to hunt out those who did not sell, and several were sent to jail. Range rides did not, in return for this stern measure, meet with violence from the Navajo; only one or two met with more than vocal hostility.[10]

The opposition to stock reduction had bitter side effects, to be seen in the rejection by the Navajo in 1935 of the Wheeler-Howard Bill, or the Indian Reorganization Act, as it was also known. This legislation was the result of John Collier's efforts to give his policies legislative force. It set out a program for Indian self-government by means of constitutions, tribal organization, and federally chartered corporations to deal with economic development and the management of industry and business on the reservations. It also included a provision by which the secretary of the interior could issue grazing regulations and restrict the numbers of livestock to or below the carrying capacity (as the government analyzed it) of the range. Each Indian tribe could accept or reject the bill by popular vote; those tribes who did not approve it would not be bound by its provisions. The Navajo were one of several tribes to reject the proposal, and they did so because of J. C. Morgan's agitation, his playing up of the provision concerning grazing. The issue of livestock burned so fiercely on the Navajo Reservation that it was enough to provide the leaders, and the people, fuel with which to feed their reaction to the entire bill, as if their resentment and frustration could be expressed in their rejection of it. The bill was not overwhelmingly rejected, and it was not clear that everyone understood the terms.[11] Many seemed to think that the stock reduction program and the Wheeler-Howard Bill were the same thing, or aspects of the same thing. As a result, the Navajo, one of the largest and by no means the poorest or least powerful of Native American groups, did not draw up a constitution, as tribes who accepted the bill were then required to do.

10

New Ventures

In 1929, Dick Simpson sold his Gallegos store, one of the largest trading posts in the area, to the Progressive Mercantile Company, a Farmington wholesale company. This sale was probably due less to the depression than to the fact that Simpson was no longer a young man and wanted to move to Farmington with his new wife, a white woman he had married after the death of his wife, Yanapah. The trading post continued to do business, but new traders or managers were often avoided by customers until familiarity or second impressions tipped the balance between convenience and distrust. Stokes was Simpson's nearest neighbor, and perhaps Carson's inherited some of Dick Simpson's customers. In any case, Carson's was one of the most firmly established and solid stores in the Gallegos region, and now it became one of the principal trading posts there.

There were several trading posts in the area, and competition was keen and business good, for sheep were numerous and many Navajo ranchers were well-to-do. Relatively unaffected by the depression, the Checkerboard muddled along on sheep, farming, and trading.

With the Carson's Trading Post firmly established and Jessie at the helm, Stokes began to expand his horizons. In 1934 he bought a small store on Behrend Street in Farmington, in partnership with Jim Pierce, and sent Freddie there to work. Navajo Trading Post, as it was called, derived many customers from a project begun in 1933 in Fruitland, a town a few miles west, to irrigate land adjacent to the San Juan River and allot acreage to Navajo families to encourage farming. The money earned by the Navajos who worked on this project was spent in trading posts in Farmington and Fruitland.

By 1934 Stokes owned a fair-sized herd of about 3,000 sheep, but he was still one of the smaller white ranchers in the area. His neighbor, Alvin Brown, had about 7,000, and Reid Coppinger and Dick Simpson (now the Mercantile Company) had 6,000.[1] In 1935 Carson bought some land in Colorado near Bayfield, east of Durango, a ranch with pastures and a few buildings, to use for lambing grounds and as a base from which to take the sheep up to the mountains. He kept them around Carson's in the winter; New Mexico was cold and snowy, but it was nothing compared to the winters in the mountains of Colorado. Around mid-May Stokes drove his herd to the ranch in Colorado, where they stopped for the lambing season. Navajos were hired to tend the flocks, which required extra care at this season. In July the sheep, with new lambs in tow, were taken to the high pastures north of Engineer Peak, where the grass was long and rich, and snowbanks lay in the meadows even in August. Toward the end of October the sheep were brought back down to New Mexico.

In 1936, two years after acquiring the Farmington store, Stokes made a deal with an Aztec man, Glen Swire, for a tiny post called Huerfano. It sat at the foot of Huerfano Butte, some ten miles east of Carson's. It was a solitary store, built on land belonging to a Navajo called Jose Antonito, to whom Stokes paid rent. Antonito was reputed to be a rough, unfriendly character, alleged to have killed his brother—it was said that he struck him in the back with an axe—and spent time in jail. In January, Stokes and Jessie drove to the newly acquired trading post, which was conveniently near Carson's, to take inventory and tidy up. Stokes decided to bring Freddie out from Farmington and put him in the Huerfano post, though he was concerned about Jose Antonito. However, Freddie and Antonito got on well together, and Antonito became a visitor at the store. Freddie enjoyed talking to him, enjoyed having company, and they never even had an argument.

Stokes later moved the Huerfano store to the south, two miles from Huerfano Butte on a small wash; it was closer to Carson's and farther from Antonito, and Jessie and the girls were able to work there, too. Freddie went wherever he was needed, Huerfano, Carson's, the store in Farmington, though for a while he stayed put at Huerfano. When the road from Cuba to Bloomfield (where Route 44 now runs) was paved several years later, Stokes moved the store once again, up to the roadside, under Huerfano Butte and south of the highway. He built a small stone trading post, a barn, and a couple of guest hogans for visitors and customers staying overnight; providing such facilities was becoming a habit among many traders from one side of the reservation to the other.

While Stokes was busy with the three small stores and his herd of sheep, Mildred, Jo, Marie, and Chin were growing up. Mildred finished high school and went to Fort Lewis College. In 1934 Jessie and Stokes rented a small apartment in Albuquerque for the girls so that Mildred, who had just finished college, and Jo could both go to the Western Business School and Marie and Chin could finish high school. The girls returned to Carson's as often as possible and worked in the stores on vacations, especially Mildred and Jo, the two eldest. Jessie kept a journal, full of the comings and goings of her family: "Stokes comes home" or "Girls go to town [Farmington]" or "Stokes goes to Aztec with wool." The sheep kept Stokes on the move too, in summer and fall. The following excerpts from 1935 are typical of the activities Jessie recorded each year:

May 1   Stokes cuts out sheep and starts bunch to mountains.

May 2   Rains.

May 3   Stokes helps sheep cross San Juan bridge. Rains and very cold.

May 4   Freddie, Marie and I go to Mama's [in Farmington].

May 16   Jo comes home. Dr. Jennie comes out. [Dr. Jennie Rohrabacher was a journalist who wrote the social column in the *Farmington Times Hustler* and a good friend of Jessie's.]

May 17   Miss Kelm comes out after Dr. J.

May 18   Stokes comes down.

May 19   Walter and Winnie come over . . . Ned Blacky [a local Navajo and a constant figure in Jessie's photographs] dies. Stokes goes back to camp.

May 28   Dr. Jennie spends day with us. Stokes comes down.

May 29   Stokes and I start to Albuquerque, leave store at 6:15 a.m. arrived in Albu. 10: a.m. Roads fine. [The journey still takes about the same time.]

May 30   Stokes, Mildred, Chin and I start for home. Leave Albu. at 9:30 roads fine.

May 31   Stokes goes back to sheep camp. Freddie, Jo and Marie go to Sheep Camp and Durango bring Joe White and Joe Chilli back. [These were Navajos from Carson's who worked for Stokes.]

and later on in the same summer:

August 2   Stokes and girls come home . . . We go to town to picture show.

August 22   Mr. & Mrs. Weed and Stokes chase a coyote. We go and eat our lunch over near Kutz Canyon [the canyon where the Angel Peaks stand and where the Southern Union Gas Company drilled for gas.]

August 23   We go to races in afternoon. Jane & Frances come out. Mildred, Jo and Patty & Jack Allen come out. We all attend Sing.

August 24   We all go to pictures in Aztec.

August 25   Girls go with Mrs. Weed and Worth to church in Farmington. We all have a picnic near Pollyanna's Lake.

August 26   Stokes goes to Durango. Jo and Marie take Shaddrack [a Navajo who works for Stokes] to town to meet Stokes.

August 31   Dr. Jenny comes out with Stokes.

Sept. 2   Bob, Blanche & Lizzie [Jessie's brother, his wife, and their daughter] come by. Stokes, Marie, Chin, Dr. J. and I go to town.

During the spring, Stokes traveled constantly to the ranch to check on the lambing, and all summer he drove back and forth between the camp and Carson's in the desert. Friends and family came out to visit at Carson's to picnic or sometimes to go to the Navajo sings. Often the girls and their friends accompanied him on his trips to Colorado. The ranch was in a dip of rolling mountain foothills; stands of fir trees surrounded by tall grass grew down the slopes. There was a long lane from the road to the cabin, narrow and rutted and constantly washed out. The ranch had what Carson's lacked, an abundance of rain, faithfully reported (almost daily) by Jessie in her diary. The family went up frequently during the summer and fall, and just as frequently they abandoned their vehicles at some spot in the road too muddy to traverse and walked in. "Have to walk part way as the snow is piled in road too deep for car to go thru," writes Jessie one June 6. Stokes went up almost every week, a ninety-mile trip on roads, still unpaved, that wound along swampy stream beds beneath the mountains. None of the family thought twice about the length of the trip or the frequent breakdowns or getting stuck in mud.

The routine did not change much in 1936:

June 19   Jo, Marie, Chin and I go to Sheep Camp. Eat breakfast in Durango at 6 a.m. Bring Oscar Jr. home.

June 22   Stokes loads out wool. 154 bags.

July 11   Stokes goes to take supplies to camp. Jo & Marie go to town to spend the day.

July 12   We look for Stokes all day.

July 13   Mr. Brown, Charles Verger and Santa Fe man eat dinner with us. Stokes is kicked by horse, two ribs broken.

July 14   Stokes, Jo & I go to town. S. goes to Dr. Moran. Eat supper with Mama.

July 15   Stokes, Jo, and Marie go to Huerfano Store to invoice.

Jessie mentions many names and visitors, most of them uncles and aunts and cousins; the four sisters remember a rather quiet adolescence, with few opportunities to meet people except at school. Farmington was still a very small town in the 1930s. J. C. Penney's was the principal store, and Hunter Mercantile, a general store, advertised "stylish Goloshes" in the local newspaper. This quiet life suited Jo, who was shy, and homesick for Carson's whenever she was not there, but Mildred, like her father, was more restless and curious, and wider horizons would have appealed to her. They all helped out at Carson's or Huerfano and drove around on errands or to pick up Stokes or Jessie, to take someone into town or collect them, or to pull them out of the mud. Their schooling reflected the pragmatic approach of their parents. A business background, at however basic a level, in bookkeeping, in record keeping, would be no disadvantage.

By the 1930s, food came in cans and jars—preserves, tomatoes, beans, corned beef—which made home curing and preserving less and less necessary. Stokes and Jessie were from an era in which almost every step of food preparation was done at home, and life without this female work was, though possible (and, for cowboys and sheepherders, unavoidable), unenviable. Stokes's parents, living on their farm near Farmington, would send out smoked bacon, salted beef, and fruit. Jessie had hens, and a cow for milk. Baking was a necessity, and a picnic with friends meant that she spent all morning killing, plucking, and cooking a chicken or two. Jo or one of her sisters would go up to their grandparents' farm to pick rhubarb, apples, or cherries. "Can berries and rhubarb," reads Jessie's diary for July 15; and the next day, "I can cherries." The children hated it when their mother put up fruit and vegetables. The kitchen was hot, and every large pot was full of steaming water and preserve jars or boiling jam. Jessie was too busy to pay any attention to them, there were no cookies, dinner was late, and the process went on for weeks.

The daughters learned these skills, too, but there was a focus on a different kind of work as well: the business of supplying goods, keeping accounts, surviving above the thin red line of bankruptcy. If Stokes ever wanted a son, he never expressed it, and his daughters received only encouragement and compliments. He made them feel important, and he never downgraded their work or puffed away their efforts as being "fine for women." Jessie's indomitable energy was obvious and necessary and Stokes knew it. Perhaps his opinion of women was further influenced by the observation of Navajo women as they herded, dipped, sheared, purchased, mothered, and ruled the roost. Navajo women traditionally owned all property and determined a good deal of what happened in the family and community, while men worked and claimed as possessions their jewelry, clothes, and horses. If Stokes had had sons, he would no doubt have encouraged them to become traders. As it happened, he turned his daughters into traders instead.

1937 was a year of much coming and going. January was bitterly cold, 4° below on the eighth, and windy; later in the month it snowed. The plumbing at Carson's (by now water did not have to be brought in from the well) was frozen, and it stayed that way until February. Alfred Eaton, Stokes's shepherd and general overseer, had his work cut out for him, driving up and down the cold roads to bring in lambs whose mothers had died or who were weak, moving the sheep camp, taking oil cake to the herds. Mildred got the mumps in January, then Marie caught influenza, followed by Chin. Helen Baldwin, a Navajo woman whom Jessie knew well and saw often in the store, died. Jessie herself went into the hospital for a week, but she recorded only the fact and not the ailment, mentioning it briefly and without details. The Huerfano day school, which had been built across the wash from Carson's and dedicated in 1935, had a fire that burned down the garage. The roads were dreadful, and the weather worse, and though the conditions did not cut down much on the travels to Huerfano, Aztec, Farmington, or even Durango, the accounts of getting stuck increased. Jessie's entry for February 7, a Sunday, sums up the winter: "Mildred and Marie arrive home; Stokes and Jo have a flat tire. Start walking. Alfred meets them. Snows and rains. Miserable for everyone."

But the winter of 1937 turned into a gay summer and fall, though the weather was windy and sandstorms were frequent. Mildred, who was teaching at the Huerfano day school, was married that December, on Christmas day, to Reuben Heflin, who was also a schoolteacher. The wedding took place in the little stone chapel that the Episcopal mission had built in 1935 across the Gallegos Wash from Carson's. The event was a small family affair. It was the first Carson wedding, but a quiet one. The family was not one for fuss and fanfare, and Jessie saw weddings only as an introduction to serious, hard work.

11

Oljato Trading Post

In 1938 Stokes exchanged Navajo Trading Post, the store he owned in Farmington, for a tiny, remote post called Oljato on the northern edge of the Navajo Reservation. Jim Pierson, the former owner, wanted to return to town, to the world outside the reservation. Oljato was off the beaten track then, and it still is. It was built under a mesa about ten miles west of Monument Valley, where the San Juan River, bending through Utah, marks the northern boundary of the reservation. The river at this point runs along the edge of a rock stratum. Creeks and washes run south—Paiute Farms Wash, Copper Canyon, Nokai Canyon, Oljato Wash—and between the washes are mesas: Hoskinni, Nokai, Paiute. The country is a place of weathered and eroded purple and rose-colored sandstone, and though the buttes of Monument Valley seem solid and durable, in reality they are wasting away, worn by wind and time, riddled with hairline cracks, skirted by talus slopes of eroded boulders, pebbles, and sand.

John Wetherill, Richard Wetherill's brother, first put up a trading post here around 1909 or earlier, of the same name—Oljato ("Moonlit Waters") —but not on the same spot.[1] In 1924 Jim Hefferman purchased Oljato, and after his death in 1926 the place was bought from his widow by the Taylor family. Jim Pierson bought the post in 1936 from the Taylors, and Stokes, in turn, acquired it from Pierson two years later. Stokes did not, however, leave Carson's for Oljato, for Mildred and Reuben bought the store from him and moved there. With his help they obtained a loan from the bank to pay for the trader's license and bond that, for a trading post on the reservation (unlike the Checkerboard area), was required by the BIA. The Heflins paid about $6,000 for the store, a little over $3,000 for the inventory, which included pawn, and $5,000 for their license and bond.

The purchase of a reservation trading post in fact amounted to a purchase of the ability to succeed the previous trader and inherit his customers, since neither the land nor the buildings could be owned. Reservation land was inalienable, the buildings immovable; only the lease and the goods belonged to the person who traded out of the store. Ownership, or rather the lack of it, was not crucial in these early years. Trading provided a living, sometimes a rather meager one, and did not require very much investment. It was more a way of life than a regular business. As time went on, inventories became larger, especially in bigger or wealthier Navajo communities. Improvements were made in the stores, expansion of rooms, new outbuildings, a little more comfort for the traders' families. The sale of a trading post was the only time a trader could make back his investment, realize some capital. Sometimes a wholesale outfit, recognizing perhaps that it was underwriting the posts it served, bought a series of trading posts and hired managers to run them. In a job that seemed to be typified by independence, hired managers did not always work out, especially in the early days, perhaps because of a lack of commitment or too small a salary and too long hours. It depended largely on the personality of the man hired. Often members of a family went into the trading business together, spreading the costs and benefits, or at any rate helping each other as they could. This was the Carson family's approach to trading.

No paved or gravel roads served the interior portions of the reservation. Farmington, small and undeveloped though it seemed in 1938, with its population of about 2,000, was far larger than any settlement on the reservation, even Shiprock. Only dirt roads ran west, through sagebrush, across washes, over sandstone, marked by stone cairns to direct the intrepid travelers who went from Shiprock to Tuba city and beyond to the Painted Desert and the Grand Canyon. The road that crosses the northern reservation, Route 160, was paved only in 1964; before then every reservation trader in that section had to negotiate whale-backed sandstone and the dry beds of washes, not only on journeys and visits but to pick up goods and deliver lambs. In winter the slick rock was icy, and in early summer the deep blown sand swallowed wheels and axles. The most difficult time was when the washes filled with water, which, especially after spring snowmelt or an August thunderstorm, turned dry beds into torrential rivers. Men who traveled the region stopped for a running wash and waited. They were not, after all, in much of a hurry. There was a tale told of a wash that ran too swiftly to be crossed. A couple of old hands watching the rain through the window of a trading post at the crossing saw a Buick approach the water's edge and, without apparent hesitation, proceed across. At the door of the post the automobile stopped, and a well-dressed young woman got out and came into the store. She asked for directions to Monument Valley. The trader eyed her gravely and just as gravely gave her the route. She thanked him and went toward the door, turning as she left to say, "You know, you ought to fix the bridge over that stream." Clearly, she was not from the region.

Mildred and Reuben moved out to Oljato in 1938. The 170-mile drive from Farmington to Kayenta was a beautiful one, through wild and open country broken by buttes and ridges. To the south lay the Chuska Mountains, the closer Carrizos, and the cliffs of Tse Awe ("Baby Rocks"), where the sandstone eroded into finger shapes like so many children clustering beside the mother mesa. Comb Ridge, a tilted bed of sandstone, ran from east to west behind Kayenta. Beyond Comb Ridge the great buttes of Monument Valley could be seen, small but startling in the distance, and far beyond them lay Sleeping Ute Mountain.

Trading posts were scattered along the route: Beclabito, dating from about 1911 and owned by one of the Foutz brothers; Red Mesa Trading Post, built some time in the early 1920s; Mexican Water and Teec Nos Pos, built by H. B. Noel in 1908 and 1906; Dinehotso and Chilchinbeto, both dating from the early 1900s.[2] At Kayenta the trail to Oljato branched off to the north, crossed a steep-banked arroyo, and wound among broad mesas until it came to Oljato Wash and the little stone store.

Kayenta, a small settlement thirty miles south of Oljato, boasted a post office, a government sanitarium for tubercular patients, and a trading post run by John and Louisa Wetherill. It also offered the closest telephone. Two volcanic plugs, Church Rock and 'Aghaała Peak, stood to the northeast, and Black Mesa, as dark as its name, just to the south.

Oljato trading post was no larger than Carson's; it sat under a lump of sandstone that resembled a giant knee, and on which, years later, the name O L J A T O was painted in large white letters to mark a small landing strip. Stokes came out to help the Heflins take inventory and make repairs and additions to the buildings. Oljato held a great attraction for Stokes—for all of them—partly because it was in country so beautiful, partly because the Navajo community was quite different from the one around Carson's. The Carson community had had considerable contact with Anglos and Spaniards and had become familiar with automobiles and towns. But each Navajo community was different and distinctive.

The environment of Oljato, both the distance between places and the relative absence of whites, made it seem that no changes had occurred, and traditional ways were still strong. Customers rode in, often from Navajo Mountain, skirting cliffs and threading the canyons on horse or burro, their wool wrapped up in a sack or a Pendleton shawl and slung over the animal's rump. Wagons were not always useful, because of steep trails, and automobiles were unheard of except among the very few whites—traders, missionaries, and Indian Service people.

Monument Valley had been discovered by Hollywood about the time that Mildred moved to Oljato. In fact, Harry Goulding, proprietor of the trading post bearing his name on the other side of the mesa, had brought Monument Valley to the attention of Hollywood. Goulding was a tall, thin, sheep rancher who had built the trading post in 1929 and settled down there with his wife, Mike, because he loved the valley. Harry heard that John Ford was planning to set a film in the Southwest. He thought to persuade him to shoot it in the landscape that lay outside the windows of his trading post and, taking a folder of photographs with him, he traveled to California. The spectacular landscape gave him the idea, and the economy that was affecting the country so adversely gave him the determination. The production of a film in the location would bring money, even jobs, to the local Navajo, as well as to Goulding's small trading post.

Though it was not easy to get into the director's office, sheepherding had given Goulding patience. Ford's secretary told him that the director was busy; Harry said he would wait, folded himself into a comfortable chair, and waited. Nothing would dissuade him from his idea, and nothing could get him to leave. Eventually the secretary called Ford and told him she could not get the stranger to go. Ford came out, impatient but polite. The photographs got to him, as Goulding hoped they would, and politeness turned to interest. The result was *Stagecoach*. The Gouldings put the film crew and the actors up in their guest cabins. Navajos got work and wages, and a chance to sell rugs and baskets to the visitors. The use of Monument Valley as a location by Hollywood was a minor economic godsend, and *Stagecoach* was the first of several movies to be filmed in the valley.[3]

Oljato, however, was not disturbed by Hollywood or its presence across the mesa despite its relative closeness. It was said that Oljato was wild, that the land from there to Navajo Mountain was full of Navajos or the descendants of Navajos who had evaded the roundup and incarceration at Bosque Redondo, who were independent, strong-willed, proud of their survival. "This Oljato country was a beautiful, wild, strange country," wrote Mildred when she had been there a few years; "The Indians were the most friendly I had ever met."

Freddie Scribner came out to Oljato to work for the Heflins and was invited to a Beauty Way Sing; his first Navajo ceremony made a big impression on him. At the store, an old singer named Tom Holliday had mentioned to Freddie that he was going to sing down the road at a ceremony. Freddie, making conversation, said idly that he would like to go to a sing. The next day old Tom Holliday came into the store, standing around, buying nothing. Freddie asked him what he wanted. "Nothing," he said. Finally the store emptied, and Freddie again asked Holliday what he wanted. "Well, I've come to take you down there to that Sing." Walter got some flour and sugar and coffee, and he, Freddie, and Holliday drove off down the canyon in Freddie's car, stopped, and walked to the top the mesa. The Sing was being held in a large hogan, and it had just begun when they entered. Freddie sat in the hogan beside Tom Holliday, all day long. The old man's son, Billy Holliday, apprenticed to his father and learning the chants from him, was doing the Sing.

Freddie described the ceremony: "Every once in a while Billy would stop and come and ask him, what should I do now? He was a pretty good medicine man, the old man. And he asked me, what do you think about this? I said I think it's good, I said, it's just like a church; I said if I'd known it was like this I'd have worn my good clothes, I don't have very good clothes on. He thought that was the funniest thing; he stopped the Sing and told them what I said. I said, see, I've got a hole here; he told them this, and they had a real good laugh. Then they went back to singing. It's like a chorus; there must have been eight or ten of them at least on one side of the hogan, and at a certain time they'd chant. It made quite an impression on me. If you're on the Path of Beauty you are all right; if you stray from it, the only way you're going to be all right again is to get back on it. That's what the Beauty Way sing is for."

Oljato, like every trading post, had its own currents and eddies, its own tides. Trading post life was (and remains) a busy life, with constant fetching and carrying, fixing and mending. There were slow days when few people, if any, came in, and full days when everyone came to buy or sell. The world outside the trading post was not forgotten; it simply never, or only occasionally, came to the door. The Heflins purchased a radio shortly after they moved out there, and it became a major attraction in the community on Saturday mornings, when the Indian Agency at Shiprock broadcast a local program. The reservation seemed another country, though it was not impervious to the news of the war in Europe that filled the

Farmington and Gallup newspapers, the war in which both traders and Navajos would participate.

The poor conditions of the roads did not prevent such activities of the outside world as mail delivery, census taking, draft registration, and the regulation of crime, of the number of sheep a Navajo might own, and of trading post operations—but it frequently slowed some of them down. The traders' preoccupation with the Navajo, with a way of life that diverged considerably from their own, gave them a feeling of being distant, of being on the boundary of their own society, which indeed they were. Changes came to the trader only a little less slowly than they came to the Navajo, though they were different kinds of changes. New machines and conveniences began to be installed, slowly but surely: windmills to pump water, plumbing, electricity. There was no indoor plumbing at Oljato; Reuben made a bathtub and sink out of concrete (Mildred set chips of fossilized wood into the concrete to decorate its austere surface). Water came from a raised tank and ran out onto the sand; the privy was an outhouse. A generator for electricity was installed in 1944.

Visitors in the 1940s were few and far between, the occasional prospector, the odd drifter. One morning Mildred glanced out of the kitchen window and was startled to see a white man walking up the wash toward the post. Reuben went out to see if he had had trouble with his automobile, but he asked only for some food. He was blond and bearded, and he seemed no ordinary tramp; his English was too good. He asked for directions to Tuba City and a pack of cigarettes (for which he offered to pay). When he left, however, he did not follow the route he had been directed to take; he instead disappeared into the rocks. Navajos said that he had stayed at one of their camps the previous night, and he was seen later around Tuba City. He was not a typical tourist, but neither was he atypical of the travelers in the area.

The country indeed seemed to attract unusual people, people equal to distance, dryness, and the unexpected. There was a missionary at Oljato named Shine Smith; Freddie described him as a free-lance missionary, but he had been with the Presbyterian mission at Ganado in the 1920s. Something had happened between him and the church fathers, though neither Freddie nor Mildred, who came to know him well, knew any details.

Shine Smith went to Kayenta and stayed with John and Louisa Wetherill at the trading post. After the Heflins went to Oljato, Shine "sort of came and stayed." Not everyone felt warm toward him: one trader said that he liked Shine Smith because it made him feel good when the man left. Shine had a habit of cooking a large pot of stew from ingredients he gathered from the trading post shelves but did not volunteer to pay for—and feeding all the customers in the store, an openhandedness at their expense that not every trader appreciated. However, the Navajos in the area liked and trusted him, and he took them to the hospital, drove them about the reservation on visits, helped them when he could.

At Christmas, parcels of food, clothing, and gifts would be sent to Shine by friends and charity groups with whom he kept in contact, and he would always give a party, wherever he was. This was a tradition shared by many trading posts. The Christmas party thrown at Carson's for the community was an annual event, dutifully reported by the *Farmington Times Hustler* each year. Oljato furnished food and coffee, and prepared it on an open fire outside for the community; Shine presided over the distribution of gifts, a tall figure in the black cloth of the missionary with a laugh and a smile for everyone. He rarely pressured the Navajo on religion, and he went to the sings and ceremonies so avoided by other missionaries. Laughter was constantly with him, and he pulled jokes out of every situation. His sense of humor was wonderful, and infectious—hence his nickname, Shine: he made everyone feel brighter.

There was a serious side to Shine, also. Once, while he sat at the trading post with Mildred, Freddie, and another frequent visitor to Oljato, C. E. Purviance, a discussion arose about religion, in the course of which Purviance said that he doubted not Christ's goodness but his divinity. Shine became apoplectic. Scarlet in the face, he began to slap the table, crying, "Purviance, you're going to hell," Purviance, a man who never raised his voice, was more concerned that Shine would have a heart attack than for his own life in the hereafter, but the incident gave a glimpse of the religious concerns, intensity, perhaps even anger, that lay behind Shine's sense of fun, the sunshine and laughter.

Shine became a frequent visitor, if not an almost permanent fixture, at Oljato. He had his own room, and when he was there he followed the routines of the house. He sometimes helped out in the store, doing odd jobs, keeping the family in good humor. At the end of a busy day, when the customers had gone and the evening had come with its customary solitude, his cheerful presence was welcomed by the Heflins, especially by Mildred when Reuben, trailing the fall lambs to Farmington for sale, was gone for weeks.

Another recurring figure in the small community of whites at Oljato who deserves mention here is C. E. Purviance. An administrator in the San Francisco public school system, Purviance was working on a Ph.D. at Stanford University; child development among the Navajo was the subject of his dissertation. He had first come to know the Heflins at Oljato, after contacting them through an acquaintance to ask if he could live at the trading post. His goal was to do a longitudinal study of children in one family, and he came to stay with the Heflins for a few weeks every summer. He became a family friend and brought not only his wife and children to Oljato but also new information from a different world, on everything from book titles to vitamins.

In October 1940, Mildred's first baby, Edie Jo, was born. Jessie became a grandmother, and Shine Smith became a babysitter. Like Jessie, Mildred went to Farmington to have the baby. There was no telephone at Oljato, and the nearest doctors were at the small hospital at Tuba City (the sanitarium in Kayenta had by this time closed down).

Hospitals for the Navajo on the reservation were few in the 1930s: there were government hospitals at Shiprock, Tuba City, Chinle, Leupp, Tohatchi, Fort Wingate, Toadlena, Fort Defiance, and Crownpoint (three of which had X ray equipment), and three sanitariums for tubercular cases, at Fort Defiance, Winslow, and Kayenta. Two hospitals were built, one at Fort Defiance in 1938 and one at Crownpoint in 1940. In addition, there was a hospital funded by the Christian Reformed Church at Rehoboth, near Gallup, and the Sage Memorial Hospital attached to the Presbyterian mission at Ganado, which had a high reputation and was perhaps the best equipped on the reservation. Medical care was provided by field nurses, and often by teachers at the schools, until the mid-1930s. The New Deal struggled to bring Public Health nurses and training for the Navajo out to the area, and to educate both adults and children about hygiene, child care, and food.

In large part the Navajo's health problems stemmed from poverty. Malnutrition and lack of sanitation contributed to disease. Infant deaths were frequent; older people died of exposure, tuberculosis, accidents, pneumonia, and occasionally from drinking home-brewed liquor. The Navajo themselves were traditionally much concerned with health; sickness was prevented by prayers and ceremonies and cured by medicine men and rites. Many Navajos, with some justification, were wary of Anglo hospitals. Given the poor quality of some of the hospitals and perhaps of the doctors who came to the reservation, the white man's way of healing was no more effective than their own. The New Deal tried to change this, and in some measure it succeeded. New hospitals, new direction in the health services to the Navajo, and new training of the Navajo all helped to make improvements. And, in an indirect way, the desperate economic situation of the depression brought a better quality of medical practitioners to the reservation; young doctors, unable to afford to start private practices, often accepted jobs from the government, jobs that in better times would seem less attractive.[4]

But government health care was only for the Navajo. Mildred, being white, was expected to use the facilities provided for whites off the reservation. In her absence, Reuben worked alone at Oljato. Mildred stayed with her parents until the baby was strong enough to survive the long trip home.

Most Navajo mothers of this era gave birth in the hogan (though by the end of World War II, they came increasingly to hospitals), and they did not have an easy time. Mildred was startled to learn that a young woman, Helen Hudgens, whose husband often worked for Reuben at the post, had been in labor with her youngest child for three days. Helen had told Purviance a few years earlier (Purviance was using the Hudgens family as subjects for his study) that she had had no trouble with childbirth, and Mildred was horrified. "What they go through at childbirth only God knows," she said to Purviance later. "The poor things simply accept all the suffering and pain as a matter of fact."

The stock-reduction program continued into the 1940s. Rangeland around Oljato, Monument Valley, and Kayenta, though arid, was spacious enough to graze sheep and cattle. The cattle were fat and the sheep were lean, and it was suspected by the government range rider that the Navajos stole cattle from the Mormons who wintered their herds on the south side of the San Juan River, where they may have strayed onto Navajo grazing land. This cattle war between Mormons to the north and Navajos to the south had been waged since at least the 1920s. The range rider, however, incensed at the misappropriation of property by the Navajo, collected evidence and sent four or five Navajos to jail in Salt Lake City. After six months they were released, and since several of them came from the Navajo Mountain area they were driven down to Oljato. A couple of Navajos told Mildred a few days later, "Well, they got home, all right. They ran all the way home to Navajo Mountain, those guys." Mildred thought somberly, "Just like birds out of a cage." The distance to Navajo Mountain from Oljato was some twenty-five miles by trail.

The numbers of sheep, cattle, and horses a family could own were still being reduced, and the Navajos continued to resent it and react against it, systematically and ineffectively. They tried witchcraft and they tried political protest, but neither worked. In 1939, witches had become more active, or at any rate more feared and more talked about. At Piñon, a remote area on the top of Black Mesa, several miles from Kayenta, a powerful medicine man was actively and effectively bewitching people in the community, especially those who were pro-government. One of the men affected by his witchcraft was Ben Wetherill, the son of John and Louisa Wetherill, who worked for the Navajo Service at Piñon.

The reservation had now been divided into nineteen areas, known as grazing districts, rather than the six regional agencies of earlier times. This was done to centralize the bureaucracy of the Navajo Service administration in one agency, and to better administer the stock-reduction program. According to Donald Parman's excellent account of the effect of the New Deal on the Navajo, the medicine man, Glo-en-zani, tried to bewitch the district employees. One morning Ben Wetherill discovered a kind of cross drawn in the sand outside his house. Though Anglos are normally thought not to be affected by Navajo witchcraft, Ben, who had grown up among the Navajo and spoke Navajo so fluently that he dreamed in that language, was overcome by anxiety. No accident befell him, however. Others had not been so fortunate; one Navajo attributed a fall from a horse, and another the death of his young son, to Glo-en-zani's powers. Ben persuaded the government officials at Window Rock to talk to Glo-en-zani. The community was so upset that Glo-en-zani was in danger of being murdered, and for his own protection Ben Wetherill brought him to Window Rock, where he was given the choice of jail or recanting (he had made open claims about his powers of witchcraft). Eventually he underwent the ceremony of recantation, and the community returned to harmony.[5]

If Piñon illustrated the emotional reaction to stock reduction, Oljato took the path of political action, sending a small delegation to Washington in May of 1941. Members of the community came to pawn bracelets and bead necklaces to Reuben in order to collect enough money to pay the fares of six people to go to see President Roosevelt: John Chief and his senior wife, from Oljato, John Fat and Neshie Yazzie from Navajo Mountain, Old Man Salt from Kayenta, and Shine Smith. Reuben lent them his truck, and they drove to Durango through Utah. Rumor had it that they would be stopped if they went through Shiprock. In Durango they met up with Stokes and Jessie, who brought the truck back to Farmington for Reuben, while the delegation left by train for Cortez, where there was an airport.

Once in Washington, Shine managed to get them an interview with Eleanor Roosevelt, though not with the president. The wife of John Chief told her, through an interpreter, "Our sheep are our children, our life and our food." The rain gods would send no more rain, she said, as there were no animals to eat the grass. Mrs. Roosevelt was sympathetic, but it was beyond her power to help. The little group returned home. To raise everyone's spirits, Shine did an imitation of John Fat in line in a busy Washington cafeteria, carefully unwrapping his money: first John unrolls a piece of calico, then a piece of buckskin; heads wave in the line, impatient, but John slowly counts out the correct change and slowly rewraps the money and returns the package to his shirt bosom. With imperturbable patience (and perhaps a private resistance, a thumb-of-the-nose to the haste and impatience of Easterners) John repeated this performance each time he paid for his meal. Shine's mimicry made Mildred and the Navajos laugh, a little piece of comparative ethnography they all could appreciate.

The trip to Washington gained them nothing. Rational action had proved no more effective than witchcraft. The demonstration of Navajo opinion caused trouble, at least for Shine. The Agency superintendent, Fryer, was not happy when he learned about the trip. An outspoken man, a good and conscientious administrator, and the superintendent of the Navajo Service from 1936 to 1942 throughout the difficult and touchy situation of the stock-reduction program, he worked hard to achieve the results that Collier saw as crucial to Navajo welfare. Upset by this expression of disagreement led by a missionary, a somewhat unofficial one at that, he drove two hundred miles of dirt road from Window Rock to find Shine Smith and threatened to "expel" him from the reservation. BIA officials once again complained that neither missionaries nor traders gave the government much support for its programs for the Navajo.

Though Navajos had no real choice in the matter of stock reduction (heads of families around Oljato were sent to jail to get them to comply), and though when confronted by the government's demands they obeyed without violence, they never ceased to speak out against it, at public meetings and family gatherings. Stock reduction was one of the major topics of conversation at the squaw dances during the summer of 1941.

At one of the dances, Jack Crank, a Navajo from Oljato, said he would kill any white man who came to get his livestock. Full of anger and liquor, he claimed that he had killed before and he would do it again. This boast came to the attention of the Navajo Service, who came to question him about it. Crank told them that he had indeed killed a "billagana," (a white man) nine years earlier, and had buried him in a shallow grave from which, so he said, he took bones when he needed certain ingredients for rituals. He could and did show the officials the spot. A solitary cowboy had been crossing the Navajo country with a string of good horses, bound for Blanding, Utah, unaware that traveling the region without tacit permission from those Navajo who called it home could arouse a certain amount of hostility in this particular corner of the reservation. In the face of the encroaching and irrepressible stranger, Jack Crank had acted as any warrior might do in the face of an enemy. The horses were both temptation and booty of war. Together with John Chief, his brother-in-law, Jack Crank followed the stranger to his evening camp, finding him as he was preparing his supper on a camp fire. The two men swung off their horses and began to talk to him. When the moment presented itself, Jack Crank hit the man on the head with the butt of his rifle. They then buried him and rode off with the horses.[6] Crank and Chief were taken to Winslow and detained, but the cowboy's relatives, who had assumed he had drowned, did not want to take up the case, and eventually the two Navajos were released.

Anxiety about hostility or violence was not, however, a constant undercurrent of the traders' lives. Mildred spent the war years at Oljato and was often alone there. Freddie went overseas to fight, and Reuben was frequently away picking up merchandise or taking lambs to Farmington, a trip of several weeks, while Mildred ran the store and took care of their small daughter. The nearest telephone was at Kayenta. "The Indians were all kind and I did not mind it," she wrote later.

Traders were sometimes openly challenged, especially in the first months of their tenancy at a trading post. No one would interfere in a fight—verbal or physical—if it occurred; a man was expected to defend himself, and the Navajo were curious to see how he would do in a test. A trader who came in the 1930s to a trading post some distance to the east of Oljato was warned by some of the older customers that there were three young men who would give him trouble, and no one would help him when they did. The youths had a bad reputation, and it was feared they were witches. They did bring trouble, cursing him to his face, standing in the store and insulting him, but the older men would always stand around and distract either the trader or the challengers. Finally, the conflict came to a head when the trader decided that the only way to deal with it was to confront them. When Dan, one of the young men, next came in and began to call him names, the trader asked him to step up to the counter because he could not hear what he was saying. Dan obligingly came, and repeated what he had said. The trader grabbed him by his old-fashioned hair knot and held his head down on the counter, keeping him at arms length. They struggled, and after a few minutes the trader managed to get him out of the store. Dan's friend Lee, deciding to take up the fight, came into the store and punched the trader, who immediately gave him two black eyes. By now the trader was apprehensive. He did not know how many of the young Navajos would join in, nor how their families would react, and he had a tense, worried day in the store.

That evening members of three generations of each family came to his door: grandparents, parents, and the young men themselves. They wanted to talk. Not without trepidation, the trader let them in, and they all sat down. Then, one by one, they spoke their piece. It amounted to an apology from the two youths, an excuse for their behavior from their parents, and expressions of respect from the grandparents. Amazed and relieved, the trader opened a case of soda pop and friendship was established.[7]

Relations across cultures are not always easy, and they are made less so if one of the cultures is taking over land, a way of life, an economy. Misunderstanding, frustration, disappointment, and inability to communicate all take their toll. A trader could be disliked as a symbol of the culture he represented, and he would have to prove himself as an individual. Not all traders succeeded. Some traders courted violence and found it. Others did not bother to get to know people, to try new goods, to supply things that the community needed. They did not care and the trading post shelves showed it. Sometimes the owner of a store would hire a manager to run it. Many managers were good, but some grew lonely, frustrated, irritable, interested only in getting paid and getting out. The solitude, the long day's work, and perhaps the absence of restraints made for a rugged individual, especially if he were without family and the softening effects of a home life.

It is not surprising that those traders who brought their families with them often did well. Another person to talk to, or to be silent with, offered a companionship not to be put aside lightly in the long winter evenings, or during the long summer weekend sings when people came in early and late for gas, for gifts, for pawn. Joint tasks made trading easier, and small jobs came up constantly: a broken pump, a flat tire, escaped chickens, sheep on the trading post roof, a sliced finger. Mildred and Reuben worked together, as Stokes and Jessie had, and they spent seven and a half years at Oljato.

12

Weddings and War

The year 1940 had brought another marriage to the Carson family as well as the first grandchild. "A very pretty wedding was solemnized at the O. J. Carson home at high noon on Wednesday, July 10, when their daughter, Miss Josephine A. Carson, became the bride of Sam R. Drolet, son of Mr. and Mrs. R. E. A. Drolet of Farmington," wrote Jennie Rorabacher, the society editor of the *Farmington Times Hustler*.[1] Sam and Jo met in high school, though they barely knew each other there. Sam's family had moved to Farmington from Pennsylvania, but the name was French and at least one of Sam's uncles spoke French before he spoke English, for their first migration had been from Canada. Sam was a trader, or an apprentice trader, and was working for his Uncle Marshall, his father's brother, at Naschitti Trading Post (also known as Drolet's) in the foothills of the Chuska Mountains south of Shiprock.

The wedding was private and formal. Jo wore a blue taffeta gown and Marie, her bridesmaid, pink silk. The living room at Carson's was full of pink roses and sweet peas. Stokes led Jo across the living room to the minister and Sam, after the ceremony and the celebration the couple went, as Jessie and Stokes had, to Denver for their honeymoon. When they returned, Sam took Jo back to Naschitti and work.

About a year later Jo and Sam left Naschitti for Carson's, where Sam began to work for Stokes, managing the store and helping out at Huerfano. The store had been Jessie's responsibility, since Stokes was increasingly preoccupied with the sheep and the ranch outside Durango. When Sam and Jo began to manage the store, Jessie joined Stokes in Colorado, at the ranch and at Cascade, where they had a cabin that provided a base from which to provision the sheep camps. That summer after putting the sheep up on the mountain ranges they began to work on the ranch. With the help of Navajos from the community around Carson's whom they hired and brought to the ranch, and by means of a disk and caterpillar rented from Farmers' Supply, a plough borrowed from a neighbor, and a home-made drag, Stokes cleared the scrub oak and brush, cut ditches, and ploughed. Poles were cut for fences, and wheat, rye, and alfalfa were planted. They also refurbished the cabin at Cascade, getting screens for the windows and new linoleum for the floor. Sam and Freddie came and helped occasionally when they could spare time, and Chin, Marie, Jo, Mildred, and "Baby" (as Jessie referred to Edie Jo) all visited, as well as a stream of friends and relatives.

No longer tied to the trading post, Jessie seemed to have more freedom and more fun. She had time to drive with one of her daughters to Durango for a permanent, to see a picture show, or to have supper at the Club Cafe with Stokes.

Stokes, by now in his mid-fifties, was as handsome and fit as ever despite a lame knee. The years sat well on him, though the ranch and the sheep camps involved hard work. His daughters, too, were all doing well. Marie and Chin were working. Mildred and Reuben were immersed in the trading post at Oljato, and Edie Jo was putting a new smile on Jessie's face. Stokes's second son-in-law was a man after his own heart, and with Sam at Carson's Trading Post he and Jessie could tend to matters on the ranch and Jo did not have to leave the home to which she was so attached.

1941 brought Pearl Harbor. The war had been present since 1939 as front page news (complete with maps and pictures) in the *Farmington Times Hustler* and the *Gallup Independent*, but distant in fact. Now it entered more immediately into the lives of the traders. Freddie Scribner joined the navy, the Seabees, and went to the Pacific theater. In 1942, Sam Drolet also went into the navy. Sam had gone to the New Mexico Military Institute at Roswell after high school, and though he had not enjoyed it very much, finding it rather too regimented for an independent Southwesterner, it prepared him for the navy's rigid discipline and the confinement. For traders, perhaps more then for most men, the change from civilian to military life was extreme—an exchange of space for confinement, quite literally, from a country of light and distance and color to a small bunk in a gray, steel enclosure bucking around in an ocean. As a trader a man could call his time his own, though it was a moot point whether a trader or his customers really played the tune to which he danced. Traders felt, at any rate, that they were independent. The military played a very different piece of music. But Freddie and Sam were young, and it was a war that seemed clear-cut on its issues, essential to be fought.

The war affected the Navajo as well, for they had been made citizens (though unable to vote) in 1924 and thus were subject to the draft. Changes in education and health care meant that many passed the entry tests. Those who did not go to fight had the opportunity of seeking employment in the variety of jobs that became available as thousands left America for the theaters of war.

If the war and service in it changed life for the white trader, an even more dramatic alteration of every aspect of life occurred for the Navajo. They were truly in enemy territory, always a situation of grave and serious danger. Navajos won a considerable reputation, not only for their courage and the stoicism that desert life had taught them, but by the use of their linguistic skills, which provided the army with a code for sending messages. The Navajo Code Talkers became legendary, transmitting information in Navajo, which the Japanese could not translate. Navajo is a rich, subtle language with a complex grammatical structure and an inventory of sounds that takes time to hear and to pronounce. The endless creativity of Navajo dealt easily with new terms for military technology and offered highly successful means of military communication.[2]

The Code Talkers were a special corps, but other Navajos fought with less attention and glamour, though with no less bravery. One young man who had worked for the Heflins at Oljato wrote to them, as many did, asking them to keep praying for him and to ask his family to pray for him. Mildred kept in touch with him, but his family was deeply concerned. In particular, they were anxious because in order for their prayers to be effective, his grandfather, a widely respected medicine man (the same Tom Holliday who had introduced Freddie to his first sing), needed a living part of the boy to pray over. One morning the family came to ask Mildred if she could send Francis a small white pebble they had brought and tell him to spit on it and send it back. Mildred enclosed the stone in a note and sent it with another to explain it to the censor. Nothing happened. Undaunted, persistent, the family brought her another little stone, which reached its destination and was returned. A Sing was held—with some success: as Mildred noted, "Francis came home without a scratch, and he was in the middle of some of the hottest fighting."

The war gave Navajos an opportunity to work side by side with other Americans, and when they returned to the reservation the tension between old ways and new increased. It was no longer easy, or even possible, to maintain a completely traditional way of life, yet the opportunities for a Navajo to obtain jobs on the reservation were few. During the war, Navajo men and women had been hired in various defense works, as well as in other employment, in Utah, Nevada, and California, because the demand for employees increased as men went overseas. Once the war was over, however, jobs were no longer so available.

The railroads continued to employ Navajos. Many traders, Stokes, Reuben, and Sam among them, were licensed railroad agents authorized to hire men for work and to fill out the cards each man would sign to get unemployment money during off-seasons. Railroads provided one of the steadiest forms of employment, with good wages and benefits, the only drawback being the distance from home that a man had to go. Usually groups were hired from the same area, and friends and relatives could work together.

The tribal government was a source of jobs, as were the reservation schools and the trading posts. But money was scarce, jobs few, roads unpaved, and prices high. Living conditions on the reservation were almost unchanged from those under which the Navajo had labored and survived for decades, but certain factors had changed. The reduction of sheep had deprived them of the structure of their own economy. Experience in the military had trained them in new skills, accustomed them to a new world, exposed them to new goods. The return to traditional herding and farming was not easy for the homecoming soldiers.

In 1944, Mildred's second daughter, Nina, was born. In May of the following year Reuben and Mildred sold Oljato and bought the lease to a trading post in the same part of the country, about fifty miles west of Kayenta. It was called Shonto ("Sunlit Waters"), by name a sister post to Oljato's "Moonlit Water."

Shonto Trading Post was located in a small red sandstone canyon between Black Mesa and Navajo Mountain. Like Oljato, the trading post was too far below the mesa top for the dome of Navajo Mountain thirty-five miles northwest to be seen. A wash ran over the sandy canyon bottom, and a grove of cottonwood trees, planted by the CCC to prevent erosion, stood between the store and the wash. The trading post sat at the foot of the cliff, on one side of it a spring, on the other a little *rincon* where sheep corrals were built. Cottonwoods and poplars grew at the base of the cliff, catching moisture, and a big mulberry tree rose behind the trading post. The previous traders, Harry Rorick and his wife, Elizabeth, had bought it in

1930 from the Babbitt Brothers, a wholesale outfit in Flagstaff that had bought several trading posts in the western reservation.[3]

The Roricks built four guest hogans and a stone cabin for themselves behind the store. Harry Rorick and a group of Navajos blasted a road up the steep eastern cliff in order to gain access to the cliff ruins of Betatakin some nine miles away. Both Rorick and John Wetherill at Kayenta would lead visitors there; indeed, for a while Shonto was called Betatakin Trading Post.

The main entrance to Shonto Canyon, when the Heflins moved there, was a steep road from the west, which the government had built over an impressive sand dune that swept down a natural break in the cliffs. In 1935, the BIA had built a day school a few yards from the trading post, and a road had been needed to reach it. For the Roricks, the sandy canyon bottom was their road, following the wash as it twisted between cliffs that slowly decreased in height until it opened into flat country below Black Mesa on the route between Tuba City and Kayenta.

Shonto was an oasis. Few other trading posts had so many trees, so green a shade, so much water. The cottonwoods and poplars rustled over it. The stone-walled buildings kept store and house cool; the cliffs kept the sun at bay. Reuben built on to the living quarters and the store itself, using the same kind of sandstone blocks as in the earlier construction. Mildred put in a garden, with vegetables, a lawn, and hollyhocks against the sandstone.

Harry and Elizabeth had separated by the time the Heflins bought Shonto, and Harry, very lame, was trading at Shonto alone. He had removed the high counter and put the merchandise where customers could help themselves, since he was unable to move around. Rorick sold the store and its inventory to the Heflins for $45,000.

In February 1946 in Durango, Chin, the youngest Carson daughter, married a government range rider in the Shonto area, Ed Smith, who had been born and brought up in New Jersey but had moved west by degrees. The wedding was in Durango and Mildred went, and stayed on there for the birth of her third daughter, Sharon.

Edie Jo, Nina, and Sharon grew up among dogs and horses, playing in the meadows along the wash, along the cliffs, and down the canyon where they occasionally found arrowheads or broken pottery. Like other canyons in the area, Shonto Canyon contained prehistoric sites, most of which were buried or barely visible. Like their mother and aunts, the three girls were each other's companions.

Sam returned from the navy, and he and Jo continued to manage Carson's, to which more rooms had been added as the family grew larger. Jo had a son in July 1947, named Raymond after his Drolet grandfather and Jay after Stokes. He was the only Carson grandson.

Marie was married, also in 1947, to Willard Leighton, a friend of Sam Drolet's and a partner at Two Gray Hills Trading Post. They were married in November at Shonto, and went to live at Two Gray Hills, a post in the Chuska foothills not far from Naschitti, Marshall Drolet's store.

In the late 1940s Stokes decided to sell his sheep; the market was no longer very good and the work was hard. He kept the ranch and ran a few head of cattle there, but his sheepherding days were over. Instead he bought Oljato in 1948, from cousin Fred Carson, who had purchased the post from Reuben and Mildred. He and Jessie traveled between Oljato and the ranch, putting the store in order. Eventually Chin and Ed moved to Oljato and managed it for Stokes until they bought it from him in 1958.

The trading posts held by the various Carson family members, Oljato, Shonto, Two Gray Hills, Carson's, and Huerfano, served very diverse communities. The routes across the northern section of the reservation tied the family together in their travels back and forth, and Farmington was the major supply point for them all. The posts covered trade in the Checkerboard area and the reservation proper, in New Mexico, Arizona, and Utah, in acculturated Navajo communities near towns and in remote communities that maintained traditional lifestyles. The Carsons traded in basketmaking regions, in places known for fine weaving, and in areas where the thick, handsome saddle blankets so prized by early cowboys were still woven. They traded in crossbreed sheep with heavy fleeces and old-style sheep with scantier wool. They all bought lambs, at least in the 1940s, though Stokes was the only member of the family who ran his own herd.

Oljato was small and remote, but the post served between one and two hundred families. Shonto was in a fairly large community of five or six hundred families who lived and traded there as well as at Inscription House, Navajo Mountain, Red Lake, Cow Springs, and Tsegi. Sheep, wool, a little mohair, and a few rugs made up the local trade. Posts whose traders were long-term residents usually did better than those whose traders constantly changed, and business at Shonto and Oljato was steady.

Two Gray Hills was a small whitewashed trading post in yellow-gray rolling flats on the northeast edge of the Chuskas in a region known for its rugs and its witches. The post was named for two rocky, clay-colored hills or small mesas a little south of the post (though gray seemed the least of their colors). It had been built in about 1897, since which time the local weavers had earned a name for the quality and distinctive style of their rugs, and, incidentally, for the trading post.[4] By the time that Willard Leighton ran the post, the quality of the weaving and the distinctiveness of the style, though it was never static and no rugs were identical, were established. The yarns were spun almost as fine as sewing thread in some of the weaver's tapestry pieces. Willard was one of the traders responsible for increasing the price of the rugs and the return to the weavers.

Two Gray Hills is an eerie place. The Chuskas rise steeply on the south. There is a point a few miles east of Washington Pass, some eight thousand feet above the New Mexico landscape, where the vegetation of the higher elevation changes abruptly from tall pines and mountain meadows to dry slopes covered with sagebrush and rocks. The land below lies bleached and pale, its level surface broken by the remnants of the volcanic core known as Shiprock. For a moment before the steep descent to the plain, the forest is at one's back, with its smell of pine needles and moisture, and the desert stretches before one's eyes, swirling with small dust devils. There are said to be witches here, much feared for their powers to do evil to those who have too much wealth. Perhaps the weavers, becoming wealthy from their fine rugs, were preyed upon, or made anxious by the envy of others. Willard, driving home late one night in 1956 in the dark, saw a figure at the side of the road; after the man had turned away from the headlights Willard realized that he stood there with wolf skins half off his body, the wolf's head over his shoulder. Startled and scared, Willard did not stop until he reached the trading post.

Trading posts changed little in the 1940s. Reservation traders had no incentive to invest heavily in modern conveniences such as refrigeration. In any case, most traders regarded the installation of generators, wells, and plumbing as modernization. Leases, though there was rarely a problem in renewing them, lasted for only a few years. Certainly, such short-term leases gave a sense of insecurity, but in the do-it-yourself days of trading, especially during the 1940s, this was not a serious problem, not a deep concern. Security of tenure became a problem by the 1950s as regulations expanded and more investment, time, bookkeeping, and paperwork were required.

Few, if any, traders were Navajo (though many white traders had Navajo wives). In 1945, a young Navajo from Shonto, H. T. Donald, tried his hand when he bought the lease for Tsegi Trading Post in Marsh Pass, halfway between Shonto and Kayenta. He was a friend of Reuben and Mildred's, and Reuben lent him some money, which he added to the loan

119

obtained from the tribe to help him start the business. Tsegi was success-ful under Donald, but other factors made trading difficult for him. One problem was the stress on cooperation and generosity in a Navajo com-munity. Business decisions ran counter to community values. Every trader maintained credit accounts that were risky, and many extended credit to a few families in extreme need who might be unable to repay in the near future. But an Anglo trader could refuse credit or request payment of ac-counts without incurring disapproval. It was the character of the Anglo, as perceived by the Navajo, to be mean; he was not fully a member of the community, and as an outsider he could not be expected to respond to pressure. For a Navajo trader, however, a refusal of credit to or request for payment from local residents or family members, however remote, was not always condoned, and he faced either heavy criticism or bankruptcy. Furthermore, success brought the possibility of witchcraft aimed at the accumulation of wealth.

In 1951 Donald was given a loan of $5,000 by the tribe to build a well. That same winter his truck slid on ice and tumbled over a twenty-foot bank in Marsh Pass. He was unhurt; his wife was cut and bruised. Two nights later the store was robbed of $200. Donald, convinced that he was being witched, was desperate and began to look for someone to lease or even take the store from him. Reuben, to whom he told his troubles, suggested that he have a Sing, which he did—apparently to his benefit: he continued to trade.

The responsibilities and pressures of a store were great and few Navajos wanted to face them. Later, in the mid-1950s the tribe made an effort to buy trading posts and install Navajo traders in them, but this effort was not successful. Had the management of such posts been handed to Navajo women, who traditionally managed much of the economic decisions, per-haps the results might have been different, but this is speculation.

Dedication of Huerfano Chapter House, 1931

Starting for the winter sheep camp from Carson's Trading Post, 1932

121

Window Rock, circa 1935

Carson's Trading Post, circa 1936

Jo and Jessie outside Carson's

Mildred's wedding, December, 1937

Hauling the wool, modern style

Freddie Scribner, probably taken
at Oljato

Part IV

1949–1974

13

The View from Outside

The war was over, but Sam, Freddie, and the Navajo servicemen did not return to the same peace and quiet they had left. The situation in Europe was anything but tranquil, and newspapers in Denver, Gallup, and even Farmington kept it on the front page. Perhaps the tension of war had made dramatic news a habit; certainly the increased speed and sophistication of media services made the news more international. At any rate, in 1947 the world, and the news of it, even in southwestern newspapers, was uneasy. It seemed that war might again erupt in Europe, and anxieties about communism were building up in the United States.[1]

Another concern, closer to home and of more direct import to the West, one that ranked with the European situation and communism, was the plight of the Navajo. "60,000 NAVAJO INDIANS IN DIRE NEED OF HELP," cried the *Denver Post* suddenly on October 10, 1947, and on October 21, "POVERTY AND DISEASE KILL NAVAJOS EARLY." Magazines, journals, and distant newspapers like the *Los Angeles Times* and *The New York Times* took up the subject. October 1947 seemed to be the month the white public discovered that the Navajo were not living at the high standards of which America was so proud. The stock-reduction programs and their effects on the tribe had never received such dramatic copy.

A campaign to aid the Navajo was launched by the *Denver Post*, lead by Hal Kirk. From one side of the United States to the other the public responded, sending money, food, and clothes with generosity and innocence. The Navajo needed shoes, it was said, and shoes they got: open-toed sandals, high-heeled, fashionable creations of thin leather, often brand new. They received clothes by the boxful, not only useful coats and sweaters but also silk slips, handbags, blouses, trousers, and short cotton dresses, which Navajo women generally would not wear out of modesty (and practicality) except as undergarments.[2]

The contents of the charity boxes gave considerable amusement to the Heflins, who received some to give out to the Navajo. Mildred advised C. E. Purviance, who was doing his part in this drive among the California women's clubs in Palo Alto, on what would be most useful and acceptable. She recommended long underwear, coats, flat shoes, warm gloves. He himself had been sending small parcels over the years to the family with whom he conducted his studies. Purviance's parcels to the Hudgens and the Shonto community were careful, thoughtful gifts, often suggested by Mildred or bought after his own observations of what might be useful: soap, a tarpaulin, a duffel bag, blankets, overshoes, lollipops for the children.

Larger groups also helped. The Red Cross collected a large sum of money,[3] and the Mormons sent several tons of flour to a warehouse in Flagstaff for free distribution. Wheat was expensive in 1947, and because of the desperate need for food in Europe in the lean postwar years, the government was shipping large quantities overseas; hence the short supply at home. Bakers were even being requested to cut down their use of flour for fancy cakes and pastries. The provision of such a basic good by the Mormons was more useful than it might seem, for the Navajo needed flour but could hardly afford the high prices.[4]

Mildred, who had observed conditions on the reservation over the years, thought 1947 seemed no worse and in some communities a little better than usual, for the war had brought work and training to many. Few rugs were being brought in, she remarked, and that was always a sign that no one was truly desperate at Shonto. Missionaries and others who lived on the reservation sometimes felt that charity was not quite acceptable, for the Navajo were independent and proud and resisted this kind of help. Assistance with writing, with filling out forms, with school entry, with any of the new and unfamiliar aspects of Anglo life that directly concerned them was one thing: material gifts from strangers was another.[5] More critically, charity was not a long-term solution. "I am not much in favor of all this charity," wrote Mildred. "While it is all right for people who really need it, it really solves none of the Navajos' problems." A shirt for today is not a livelihood for tomorrow. In some communities, however, the situation was very bad. At Piñon, for example, up on Black Mesa toward the Hopi villages, there were several deaths attributed to starvation. The people there had no sheep, and the land was too poor to cultivate. In such desperate cases, the aid was received with gratitude.

For once the newspaper stories followed rather than preceded action. The Navajo Tribe and the U.S. government each had already taken steps to deal with the situation. The tribal council appointed Norman M. Littell as tribal attorney in July 1947. Littell was a former U.S. assistant attorney general, and because he kept his base in Washington, D.C., he had knowledge and contacts the tribe needed in order to participate in programs for its own development. Still subject to control by the secretary of the interior, still without a constitution, the tribe had problems even getting funds. Royalties went into trust and had to be approved by Congress, and one request for funds ($18,000) for a tribal delegation to go to Washington was refused by the commissioner of Indian Affairs who had succeeded Collier. The BIA had completed a postwar planning report for the rehabilitation of the Navajo in 1947, a plan that included the Hopi also, and in the wake of this and other reports the secretary of the interior, J. A. Krug, requested a study for a long-range development program.[6]

An industrial consultant with the Department of the Interior, Max Drefkoff, came to the reservation in the summer of 1947 in order to make observations for an economic report and recommendations that were to be part of Krug's study. The result of his visit was a suggestion that forty-nine small industrial plants be established on the reservation for the processing of wool, leather, lumber, and other resources. The cost of this plan, to come out of tribal funds, would be an initial investment of about $2 million, which would produce 1,600 jobs in three years. After ten years and another $5 million, an additional 3500 jobs would be provided, as well as training for 3500 more Navajo (primarily for the garment manufacturers in California). Besides the recommendations of small industries, Drefkoff suggested that a tribal credit union be set up, that traders begin to pay rent based on a percentage of sales, and that missions be taxed. A report on education was made at the same time, and the entire study was completed in December 1947. In March 1948 Secretary Krug came out with the final report, *Report of the Navajo—A Long-Range Program of Navajo Rehabilitation*, which endorsed, among other things, the suggestions of Drefkoff.[7]

The Drefkoff plan did not delight the traders. Since the early 1930s the Navajo tribal council had talked about a tax on traders and payment, or rent, on their lease. In 1948 the council passed a resolution to regulate trading that controlled prices and required traders to pay 2 percent of their gross sales to the tribe. Since the matter of trade with Indians was strictly a federal responsibility, this resolution had no strength without concomitant federal approval. The BIA had undertaken to make a survey of trade and traders, but in the meantime Drefkoff's report gave backing to the suggestion.

Drefkoff was not in favor of either traders or missionaries. He claimed that traders were "usurers" and missionaries more interested in stopping Indians from drinking than in relieving starvation. The distrust was mutual. The United Indian Traders' Association questioned his loyalty as an economist. The missionaries bluntly called him a Red, according to a journalist writing one of the investigative articles on the Navajo for the *Denver Post*. The traders did not favor the idea of paying rent, nor many regulations Drefkoff had drawn up, but they were above all incensed by his criticisms of their general practices. Following the announcement of Krug's acceptance of the plan in March 1948, the United Indian Traders' Association sent a delegation, headed by Ralph L. Carr, an attorney and ex-governor of Colorado, to Washington to present their point of view. The congressional committee that was investigating conditions on the reservation suggested that the traders and the tribal council sit down together and discuss the regulations and the assessment for rent. In April 1948 Drefkoff was removed from his position as economic consultant to the Department of the Interior, and no action was taken on his report. However, the idea of rent that he had introduced and that the tribal council had endorsed was eventually put into practice.[8]

Mildred, writing to Purviance to keep him up to date with the reservation news, commented that the articles and reports on Navajo living conditions that filled the newspapers in 1948 seemed exaggerated, at least as far as the situation at Shonto was concerned. However, she felt that the more dramatically the newspapers presented the Navajo situation to the public the more likelihood there was of *something* being done, and there was no question that something was needed. Congress was planning to appropriate funds to carry out plans for a ten-year program on the reservation, though this would not occur for another year. This did not sound to Mildred like the immediate aid the Navajos warranted; "Poor Indians," she wrote to Purviance, "Always the ones who 'get it in the neck.' "

The newspaper reports from Los Angeles, Denver, and Albuquerque, among other places, had emphasized the economic struggles of the Navajo, the conditions of reservation life that resulted in poor health care, the difficulties of getting to school, the problems of sanitation, distance, joblessness. They did not describe the Navajo tribal headquarters, the tribe's political growth, the increasing activities at Window Rock, the Navajo struggle to achieve power and influence in the U.S. government in order to try to run their own affairs. The public's perception of the Navajo did not take in the political activists, the acumen of tribal leaders—Sam Akeah, Thomas Chee Dodge, J. C. Morgan, Marcus Kanuho, Henry Taliman; it centered less on the "educated" Navajo than on the "traditional." Native Americans were beginning to become a symbol of heroic survival in the face of a faster progress. At the same time, whites perceived accurately that the Navajo lacked the opportunities offered to everyone, and they were shocked that Navajos lived in conditions, as the newspaper reported them, of "squalor and disease." Journalists and public alike suspected government neglect.

Opportunities did not come to the Navajo. They lacked jobs, incomes, insurance, easy access to schools, and health care. They also lacked sheep (a fact that the newspapers did not expound on) and grazing lands; lacking these they thereby lacked the basis for their traditional way of life, which persisted though it did not mesh with standards of living of the rest of America. The life was, as the traders knew, a hard one with a large share of dangers, hunger, sickness, and poverty. Nonetheless there were dances, ceremonies, feasts, family strength, and a sense of place. The rewards were as rich as the trials were hard.

Traders did not see the conditions with quite the same horror as the newspaper reporters, partly because they had become accustomed to them, partly because they saw more than just the negative aspects. Most whites who had lived a long time on the reservation realized that Navajo life had its own values, logic, and strength. Change of lifestyle occurs slowly, accelerated partly by change in economy, partly by communication and exchange across different cultures. The very goods the traders sold (whether they knew it or not) brought change. Furthermore, traders encouraged white education—reading, writing, and mathematics—some traders overtly and others merely by making a job at the store available to Navajos who had these skills. Through trading posts, Navajos learned how to use new tools, new clothes, new foods. Traders strongly discouraged drunkenness, and they saw no harm in Christianity (though the relations between missionaries and traders were often uneasy; not all traders were churchgoers, and occasionally they felt that one or another group of missionaries might be doing more harm than good).

Heading one series of articles, the *Denver Post* said, "TRADERS CALLED BOON TO NAVAJOS."[9] But attitudes toward traders were becoming more critical. As Anglo opinion grew warm toward Navajos, it turned correspondingly cold towards traders. Outsiders saw the high prices, but they did not see the daily services and cooperation of many traders, and when they did they romanticized them. The fact that traders made a profit from the disadvantaged made them suspect.

From the other side of the counter, traders felt unfairly criticized. They lived in Navajo country, supplying Navajo needs, when few people cared to. They could not make a living from a destitute community. Accounts receivable, no matter how good they might look on the books, were worthless without income. Credit, extended in hard times, was a practicality common to small general stores everywhere. At any rate, traders attempted to bring what work and cash they could to the community. Mutual self-interest made them practical harbingers of material change, while their tendency to maintain more old-fashioned, conservative attitudes of their own culture made them preservers of Navajo traditional values. The balance was an interesting one.

The Heflins' life at Shonto reflected local changes, as well as those on the larger national scene. In 1945 sickness hit the Hudgens family, and the father, Elmer Hudgens, died. Purviance, much saddened, continued to come out to study the children, Johnny, June, Billy, and a younger crippled child. Helen, Elmer's widow, lived in her parents' camp for a while, moving with them to take advantage of the seasons. She wove rugs, kept sheep, and from time to time worked for Mildred.

Every year, Purviance made arrangements to come out to Kayenta. "Just a note to tell you that we are having heavy rains, and the roads are quite muddy in some spots," Mildred wrote hurriedly before his trip of July 1946. "The point I want to make is that it will be best to call us from Tuba City when you start this way. . . . if you do not reach here at a set time we will come out to look for you." Purviance came from California by bus, often hitchhiking the last few miles. Though he was then in his early fifties, a man of moderate means with a family, he was obviously adventuresome, and the summers on the reservation must have added spice to his life.

The Heflins enjoyed Purviance's visits, too. He brought them the outside world—books and magazine articles and conversation, sleeping pills for Reuben, vitamin C and candy for the three children. Even Reuben, busy and not much given to correspondence, had written to Purviance when Mildred was away, saying that he was looking forward to seeing him in August. Mildred especially enjoyed contact with a teacher (her own profession before marriage). Purviance sent her books on the Navajo, books on philosophy, books on travels and on ideas, and he recommended authors and subjects of interest. He provided the intellectual stimulus that, so far from libraries, book stores, and universities, Mildred missed. Isolation from such amenities was an occupational hazard for trader families.

In February 1947 Mildred wrote to tell Purviance that Helen Hudgens had been very ill, possibly with pneumonia: "I was down to see her today, and she looks very bad although she is much better. I suggest she go out to see the Doctor at Tuba but she said she felt too weak to go and I really think the long trip down there might do more harm than good." The children, by now about eight, nine, ten, and twelve, were well, she added, though they all had colds. "They have quite a nice camping site on a south hillside mid piñons and cedars. There are two nice hogans, a large sheep corral and a lean-to. They have to haul water about seven or eight miles from black Mesa."

That summer Purviance spent the month of August between the Hudgens' camp and Shonto Trading Post. His annual visits brought in a little income for the Hudgens, for he paid them for his sojourns at their camp, in addition to which he sent Christmas gifts and care packages throughout the year. Mildred wrote to Purviance to assure him that his payment was acceptable: "Helen and Stones [her parents' and brothers' name] were quite satisfied and expect you back next year." "I have a suggestion as to what you might put in Helen's Xmas box for Helen herself," Mildred told him that September. "A mirror, a small one that she might stand up or hang up. The reason that I am sure that she would like one is that she asked me if she might have an old broken one which she saw out in one of the guest hogans."

In September 1948 Tom Stone, Helen's brother, died. He had been in the hospital at Fort Defiance but had wanted to come home, and his parents and brother came with a missionary and drove him back to their camp. "He seemingly made the trip all right," wrote Mildred, "but lived only a few hours after being carried into the tent. All the family was deeply rent by grief. Poor Helen—we will try to get her on relief tomorrow. Would have had her on before but our supervisor is so conscientious that he doesn't want Uncle Sam to give away a nickel."

The federal and state governments were now beginning to bring more concrete aid, in the form of welfare checks, to the most needy Navajo. Later, as mineral royalties began to pour in in the 1950s, the tribe developed its own programs to train and employ Navajos and to give aid to mothers of small children. A scholarship fund had already been set up. In 1948, Indians in New Mexico and Arizona were granted the right to vote. The Navajo population in New Mexico was approximately 20,000, and in Arizona 35,000; clearly, such a vote eventually would be heard.[10]

The relations between traders and the government were somewhat am-
biguous. Traders and Indian Service employees were sometimes friends,
when distance and work permitted. Sometimes they looked on each other
with distrust: the trader for the agents' and schoolteachers' unfamiliarity
with, even ignorance of, the region; the BIA employees for the traders'
failure to support government policies in the community. In earlier days
some traders, the smaller ones, brought in liquor to sell to Navajos.[11]
Sometimes Navajo fugitives from the law would be given refuge and advice
from the local trader.[12] Both activities had strained relations in the past.

BIA employees were expressly forbidden to have any commercial interests on reservations, for obvious reasons. For their part, traders saw regulations as unwieldy attempts to codify the subtleties of the cross-cultural
situation. Furthermore, trading was a struggle with both nature and culture.
The former contributed mud, snow, drought, and blown sand to the day's
work; the latter provided endless challenges of language, personal tribula-
tions requiring aid, advice, or credit, and misunderstood arrangements.

During the 1930s the Navajo Service had assumed the duty of regulating trade with the Navajo. The ultimate authority was the commissioner
of Indian Affairs, who oversaw all business between Native Americans
and other Americans. The Navajo Service devised rules for pawn, for
inspection of weights, for bonds and licenses. A trading inspector checked
scales and investigated complaints against traders. When Reuben and
Mildred moved to Oljato, Horace Boardman, inspector in 1938, came out
to the post, watched, looked about, tested the scales. A few days later he
returned and rechecked them. He found no fault, though his second visit
made everyone feel slightly nervous. However, when asked about trading
irregularities in a radio broadcast, Boardman said that he thought traders
were probably glad to have their scales checked and added, "They like it
better whenever there happens to be a crowd of Navajo in the store doing
their trading."[13]

The BIA had made a study of trading, comparing prices and markups
across the reservation in all kinds of goods, as well as trade items, account books, bookkeeping records, and services to the community. This
study, prepared by Dr. Bonney Youngblood, an agricultural economist
with the Department of Agriculture, noted the problems: delivery, roads
(or lack thereof), isolation, credit problems. Prices were high, but Youngblood felt that they resulted from the conditions and the necessity for the
highly varied but small inventories. He suggested a few changes in regulations and recommended that the traders train community residents in
good consumer practices.[14]

The BIA's 1948 survey of trading that followed Drefkoff's report and the tribal council's motion for rent also went into operation under the auspices of Dr. Youngblood and was carried out and written by Morris S. Burge, who had been active in Indian affairs since the 1930s.

The tribal council felt that their own resolution was all that was appropriate and that the survey was an unnecessary delay to action. Despite this criticism, the investigation began, with arrangements for local Navajo representatives to observe the operations of the survey parties as they inspected each post. The conclusions of the final report of April 1949[15] were that travel and living conditions on the reservation resulted in many services being offered by traders because they were not available elsewhere. The extension of credit and the offering of these services resulted in high prices, and there was not sufficient business on the reservation to make more stores and thus more competition efficient or profitable. The report mentioned that of the twenty stores surveyed, five made less than $5,000 net profit a year, and seven made over 15 percent after deducting $5,000 for the trader's salary. The average net profit given by the report was $9,262 per store. With the development of the reservation, the report went on, traders would not be the sole source of all services and traders' prices would fall. A maximum markup of 25 percent was recommended, limits to interest rates on credit were suggested, and a rental fee schedule to the tribe was put forth. The suggested schedule was $100 on an annual volume up to $25,000, and for volumes over that amount $100 plus ½ percent on sales over $25,000. In return, traders were to receive the security of a longer lease.[16]

Sales of imitations of native crafts were to be prohibited. The United Indian Traders' Association had been created in 1930, among other things to ensure the sale of genuine native goods at all trading posts. That, after all, was their business, but a number of less reputable stores used their location to sell imitation goods at high prices. The survey included suggestions for rules covering peddlers and "carnival companies, circuses, theatrical companies"; they too were considered "traders" and required a license. No Skakespeare at Shonto. The survey commented on the increase in roads and cash on the reservation, and on the approval of the survey by Navajos and the cooperation of the traders. It predicted that trading would continue along the lines of the present system and that a change in the type of stores established (such as supermarkets or Navajo enterprises) would be slow in coming. The final report, published in 1949, was a less negative view of trading than Drefkoff's, and the proposed rent schedule and revised regulations both went into effect. In return, the tribe began to grant longer leases. By the 1950s, the new leases were made for twenty-five years, which was felt to provide traders with the security they so sorely lacked and which would encourage improvements and modernity.

The lack of modernity was to be one aspect of trading that the next investigation would be concerned with. Another, more serious problem would be the handling of welfare checks by the trader. However, there was not to be another report for twenty-four years. The underlying problem, which would grow more and more important to the Navajo, was that modernity, for which America prided itself, was not available, in the form of goods and choices of goods, to the Navajo, as it was to everyone else.

As the 1940s waned, the news of the Navajo Reservation died down, and traders and Navajos sank into oblivion once more. Impressions from the outside of life at the trading post varied from the romantic to the disapproving. The trader was either an altruist or, if he made a decent living, a villain. The more traders failed as businessmen, the more heroic they became. The reservation seemed one place in America where success was perceived negatively. If a store was poorly stocked and the trader made no attempt to learn the needs of the community or to offer any of the traditional services that helped to integrate Navajo and Anglo economics, there was reason to question the trade. The post was not just a store, it was a service center.

Traders, isolated by distance, began to feel isolated as well by the attitudes of their own society. Mildred wrote to Purviance, telling him approvingly of the investigating committee of 1948, and of the many articles on the plight of the Navajo; "The only thing I do resent," she added, "is being called a thief, a cheat, and liar when I am not."

14

Inscription House
Trading Post

After buying the lease on Oljato in February, Stokes spent much of 1948 traveling between Carson's, Huerfano, Durango, the ranch, and Oljato accompanied by Jessie, often one or two of his daughters or sons-in-law—usually Chin and Ed—and even grandchildren. That spring, Stokes planted alfalfa, wheat, and rye at the ranch, fenced, and bought livestock—cattle, sheep, pigs, horses, mules—which would fatten in his pastures and be sold in the fall. In August after harvest he and Jessie began to go down to Oljato every two weeks throughout the autumn. They took Ed's family, who came out from New Jersey to visit, to Oljato and toured the country with them. In October, Chin and Ed tended the Oljato store.

At the end of October a fierce storm hit Durango, harbinger of the winter to come. Jessie was at the ranch, but Stokes was in Durango and could not get home until the next morning. The roads were all snow-bound and Jessie was worried about Marie, who had left Carson's with her children for Shonto the previous day. November was cold but dry, and again Stokes and Jessie went to Oljato, to give a Thanksgiving dinner for the Navajo community. Snow began to fall as they left a few days later. Stokes brought several Navajos back to Colorado to work in the logging camps above Bayfield. He frequently took people from Oljato to Carson's to rendezvous with a railroad gang, to work in the Utah beet fields, or, as now, to work in Colorado lumber camps. Sam, Reuben, and Willard also took men to work.

In December, Stokes and Jessie went to Carson's, and Jessie spent most of the time at the Huerfano store. There were Christmas parties at the missions—at the Huerfano Methodist mission on December 23 and at Carson's mission on December 25. "Big crowd," wrote Jessie, "R[euben] & M[ildred] & girls come out bring Winnie [Jessie's sister-in-law], Willard, Marie and Freddie come. I cook two turkeys." The next day Stokes drove to Farmington to bring his mother and Miss Wilcox to Carson's, and they had their own family Christmas on Sunday. "The Browns come with Miss Kelm, Anna Mae and Barbara McCullock with them. We have 26 for dinner." After it was over, Stokes and Jessie went (perhaps with a sigh of weariness, undoubtedly with content) to Huerfano, driving the few miles over the bumpy road in the dark December evening to the peace and quiet of the little store.

January 1949 was bitterly cold on the reservation, especially in the Kayenta area. The Heflins were snowed in at Shonto for two days, and it continued snowing into February. There were heavy losses in the Navajo herds. The Navajo Service made air drops of bales of hay and supplies, but with so much territory to cover it was often difficult to make the drops at the right places. Until they began to use parachutes, the packages of food would break open when they hit the ground. There were reports of outbreaks of pneumonia, measles, and diphtheria. Mildred had left her children with Jessie (who was once more back in Farmington), but she was worried for the families in Shonto. The Indian Agency sent a team of nurses and army doctors onto the reservation to pick up anyone who was seriously ill, but Shonto had no sickness apart from the usual bad colds. Snowplows came out several times to the Kayenta region to clear the roads. "They are really working around the clock to help these people," Mildred wrote to Purviance in February, "and we have nothing but praise for them. The snow is still 3 and 4 feet deep around here."

There was one casualty of the winter at Shonto: Raymond Stone, Helen Hudgens' father, died. In March he ruptured an abcess on his lung while carrying home Red Cross supplies, and, after thirteen days of coughing up blood, he died at the Tuba City Hospital. Helen had spent the winter tending new lambs—she would not let her children miss school to herd sheep in the cold. Mildred told Purviance that Helen looked bad: "Too much work and too much grief," but at least she and her mother, Old Lady Stone, were on relief.

In March, Jessie's brother Bob died unexpectedly. Jessie and Bob had been very close, and the family was worried about Jessie, who, with Stokes, was back at Oljato. The Carsons had no phone there, the roads were impassable, and though in an emergency a family friend who was a bush pilot could land on the wash bed, it was now too wet to do so. However,

Mildred managed to get the pilot to drop a letter to let her mother know about Bob's death. The four daughters went to their uncle's funeral, though with great difficulty, especially for Chin, who was at the ranch. Jo sent her mother a comforting letter by a series of messengers. Perhaps it was better for Jessie that she could not get to the funeral. But the situation made the family think hard. In a grave emergency that coincided with bad weather, Oljato would be unreachable. That summer, Ed and Stokes cleared a runway on hard ground above the wash on which small planes might land even in the rain. They discovered that burros liked to wander across the runway, but they were easier obstacles to deal with than water and mud.

Jessie was now in her mid-sixties (though she never revealed and never dwelt on her age; she was a few years older than Stokes and sufficiently aware of the fact that she removed her date of birth from the Smith family bible). Mildred wrote to Purviance, full of concern for her mother: "She has always worked very hard all her life, and now when she could and should be taking it easy refuses to let up on the work." But Jessie was incapable of taking it easy. As Mildred put it, she was made that way. She came from an era when work was hard and continual, and to let up on it was to let up on life itself, a point of view the Navajo knew well.

Mildred herself was kept busy by the store, the bookkeeping, and her children. In order to send her daughters to school—Edie Jo was now nine—the Heflins had bought a house in Farmington, and they faced a major hardship of a trading family—the separation and travel that accompanied their children's education. Mildred drove back and forth between Shonto and Farmington, between her daughters and Reuben, managing two households.

There was plenty of news on the reservation in the year of 1950, all of which Mildred relayed to Purviance, who planned to spend the summer in Flagstaff doing research at the Museum of Northern Arizona, a change from his annual fieldwork at Shonto. John Nichols, the latest commissioner of Indian Affairs, resigned, somewhat to Mildred's surprise and disappointment, and Dillon Meyer was appointed in his place. In the fall, Meyer toured the reservation communities and spent a night with the Heflins at Shonto. Mildred barely had time to settle the girls in Farmington and school—even Sharon was in kindergarten—before returning to the trading post to arrange for the visitor. She was, however, impressed by Meyer and had the opinion that he knew the West, having been involved with work in soil erosion, and seemed sensible. The Heflins also learned that the tribe was finally about to grant longer leases in return for improvements. Traders would have to meet certain standards of cleanliness, prices, and treatment of customers. "We have installed a diesel [generator], a deep freeze, and are getting a meat counter," Mildred said. The security of a longer lease made the investment worthwhile. There was family news also: Chin and Ed had a daughter, Wyona Marie, that year.

In June 1951 Purviance wrote to tell Mildred that the doctoral thesis for Stanford on which he had been working for so long was, as he put it, "out." His deadline was January 1952, but he had given up hope of finishing. The demands of his children, now young adults, his wife, his house, and teaching left him too little time. "Stanford has been very good to me," he wrote Mildred, "and they are right: The Ph.D. is for young men to go forward on." He was in his fifties and he had struggled valiantly to juggle family, job, and intellectual pursuits. He was perhaps ahead of his time, for thirty years later it became more common (if no easier) for men and women to take up the challenge of graduate work late in life. But Purviance, though no longer working on his thesis, could not put away his interest in the Navajo, in Helen Hudgens, or in traders. He continued to visit, to communicate with Mildred and the Hudgens family, to send clothes to Shonto for Navajo families, packages to Helen, lollipops to the younger Heflins, and books to their parents. Life on the reservation in general, and at the trading post in particular, continued to interest him.

Stokes, like Purviance, also began to feel that what he was doing was for younger men. Ed and Chin were now managing Oljato for him, and with his children all settled in trading posts he decided to sell the ranch. He knew he would feel a mixture of regret and relief when it was sold, as he had with the sheep, but he accepted the practicality of letting it go. He resented not his years but the slowing down of his body, which made the work on the ranch more and more taxing. Sam and Jo bought Carson's from him in 1952, and Huerfano was put on the market. Stokes and Jessie bought a house with a garden full of fruit trees on North Wall Street in Farmington and prepared to settle down to a quiet urban existence in the town they had both grown up in.

In September 1952, Stokes, always restless and curious, decided to go with Mr. Brown (from whom he had bought his sheep herd, and who had remained a friend) on a trip to Alaska. Perhaps it was a last adventure before retiring, perhaps it was a longing to see a different landscape, one that would be a contrast to the desert. He had hoped that Jessie would travel with him, since the trading posts and ranch were no longer responsibilities. But the trips to Durango and Farmington, bank and forth to the ranch, the suppers at the Club Cafe or an evening at the pictures were excitement enough for her. So Stokes and Brown drove north together, through Colorado, Wyoming, Montana, and across Canada to Fairbanks and Valdez.

"Dear Jessie," he wrote as soon as he got to Valdez, "We got to Fairbanks. Yesterday 11 a.m. went to the Bank, had some traveler checks cashed, and went to see the Masons and the Elks. They were very nice to us. Was invited to a Mason Dance last night, but we came on halfway to Valdez. Had a good hotel last night. Getting cold at Fairbanks 4 below last night while it did not freeze here . . .

"Have been down watching them unloading cargo. We are on a port on the gulf of Alaska. We are going to take a boat back to S[eattle] if we can get on, Will know tomorrow I think. Was interesting to see them unload. This boat came, 10,000 tons and it was loaded. Freddie should have been here to check it. [After loading so many trucks with wool sacks, unloading so many trucks of goods, Stokes could not quite turn his hand in, and loading was a feat of both strength and the organization of space that he appreciated.] The road was good all the way we never shifted gears from the time we left Durango to Fairbanks. It is just an old Frontier town. Love Stokes."

They spent about ten days in Alaska and then turned back from the foggy beauty of the far North to the Southwest and home.

Peace and quiet, however, did not suit the Carsons. Urban life was pleasant, Farmington was familiar and pretty, and with a population of 12,000 it was hardly a big city; but they missed the country, missed the open space, and above all missed the Navajo trade. They felt they should be doing something useful, and though Jessie often looked after her grandchildren, it was not quite enough. Within a year they were restless, and when Stokes heard that the lease of a trading post on the reservation was for sale, he was interested immediately. The post, Inscription House Trading Post, was near Shonto, and in 1954 Stokes completed the purchase of the leasehold from the owner, S. I. Richardson. The Carsons went back to trading.

S. I. Richardson had built Inscription House Trading Post in 1929. Besides a trading post he had built guest houses, and he ran pack outfits to Rainbow Bridge and the Anasazi ruins in the surrounding country for the adventuresome visitor. Inscription House was the name of a cliff dwelling in Nitsin Canyon to the west of the trading post. The ruin was named for an inscription, scratched on a wall inside one of the rooms, that was all but illegible but was thought to read "1661 AD." The cliff dwellings of Betatakin, Scaffold House, Swallows Nest, and Keet Seel were fifteen miles east, Navajo Mountain thirty miles north. The post and its cabins were built among the piñons of the Shonto Plateau in full view of the mountain, and the trail to Rainbow Bridge wound around the spider's web of canyons that threaded the plateau.

Navajo Mountain, known to the Navajo as Naatsis'ann ("Head of Earth"), had been the refuge of a small band of sixteen Navajos, lead by Hashkéniinii, during the years of Bosque Redondo. The mountain became a refuge for the Navajo, and correspondingly it increased in importance to those living in the western corner of the reservation. The Holy People of Navajo legend clustered in the canyons at its foot, and Rainbow Bridge itself was thought of as a pair of Rainbow People—Holy People with rainbow bodies—bending together.[1]

This was the country that S. I. Richardson hoped would bring travelers to stay in his cabins and take his pack train tours. Providing lodging and tours for visitors was a sideline of many traders of the 1930s: Harry Rorick and his wife Elizabeth at Shonto; the Gouldings near Monument Valley. Stokes, however, was lame, and he was more interested in trading than in tourists. The guest cabins behind the trading post became spare rooms and storage rooms; one of them known as S. I.'s house, his to come and stay in whenever he wanted to visit.

Stokes and Jessie moved into Inscription House Trading Post, but they did not plan to leave Farmington permanently. They wanted to put the trading post in order and hire a manager. Jessie went to work in the garden. The soil of the area was good and Navajos planted corn and melons in every wash and arroyo bottom. Carson's soil had been alkaline, and the dry winds discouraged plants, though Jessie had coaxed tomatoes and flowers behind the house. At Inscription House, anything would grow if it was given water, and she planted hollyhocks and roses, lettuces and squash.

The trading post was a long, one-story stone building facing a dirt road. They painted the name "Inscription House" in red in large neat letters across the front of the building just below the roof beams. An old gas pump stood across the road. The store itself was bigger than Carson's, and the living quarters lay behind it, small rooms opening onto one another— the store onto the office, the office onto the living room, living room to kitchen, kitchen to bedrooms. Though anything but luxurious, it had the same atmosphere about it that many of the trading posts had, especially those in the Carson family, comfortable and unpretentious. Jessie had had a refrigerator at Carson's in about 1935. It burned kerosene and was a modern wonder. At Inscription House there was a gasoline-powered generator for electric lighting but no refrigeration, which was still not common to all trading posts, though electricity from some kind of generator was to be found at most stores. Later Stokes installed a diesel generator and they were able to get a refrigerator.

The walls of the post were as thick as those at Carson's, and the windows as small, to keep the sun and dust out and the cool in. The rooms were full of Navajo rugs, in layers on the floor, over the backs of the large armchairs. Many were kept because the Carsons liked them, others because they had not sold and were more use in covering a worn out spot on the upholstery. There was a big rolltop desk in the office where Jessie put receipts, bills, orders, accounts, daybooks—all that she needed to keep the books once again for the store.

Stokes began buying sheep, wool, rugs, and baskets. The market for wool was unpredictable and no longer very good. Synthetic fibers had become popular for clothes and carpets, and wool was less and less in demand. Stokes hoped for a year when the demand and the price would surprise everyone, and he could make a profit. The traders of the 1950s usually contracted with the wool dealer to supply a certain amount of wool at a fixed price, thus protecting themselves from the vagaries of the market and setting the limits of the buying price to the Navajo. Since the trader had to provide a certain quantity to the dealer, his price had to be competitive with other local traders in order to make sure that enough wool was obtained. Profits were small, though steady. The market for sheep continued to fluctuate. Stokes sent the livestock bought at Inscription House out with Reuben (or sometimes Willard) when he trailed the Shonto sheep to the railhead at Farmington, often fifteen hundred or more animals.

The Shonto Plateau and the region from Kayenta to Navajo Mountain was thick with piñon, and piñon nuts were another commodity bought at Inscription House from the local Navajo. There was always a market for them in Albuquerque or Flagstaff, not only for local consumption but also for sale to the East Coast, where they were in demand. The nuts were gathered in the late summer and fall and brought for sale to the trading post, providing an additional source of income. There were summers when the piñon crop was abundant, said to be every seven years, and families left their friends and sheep whenever they could to gather up the small smooth nuts that lay in quantity under every piñon tree. In a good year Stokes would buy several thousand pounds of them. Mildred and Reuben, also in piñon country at Shonto, bought about 10,000 pounds of piñons at 45¢ a pound the year Stokes and Jessie moved to Inscription House.

Rugs at Inscription House were frequently large, with a design known as a storm pattern. The local weavers also made many saddle blankets, which Stokes liked and bought in quantity. Saddle blankets were not sought after by rug collectors, but they were used by Navajos and bought (and admired) by visitors who could not afford the finer rugs. The saddle blankets were usually striped with stepped designs or some other small pattern in each corner, so that where the saddle curved and the blanket hung square a piece of fancy design caught the eye. The colors were often bright— red and black and white; brown, gold and yellow; turquoise and gray. Besides commercial dyes, natural sheep colors of brown and gray were used, as well as vegetal dyes. Double-size saddle blankets were popular, because folded in half under the saddle they were very thick. In many, the wool was teased after weaving to a soft fluff, which made an exceptionally good protection for the horses, absorbing sweat from their backs and preventing the leather from chafing. The saddle blanket was one piece of weaving the Navajo themselves continued to use. Rugs were woven solely for trading, but saddle blankets had a function, and their color and thickness were appreciated by the Navajo themselves.

A saddle blanket was a practical item of trade. It took little time to weave, required only a moderate amount of wool, and was usually marketable for the Navajo and the trader. Rug experts tended to look down on saddle blankets and ignore them, and the feeling was that the trader who had many saddle blankets did not do enough to encourage finer weaving. Saddle blankets, however, not only brought ready money, but were something that even an untalented or novice weaver could make. Furthermore, they had a vitality, and the finer ones were as well woven and as attractive in their own way as the larger, fancier rugs. True, stripes are a simple design form, and some of the bright colors did not always appeal to the Anglo eye in search of natural shades or the softer vegetal dyes. But the saddle blanket seemed to carry on the fondness of Navajo weavers for brilliant colors, a fondness demonstrated in the "eye dazzlers," as the aniline-dyed rugs of the late nineteenth century were called, and earlier in the use of red Spanish bayeta (woollen cloth) carefully unraveled and rewoven. Although the saddle blanket was not always appreciated by outsiders, Navajos continued to weave and use them, and Stokes continued to buy them, realizing that they brought in a little money promptly to anyone who could weave, however young or old.

Though Navajo life in this area of the reservation, and in many other remote places, remained traditional and, like the traders themselves, old-fashioned, there were continuing adaptations to the changing economy. In the 1950s the tribe took over control of the stock reduction, with a consequent decrease of pressure to reduce. But the big herds were already gone. Sheep were still important, but so too was some form of wage work, and schooling was encouraged by many Navajo families. Helen Hudgens had herded her sheep so that her children (who, a few years earlier, would have been expected to take care of them) could stay in school. "She is an unusual woman to do this for her children's education," Mildred wrote to Purviance.

The economic strategy of Navajo families was to some extent planned around the expectation of trading post credit. By now, virtually every trader gave credit, though the limits were carefully watched. Stokes extended credit to the families around Inscription House Trading Post as he had at Carson's and Huerfano, and as did his daughters and sons-in-law to families they knew and whom they knew to be reliable. Credit had become a way of life that no one really questioned. Stokes thought the Navajo were reliable, paying their bills if and when they could. Income was by now evenly split between cash, in the form of wages and welfare checks, and commodities—the old staples of wool and sheep, as well as piñon nuts, rugs, and baskets.

The postwar reservation economy of the 1950s depended far more than in the past on money and on the dollar value of commodities, yet cash itself was still not much in evidence. The Navajos had long been accustomed to an exchange of commodities, which by the 1950s was no longer strictly barter. All commodities were valued in currency and thus were susceptible to some fluctuation. However, the trading post business still superficially resembled trade: lambs, wool, hides, rugs, and so on were brought in, evaluated, and exchanged for groceries and supplies or credit payments. Little cash changed hands, any more than it had in the 1920s or 1930s. Checks were treated as a counters of exchange also, to be paid not in cash but in food, clothes, and hardware. Welfare checks were now common, and along with the railroad payroll or unemployment payments they came to individual Navajos in care of the trading post, which was also the only place to "bank" checks. Banks remained nonexistent on the reservation. Traders thus knew exactly how much credit to allow those whose income came from wages and welfare, and they were careful not to let the amount of the bill exceed the amount of the paycheck or welfare check. There was frequently no cash given back for the check, since it paid the bill exactly.

Inevitably, most checks were spent at the trading post, which was the main, if not the only, supplier to the small reservation communities. Where there were several trading posts within reasonable distance, Navajos might stop at each; they sometimes had credit at more than one store, though usually if the trader knew a customer had other accounts he would refuse credit. In a radius of thirty to forty miles around Shonto, for example, there were Inscription House, Navajo Mountain, Red Lake, Cow Springs, Tsegi, and Kayenta trading posts. For Navajos living on Black Mesa or below Navajo Mountain, the distance between stores was far greater.

Nonetheless, each trading post had a certain natural territory from which it drew its customers, and in which it was the convenient place to shop, bank, trade, and receive mail. Moreover, credit accounts resulted in a tendency to shop at one post. Trading posts near the reservation border faced competition from a wider variety of stores and goods, but in the reservation interior the local trading posts were the only places to spend money and they had a virtual monopoly of local trade. If there was nothing left over from a check, this seemed in 1957 of no great consequence. There was little or no money "saved." The only savings, or the equivalent thereof, was in the form of silver jewelry, which could be sold or pawned. Sheep, perhaps, had been a type of savings in Navajo economics: they increased over time, they were there to fall back on in lean months or leaner years, they provided a family with visible (and countable) wealth, and their wool could be sold or woven into rugs for sale without touching the principal; but the Navajo had not been allowed to keep large herds of sheep. The trader supplied goods, but savings were not his métier either.

However, the new system of economics, of owing and paying bills, was familiar to Navajos of the 1950s. The traders did not hesitate to remind their customers of accounts due, but those men who went to work on the railroad in places far beyond the reservation boundaries sent money home to pay bills as well as to support their families. Bert Carter, from Shonto, working on the railroad in Barstow, California, wrote in fine, elegant handwriting to Reuben Heflin to settle his account: "Dear Reuben: I am going to enclose hundred dollars to you to pay my pawn and accounts. You must tell me about my account after I pay this much so I will know how much my account is. I know it was a hundred and thirty when I left there. I don't know how much it is now. . . . I am very happy about that I cridet there when I don't work. I hope you don't stop my wife cridet on my book. I am appreciate to let us cridet at your store."

Bert was not the only one. Henry Lee wrote from Los Angeles, sending $60.00, "while I have pay day today. And please let me know again." Foster Crank sent $35.25 from California: "If still life [leaves] some, tell me again."

Trading post customers had a very clear idea of adding and subtracting, and of asking for information on their accounts. Railroad workers were the big earners in these days, and their families were allowed to put groceries on the man's account while he was away.

Changes took place in the trading operations, too. At Carson's in the early days Stokes took all the items he traded for to the wholesale company, where they were accepted against his credit. Now he found his own dealers for each commodity. Salesmen also came to the trading post from companies selling coffee, drug store products, dry goods, and novelties. The trader was his own commodities exchange, though he had no difficulty tapping into the market since the network was already set up. Stokes continued to use one wholesaler for the bulk of his goods, but gradually he began to rely on many small firms to supply a greater variety of items.

The inventory carried by the trading post of the 1950s depended on location and the trader. Border stores carried basic items of food and the kinds of hardware that were always in demand: tin cups and bowls, lanterns, fabric. The more distant the store, the broader its inventory. Inscription House rarely carried many brands of the same product; instead it stocked a wide variety of goods. Neither the space nor the investment permitted a large inventory in one category. Stokes carried canned milk, canned peaches, and canned tomatoes, cornmeal, coffee, kerosene, calico, rope, buckets, coffee pots, and all the items he had carried in the past. But there were new products as well: pancake mix and sardines (fish was taboo for Navajos in the early days), tea bags, orange juice, and chairs. As well as horseshoe nails there were truck tires and brake fluid; as well as can openers there were toothbrushes, Kotex, watches, powder puffs, and billfolds. There was all the equipment needed to repair wagons, harnesses, and increasingly, pickup trucks. There were clothes of all varieties, including baby clothes, baby blankets, and baby powder. The store was crowded with goods; every corner, every shelf, every hook and beam on the ceiling was occupied. Inevitably, however, inventory ran low, sometimes ran out altogether, especially in basic foodstuffs. Though deliveries were now made to the post by wholesale firms, they were often delayed by storms or bad roads, besides which the rate of consumption was not easy to gauge. These were the travails of trading.

A manager came to Inscription House, but Stokes and Jessie never left. The family gathered at Thanksgiving and Christmas in Jessie's kitchen. Stokes was content to be busy. That, he thought, was the way to stay happy. The idea of returning to Farmington receded behind the tall hollyhocks and bright zinnias in Jessie's garden.

In 1956 Reuben bought the old Wetherill post in Kayenta. Sam Drolet

147

and Willard Leighton went into partnership to buy Shonto from Reuben. Willard was still a partner in Two Gray Hills Trading Post and was also interested in prospecting. When uranium was found on the reservation, both he and Reuben became excited enough to take out prospector's permits. "They now have an instrument on the market which definitely tells you, except when they set off atomic blasts in Nevada, if there is anything in the ground," wrote Mildred to Purviance. "We have had lots of fun anyway if we never make any money." The fun disappeared when it came time to do the accounts and buy wool, and the money always seemed to come in on the claim next door.

In 1956 Purviance retired from the San Francisco public school system, where he had taught for thirty-one years. He came out to Kayenta for a visit the following summer, and Mildred took him to Inscription House to meet Stokes and Jessie. He endeared himself to Jessie by washing the dishes for her. The kitchen at Inscription House had a window with a view into the garden behind the store, and Purviance could see the flowers and juniper trees and hear the conversation at the table behind him as he washed. Jessie had a rich sense of humor, quite equal and complementary to Stokes's. She later wrote to thank Purviance for his Christmas present of walnuts from his own trees and fruit cake: "Mr. P. your ivory soap is waiting for you to come back and wash dishes." She added more seriously that they had a new well, 930 feet deep; "Good water too." The important things were still water and roads.

The goods at Inscription House, as at most trading posts in the late 1950s, were still behind the counter. Each can of milk or axe handle had to be brought to the counter by Stokes, Jessie, or a clerk, the amount written down, either subtracted from the agreed value of the trade or added to the account, and then another item requested by the customer. Trader and customer would shift along the counter to different areas—to the hardware section, the dry-goods section, the fabric counter—so the purchasers could see exactly what they were getting and decide how much or what color. It was a careful process, with much pause for thought. Other customers would gather around a counter so that they would not be forgotten. Stokes would crack a joke—dry, gruff, good humored. Patience was a requirement, and Stokes had nowhere to go. He hired Freddie, who by then had a family, and when Freddie returned to Farmington he hired local Navajos. Sometimes the long purchase, the longer day, was wearying, but when in later years the shopping became quicker and adding machines computed faster, Stokes and his daughters found that they missed the exchanges that had taken place over the counter in slower days.

None of the Carson family claimed to speak Navajo; in fact, all spoke "trader Navajo," a jargon that made trade possible when a customer spoke little or no English. Trader Navajo was limited, both in grammar and vocabulary, but the Navajo put up with it, amused by the mistakes and mispronunciations, as the traders well knew. One got accustomed to being laughed at, and not merely for mispronunciations.

Every time the door opened into the store, a blaze of sunlight reflected off the white sand outside into the relative cool and dark of the store. Thick walls kept the heat at bay. The interior of the store seemed like another world. It smelled different, of leather, kerosene, and soap. The murmur of conversation filled the storeroom, quick-clipped English language, the rise and fall of sibilant Navajo phrases, all cut across by the old cash register bell. A vague hum came from the electric generator. There was no wind inside, and only when the door opened did its dry sighing and the rustle of sand blown over the doorstep make its constant presence felt. By the end of the day, Stokes's knees were weary and every pencil seemed to be too dull to write with. Every brown paper bag had columns of figures scribbled on it, and scraps of paper, bottle tops, and candy wrappers lay about the floor. After locking up, Stokes would turn out the lights in the store and limp back to the kitchen, to read a paper, eat supper, and enjoy the quiet evening and the cool air.

15

Skirmishes in the
War of Change

Chin and Ed, after ten years as managers, bought Oljato from Stokes in 1958. The trading post had fewer wool and sheep accounts now, and it remained small, basically unchanged from Mildred's days there. The store was the same tiny room, shelved from floor to ceiling, with goods under the counter and hanging from hooks on the beams and wooden posts. A cast-iron stove stood in the center of the floor; the entrance was small, and it was necessary to stoop slightly to enter. The only change, other than the airstrip, was the growth of tamarisk and bushes all around the store.

Despite the size, despite the shrinking livestock business, the store kept busy with those families who had other means of income. The seasons were marked not by wool and lambs but by the goods sold: plows, fencing, metal staples, and seed in spring; lumber, paint, stovepipes and occasionally stoves, quilts, and corn grinders in fall. Chin wrote to Purviance describing an average day at Oljato in 1959:

"Opened the store at 8:00. 1. One car waiting for gas. Bought $2.00 worth and went to Uranium mine to work. 2. No one in store until 8:30. Small boy brought in two goat skins. Paid him 25¢. He bought Cracker Jacks and gum. Asked for mail for his mother. 3. Man came in car to get gas, $3.50, and wanted to borrow hose (lending hose for that purpose) to fill water barrel at missionary's well. 4. Man and wife came in wagon. Had letter from daughter in school in Oregon. Wanted letter read to them, and also a letter written to her. Pawned a hat band for $8.00 to buy a basket and cloth for a Sing. The lady's mother is very sick. Everything quiet; no one around for about half an hour. 5. Boy brought in saddle blanket. Paid $3.00 for it. He wanted to buy a large sack of flour which cost $3.75. Bought coffee and sugar, salt and baking powder instead. Took all his groceries and left. Came back later to pawn bracelet for flour. Told him that he could go to school in two days, if he wanted to, but did not wish to go to school."

The morning had a dozen more small purchases, requests and pawns, until noon. "16. Another man came in to see if father had relief check. Wanted me to write to Tuba City Hospital to see how his brother-in-law was getting along. Broke his leg at squaw dance when he fell from his horse. Now about 12:30 so closed for lunch. Opened about 1:15. 17. One old man from Monument Valley waiting to get in. Didn't think much of the idea of being closed. Pawned a bracelet several months ago. Paid $5.00 on it. Wanted to buy a hat which cost $12.00. Only had $10.00, so charged the other $2.00 on the bracelet."

The flow of customers with minor purchases and exchanges continued until 6:00 P.M., when Chin closed the store. The major event of the day was a visit from a man from the uranium mine, who bought $15 worth of groceries and a $30-leather purse for his wife and paid $20 on his year-old account, but the trickle of customers who came for two or three items was typical. These were the daily operations of a post, except at times of lamb sales and shearing, when families shopped in quantity.

There were changes in the late 1950s at Carson's Trading Post that made it very different from the reservation posts. Much of the land surrounding it was owned by Navajos who had homesteaded or made claims for ownership, something that both Indian agents and Stokes himself had encouraged and helped with. In 1950, oil exploration and discovery increased and, by 1957, many families, or their descendents, who owned land were receiving money from leasing, royalties, as well as bonuses sometimes paid by oil companies. Much time and research was required to track down the Navajo owners. Families grew and moved, and often no one remembered ownership since land had always been there and had always been used by them. Like the BIA agents, oil companies used the trading post as a contact to help in finding someone from whom they wished to lease mineral rights. On the reservation, oil money went not to individuals, who could not own land, but to the tribal government, which used it for social programs.

Navajos in the Checkerboard region had increasingly greater access to work and to stores other than trading posts. However, the provision of credit and other services, gas and food, hardware and dry goods not stocked by Farmington stores, and in particular the purchase of rugs, wool, and sheep, kept Carson's in operation in changed times.

Developments surged on the reservation. A power plant was to be built across the San Juan River from Fruitland, from which the Navajo were to receive royalties and industrial potential. The Glen Canyon Dam was almost finished and had spawned a new border town called Page, sixty miles north of Shonto, with churches, liquor stores, motels, and supermarkets. Virtually every Navajo child in the 1960s attended school, and the tribe had been offering college scholarships to encourage their own professionals. For several years, X rays, polio vaccines (begun in 1955), blood tests, and prenatal care were taken into remote areas by mobile units as part of a concerted effort to improve the health of the Navajo. There were still many early deaths, accidents, suicides, and cases of alcoholism and related ills, but small victories over tuberculosis and trachoma had already been achieved.

In 1963 an election took place among the Navajo for a new tribal chairman. Raymond Nakai, who had been an announcer for a Navajo-language radio program from Flagstaff, was elected. During the next few years there followed struggles between the new party in power, headed by Nakai, and the "old guard." Norman Littell, still the tribal attorney, was allied with the old guard, and Nakai consequently wanted him banned from tribal council meetings. There were also court cases between the Department of the Interior and Littell in connection with his services to the tribe and the limits of his power. The struggles and power plays were part of the increased political activity—increased desire on the part of the leaders to wrest some autonomy from the BIA. Window Rock, the Navajo capital, was bustling, and tribal funds were growing larger from oil, gas, and uranium royalties.

At the trading post level, time brought other changes. The Carson grandchildren were now entering college. The two oldest Heflin daughters were at the University of Arizona, and Sharon Heflin and Raymond Drolet were in their last years of high school. There were more pickup trucks outside Inscription House, and more tourists; new roads were finally being built across the reservation. The highway was being paved from Flagstaff to Kayenta, and from Kayenta east to Shiprock. A few years before, Reuben had built a motel, the Wetherill Inn, in Kayenta, which provided accommodations for people who came to see Monument Valley and the ruins in Tsegi Canyon—Keet Seel and Betatakin—of which the National

Park Service, under agreement from the tribe, was guardian. The Wetherill Inn was one of the first regular motels in the interior of the reservation. Before that, visitors camped out, stayed with friends, or were put up for a small fee by those trading posts with guest hogans or cabins. When the new highway was begun a mile from Kayenta, Reuben applied to the tribe for a permit to build a motel on the highway. The route led to the Hopi Mesas and the Grand Canyon, and the gradual increase in tourists and other travelers made the proposal seem timely and practical.

At Oljato, Chin and Ed also saw more tourists, who came in small chartered planes to visit Monument Valley. The trading post, with its curio room full of baskets and rugs and jewelry as well as Ed's collection of firearms and Chin's miniature baskets, was cool and dark and as unfamiliar to the visitor as the scenery. Of the background of finance, deliveries, leases, regulations, distances, and weather, outsiders saw nothing. The old-fashioned charm of the long room full of armchairs and antiques and dark cedar beams seemed to come from a world without economic underpinnings. Ed would talk to visitors about stock reduction and its unfairness to the Navajo, but it was a problem of the past, with the patina of history, and few tourists realized how much it had affected the Navajo.

C. E. Purviance visited the Heflins in the summer of 1963, and he again went to see Stokes and Jessie, as well as Helen Hudgens. Helen had remarried several years earlier and was now the mother of another small daughter. Purviance faithfully continued to send presents. June Hudgens wrote that December to thank him: "Don't be surprised," she wrote, "I am married now and got a little baby girl, three months old." She lived at Kaibeto, she went on; her brother John was in Los Angeles; her brother Bill, also married, still lived at Shonto. She sent greetings from her mother at Shonto.

In many ways 1963 was a watershed year, for the traders and for the reservation, a year in which small changes began that would influence both in the years ahead. A hint of a change in attitude toward traders appeared in a Ph.D. dissertation written by anthropologist William Y. Adams in 1957 and published by the Smithsonian Institution in 1963 under the title *Shonto: A Study of the Role of the Trader in a Modern Navajo Community.* The book discussed trade and trading posts, describing details of trading and the community in depth, the daily routine, the credit system, pawn, mail, exchange of commodities, the details of railroad hiring at trading posts, and the life of the Navajo community around the post. Adams outlined the work, the community involvement, and the very specific position of the trader both as a supplier of foods and a point of contact with the Anglo society and jobs.

Adams perceived the role of trader as occurring in a colonial situation in which a dominant society, in the figure of the trader, behaved with classical paternalism toward another culture. Adams wrote that the trader had no time to be an anthropologist: "Every trader is physically a prisoner of his store day and night—the endless complex of activities connected not only with operating the business but also with looking after the physical plant."[1]

Adams discussed the traders' attempts to increase both the productivity and the purchasing power of their communities, attempts that were characteristic of traders in the remote areas. Traders near border towns, as Adams pointed out, were different, since they faced heavy competition and the long-term viability of their positions was always in question. The positive aspect of traders who worked to better the economy of their communities was in Adams's view balanced by the negative aspect of the dependence they tried to create and perpetuate among the Navajo. The role of the trader—of "culture broker"—was seen as powerful. Through his hands came not only the necessities of life but the opportunity for jobs. The trader was used to translate not only, in a literal sense, documents, but Anglo culture. For all these reasons he was a figure of heavy influence in any community. Yet he was to some extent a stranger to his own society, walking between two cultures, not quite immersed in either. In Adams's view, traders, sensing that change was coming, that the Navajo were becoming increasingly independent of them, strained to keep the old ways, the traditions, and the imbalance of power. The study of Shonto saw the trader of the 1950s as a conservative force, though he had been an agent of change in earlier decades. Not only did traders encourage tradition, concluded the report, they also kept the economies of the two societies apart. Adams wrote that "in advanced stages of culture contact, therefore, the trader may become the most influential single agent, either European or native, for the preservation of indigenous culture."[2]

Adams had grown up on the reservation, and his mother had been the director of education at Window Rock during the New Deal and later the director of placement and welfare. He had worked for Reuben at Shonto off and on when he was in college. While collecting data for his dissertation he had returned to the trading post to work. He mentioned to Reuben that he was studying the store, but for the most part he made unobtrusive observations of the behaviors of both the Navajo and the trader, no doubt because the study of behavior is made more difficult if its subjects are aware

155

of the observation. He did not feel totally accepted by traders in general. "My status as 'college kid' allowed me considerable leeway," he wrote in the opening chapter. "At the same time it undoubtedly stood in the way of full acceptance by traders as 'their kind of people.' "[3] He also set forth in the introduction his own biases: neutral toward the government, negative toward the Navajo tribal organization and many councilmen, positive toward Navajos collectively. He viewed change ambivalently, realizing its inevitability, realizing that for their own benefit the Navajo must adapt in order to survive.

Adams's thesis on Shonto was the first anthropological study of trading and traders as a bona fide dynamic cross-cultural situation, the first to perceive the subject as one worthy of academic observation. The study of culture and personality was a popular one in anthropology in the mid-1950s. The focus in Adams's work was not only on the cross-cultural situation in which the trader figured, but on the position of the trader himself. This concentration on the trader's role made the trader seem omnipotent, and in many ways he was. But in restricting the focus to this role, the study never showed the areas of Navajo life in which the trader took no part, nor the subtle ways the Navajo played against Anglo psychology and not infrequently won. Adams had, by virtue of his situation at the trading post, a deeper exposure to the trader than to the Navajo, a fact that gave the study a one-sidedness. As he himself pointed out, "The greatest danger of personal bias to the present study is that it may have led me to overestimate and overstate the importance of the trader in Navajo life and in Navajo–White relations. If this is so, it must be because I have not even yet entirely shed my own role as trader."[4]

The trader was powerful in the economic sphere, and in the transitional economy of the Navajo—between Bosque Redondo and tribal oil money—he was an important link between two economies as well as two cultures. Economic influence leaks into most compartments of life, but it is not the sole influence. Certainly traders themselves felt that they were not the ones in control. As Mildred wrote to Purviance, "We always felt like we were walking a tightrope in keeping on good terms with the Indians, the government, and the outside world." The Anglo society was unquestionably dominant, and traders represented it. Beyond that, they earned respect from the Navajo (if they earned it—many did not) on personal grounds. Only the Navajo decided which traders they liked and why, and their attitudes colored their trading patterns and behavior.

The study of Shonto, however, was a small part of a general change that led to the new points of view, the political actions, of the 1960s and

1970s. The new activism became powerful and dramatic, especially with regard to the struggle of minority groups for a voice and for power, as well as for a part of the affluence. The Navajos were not left out of this activity, though it reached the reservation relatively late. The actions most relevant to the Navajos were the attempts by minorities to fight old attitudes, to gain economic and political equality. The reservation was affected by the general stirring, though it was somewhat distant from the scene and received the news of the Vietnam War (though some Navajos fought in it), the demonstrations, and the sit-ins at universities, only through newspapers rather than direct experience. Adams's thesis might have been no more and no less than any other academic work on an interesting but remote topic were it not for the period in which it was published. As it was, his view of the trader, a somewhat negative view of a figure in a colonial situation, was adopted by those who took the new politics onto the reservation—Navajo students, the legal service for the tribe, researchers, and investigators.[5]

However, activism on the reservation was a few years away. In 1964 the main road across the northern section of the reservation, Route 160, was completely paved from Shiprock to Tuba City. Fueled by increased royalties from gas, uranium, coal, and oil, the tribe concentrated on social services. Schoolchildren were getting allowances for clothing to go to school—modern, new clothes as opposed to traditional dress or hand-me-downs. Mr. Purviance, who had for years arranged for a local church to send used clothing to the reservation, wrote in April 1964 to ask Mildred what was most needed. "I hardly know what to say," she answered. "At Oljato . . . each child has had five new outfits this year. . . . The situation in Kayenta is a little different but most of the children are in school and well clothed. However, I am sure coats and some warm underwear for the older people would be welcome. Reservation is changing fast."

Reuben and a partner were busy completing the new eighty-unit motel on the highway, and the Heflins had put the Wetherill Inn and Kayenta Trading Post up for sale. The Monument Valley Inn, as the new motel was called, opened in May 1965 with a ceremony attended by Philleo Nash, the commissioner of Indian Affairs, Raymond Nakai, and Norman Littell. The venture was an ambitious if solid one.[6] Tourism was increasing steadily across the reservation. The motel employed twenty Navajos at the time it opened, and the tribe was to get 7 percent of the profits. Reuben did not enjoy the success of his new motel long, however. Already the victim of one heart attack, he died in 1969 of another.

In economic matters the tribe was beginning to do well. Its return from oil and gas resources had been approximately $33 million in 1964, though the Department of the Interior claimed at the end of that year that the tribe's financial affairs were in chaos. The general superintendent of the Navajo Agency, Glenn R. Landbloom, was to work on sorting out the problem. For good measure, the BIA itself was to be given a routine audit. In part, the discordance between Nakai and the old guard in the council had resulted in less time and energy being available for the task of planning and organizing routine affairs.[7]

At the beginning of 1965, Lyndon Johnson was inaugurated, and both Raymond Nakai and Annie Wauneka, daughter of Chee Dodge, the late chairman of the tribal council, and an influential figure in the Navajo council, went to Washington for the ceremony. In March, as part of President Johnson's war on poverty, the Office of Economic Opportunity (OEO) made an anti-poverty grant to the Navajo tribe of $20,400. A special OEO office, the Office of Navajo Economic Opportunity (ONEO), was set up in Fort Defiance to serve the Navajo, and it channeled considerably more money onto the reservation over the next few years.[8]

In the border towns of the reservation, stores did a good business supplying Navajos who were better off or who lived nearby with those goods they could not get in the interior—automobiles, furniture, cheaper groceries, fashionable clothes, records, as well as modern conveniences such as toasters, hairdryers, and ovens. Many of these goods could be ordered through the trading posts, but they could not be stocked. The department stores now did for the Navajo what the trading posts had once done: they gave them a view of the way the other world lived.

Farmington, Gallup, and other border towns had had a long and uneasy association with the Navajo. Merchants had welcomed Navajo dollars and crafts, but not their presence, and they did little to make the Navajo feel welcome. Navajos who went to these towns often had to deal with hostility, discrimination, even violence. Newspaper accounts in the border towns form a tragic accompaniment to change: accounts of bar brawls, muggings of Navajos, and intoxicated Navajos killed or injured in road accidents, or occasionally frozen to death. The presence of liquor stores, not allowed on the reservation, was an added ingredient, and one that made some individuals quick to pawn, less careful where they went to do it.[9] Of unfair, even shady, dealings towards the Navajos, needless to say, there is no documentation.

Traders near Gallup and Winslow served communities that were quickly becoming acculturated. Sometimes these communities were better off because jobs were more accessible, sometimes poorer if those jobs failed to materialize or if the appeal of new goods as well as credit payments on automobiles left the people in debt. Frequently the traders near border towns survived because they gave credit and worked hard for a share of the Navajo dollar. But there were also stores with an atmosphere of hostile contempt, where the trader surrounded himself with a billy club and a gun, made certain that cash was never exchanged for a welfare check but only for pawn, was lax about regulations, especially those concerning the sale of pawn items, rarely bought rugs, saw no reason to stock fresh goods or new items, and, in short, made a travesty of the normal practices of posts in remote areas that enabled both Navajo and trader to benefit.

Nothing at Inscription House altered radically in the 1960s, although the clerks in the store were now Navajo and Stokes was proud of his progressive—and successful—hiring practices. The diesel generator, which powered not only lights but a refrigerator, and the modern gasoline pump outside the store, had been installed in the 1950s. Stokes had grown up in a time when one built or fixed whatever one needed. Telephone poles had to be cut and placed along the line, new outbuildings constructed, shelves and counters put in. Once, at Carson's, in the 1930s, Stokes wanted to move a small barn and had figured out how to do it with levers, a small piece of engineering that he and four or five Navajos had worked on together, and of which they were justly proud. Now that he was almost eighty, his troublesome knee no longer permitted him to build and fix, or to ride or walk around the corrals. He had no patience with the packaging of modern life, the superficial garnish, which only covered an old idea with a new guise; but technology brought comfort, saved time, kept one in touch, and Stokes approved of it.

Some modern conveniences were coming to the reservation. Electricity was slowly becoming available via lines from the new power plants. As the Navajo Tribal Utility Authority put it in a cartoon advertisement in the newspaper: "Electricity is the Key to Modern Living." But the spread of businesses was less speedy. [10] Large firms were beginning to look thoughtfully at the Navajo, but they needed the infrastructure of roads, lights, and a large pool of either literate labor or customers. Navajos themselves had no easier time setting up businesses, for, despite the availability of aid from the tribe, leases, insurance, and loans were still difficult for them to obtain. [11] H. T. Donald's problem at Tsegi in the 1950s continued to be a deterrent in the 1960s, a decade that saw few Navajo traders.

In 1966 the papers were full of Littell's legal struggles with the secretary of the interior, the competition for Navajo Beauty Queen, and the problems of the BIA. The Bureau seemed to be under attack from all around that year: from the tribe, from the Senate Interior Committee. There was a new commissioner for Indian Affairs, Robert Bennett, and the secretary of the interior hoped that there would be "new winds blowing" from the BIA. Stokes, like most traders, had no great regard for government bureaucracy, though he might like an individual agent. Too much paperwork was involved, with too little apparent result. The BIA staff came and went and seemed to know more about typing reports than about the Navajos.

In February 1967 OEO funded a legal-services center for the Navajo tribe: the "Dinebeiina Nahilna Be Agaditahe" ("Lawyers for the Restoration of Navajo Life") was set up in Window Rock to provide free legal services for reservation residents and to prepare cases for trial. The Civil Rights Act had been passed, and the DNA (as it was known), staffed by attorneys, law students, and Navajos, provided the legal instrument for ensuring these rights. Also in February, Norman Littell resigned as attorney for the tribe. (The U.S. Supreme Court had ruled on three years of litigation stating that the secretary of the interior could, if he found cause, remove Littell from his position). The tribe was divided over their opinion of their attorney, but the ruling upset many of them. It was, in effect, another example of the authority of the U.S. government over tribal affairs.

The next two years were full of motion and emotion, at least in Window Rock. The DNA was not universally approved of by the tribe, and its director, Theodore R. Mitchell, was expelled by them in August 1968—because of "personal, obnoxious conduct," as the *Navajo Times* put it, though it seemed possible that there were other reasons of a more political nature. "The Tribe has a right," said the paper, "to protect itself from obnoxious outsiders." More litigation over lawyers ensued, and the federal district court of appeals ordered Mitchell restored the following year. Mitchell offered his resignation to the OEO in Washington, and the board of directors of the DNA voted by a narrow margin to retain him. It seemed that the Navajo were to get liberal legal aid whether they chose it or not. Mitchell eventually resigned as director in 1970 and worked in the Law Reform Department of the DNA; Leo Haven, a Navajo who had been an administrator in the DNA, became the new director.[12]

Walter Hickell was sworn in as secretary of the interior in 1969, and the subject of termination—termination, that is, of the special status of the Indians and their reservation—was brought out again for discussion. The Navajo tribal council, which opposed termination, called for Hickell's removal.[13]

In September 1969, Gallup began to prepare, as it had for well over forty years, for the Intertribal Ceremonial, the centerpiece of tourism that drew people to the city from far and wide to watch the dances and rodeo events and to buy native crafts. This time, however, Navajo students took exception to what they increasingly began to feel was exploitation, a commercialization of ceremonies that were not meant for such purposes. Several students began to distribute leaflets entitled "When Our Grandfathers Carried Guns," and the city officials immediately ordered them to stop. Backed by the DNA, the students took the case to the district court. The following year, the suit was dismissed by the judge, but the *Gallup Independent*, which annually published a special edition for the Ceremonial containing articles on the history and culture of Southwestern Indians, mentioned that the 1970 Ceremonial was beginning "on an uncertain note." Student demonstrators continued their protest against the Ceremonial.[14]

Developments on the practical side included the growth of industry on the reservation. Fedmart, a large, low-price supermarket and department store, opened a branch in Window Rock in 1968. Fairchild Camera and Instrument Corporation completed a plant in Shiprock in 1969, hiring Navajos whom they planned to train to manufacture printed circuit boards. Long before the plant opened, Fairchild had been supporting entries in the Shiprock rodeo and advertising in the *Navajo Times*. In 1969 an electric power sub station was built at Kayenta, and electric lines were run to Gouldings and Oljato. The tribe granted a lease for a power plant at Page that would be fueled by coal from the Peabody Mine on Black Mesa and would supply Navajos with jobs and light.

Inevitably, the traders' operations came under fire. The Trading Committee of the tribal council, a group formed to oversee trading, though it was not very active, stirred into wakefulness and requested the traders, through an article in the *Navajo Times* in June 1969, to abide by the trading regulations.[15] It reminded them that their leases and licenses could be terminated if they violated these rules and pointed out three problem areas. First, the traders should not charge state sales taxes. Second, there could be no thirty-day deadlines on pawn, as were now common. The committee briefly outlined pawn regulations. A written receipt was required showing the transaction date, description of the pawn, the amount loaned against it, and the "true" market value. The pawn had to be held for a minimum of six months, unless the owner of the pawn had paid at least 25 percent of the amount five months after the date of pawning, in which case it had to be held for another two months. For every additional 25 percent of the amount due that was paid, an additional two months was added to the length of time the pawn had to be held. If the time had elapsed with no payments (i.e. eight months from date of receipt or two months from last payment if that payment brought the amount paid on the pawn up to 25 percent, 50 percent, or 75 percent) a pawn piece had to be displayed conspicuously for thirty days before it could be declared dead pawn and sold. Third, traders must pay in cash all checks mailed to them for individual Navajos, and no part of it could be held back by the trader to pay on accounts. The committee added, as a last point, a request for sales: "It seems strange that businesses outside the Navajo Nation often have sales, when they are over-stocked or when a special selling season has passed."

In August, the DNA filed a suit in the U.S. district court in which Theodore Mitchell charged the traders with credit saturation. This was the phrase William Adams had used (the brief quoted Adams) for the granting of credit by traders, describing it as a practice that absorbed most of the income of a community. From the traders' point of view, credit management (Stokes's own phrase) resembled less a sponge than a dam, to prevent the overextension of their customers' accounts. The DNA brought the suit against the secretary of the interior, Walter Hickell, the area director of the BIA, Graham Holmes, and the commissioner of Indian Affairs, Louis R. Bruce. Technically the responsibility for regulating trade and traders lay with the agencies these three men represented. No one trader was charged. Rather, the brief laid out the basic criticisms that would be taken up over the next four years: inferior quality of goods, high interest rates, dishonest weights, manipulation of the mail, monopoly over the area in which the post was located, and, due to an "egregious failure" by the commissioner, freedom of the traders to charge whatever price they chose. The court ruled against the suit, and the DNA took it through the long process of the appellate court.[16]

During the summer of 1969 a study was done under the auspices of a Window Rock Navajo-run research and development group, Southwestern Indian Development (SID), in which eight Navajo students went through the reservation to investigate trading posts. They studied fourteen of them: Greasewood, Beclabito, Ashcroft's (in Fort Defiance), Rough Rock, Rock Point, Piñon, Low Mountain, Red Rock, Toadlena, Brinks (halfway between Gallup and Shiprock), Shiprock, Steamboat, Cross Canyon, and Wide Ruins. The student investigators looked at the sanitation, physical premises, and, if the trader permitted it, account books, just as the government report of 1949 had done. Where the government investigators had found the traders cooperative, in fact almost eager to prove that their business was fair, the SID investigators found them, in the words of the report, "defensive and suspicious."[17]

The report, put out shortly afterward, claimed that trading posts were unsanitary, unsafe (because of the goods, including hardware, that hung from the ceilings), and expensive. Community members had told the investigators that traders were mean, and some said they could even get violent.[18] The investigators concluded that through his control of the community, and the high percentages of the markups, the trader could successfully "eliminate any risk of credit loss." The report listed comparative prices from each post, with percentages of the markups on each item. The latter ranged from 30 to 120 percent, as they had in the report of 1949. Pawn transactions were criticized as too vague, and time periods for redemption as too short. It also claimed that traders used the checks mailed to individual Navajos to pay the accounts of those individuals, and that the checks were never paid in cash in the full amount. "Navajo trade is the only retail business in modern America where the customer is always wrong," the report commented—and quoted a trader's joke from William Adams: "If you don't like it you can go to the store across the street."[19] The BIA did not enforce the regulations, the Trading Committee of the tribe had been inactive for years, the report found, and community residents were afraid to complain or protest. *Traders on the Navajo Reservation: A Report on the Economic Bondage of the Navajo People* was, in effect, a political statement. The directors of SID added a "Letter to the Reader" in which they denied a charge that the DNA had written the report or that "outside Anglo agitators" had conducted the investigation.[20] SID was, they insisted, entirely responsible for the contents. No matter what the Navajo did, they seemed to be questioned as the final authority, whether as employer, researcher, or political entity.

Such was the news that filled the local scene. Stokes, however, was interested more in national news than the activities of Window Rock, which were, in his view, tiresome, endless struggles. Washington had plenty of problems, the bureaucrats were making enough mistakes to fill a barrel, and he liked to grumble about them. The delivery of gasoline to Inscription House was made by Keith Red, and he and Stokes became friends over the signing of receipts grubbily fingerprinted with grease. They discussed America, Washington, government, and regulations with the insights and unhampered goals of the common man unrestricted by the red tape, paperwork, and codebooks. "Wait till I get to Washington," Stokes would say cheerfully, limping out to see Red to his tank truck, "We'll straighten things out."

If Stokes read about the SID report on trading (it was not widely published), the Trading Committee article, or the DNA case, he did not say much about them. Traders were becoming almost inured to criticism, referring to themselves with twisted amusement as "crooked Indian traders." Besides, Stokes had a clear conscience and a long one. The rules he abided by were his own, and they too were rigorous, though considerably less complicated than pawn loan percentages. Customers were to be treated fairly, and bills were to be paid. Life was difficult, and you needed all the help you could get, in return for which you gave other people help. He had been able to bring in a little work, money, and food to the community—to two or three communities—over his fifty years of trading and sheep ranching, and he was proud that he had been a help to his customers.

In the long run, Stokes believed that he owed his business all to Jessie; without her, without her work, he would have been a pretty sorry figure, he thought, not much of a man. Jessie was tough and loyal and she worked hard, and as a result they had traded and ranched and had four daughters working at four trading posts. So often the women ran the store. Remembering the days of scrubbing and fixing and counting and selling at Carson's, not to mention burying Navajos and waiting for customers and traveling about, he would say with a laugh, "Jessie made a mistake when she married me, and she knows it. Only she's too stubborn to admit it."

16

The Federal Trade Commission Goes to Battle

The political activity that began in the late 1960s continued into the 1970s. The DNA, acting for the tribe, brought suits against specific traders, and in April 1972 the BIA admitted that its regulations were "both inconsistent and ineffective," and that it was not an agency set up to deal with business practices.[1] Consequently the BIA decided to call on the Federal Trade Commission (FTC) to bring its expertise to bear on the situation and examine the business of trading posts. The FTC immediately began an investigation. Once again observers went out to the trading posts on the reservation, and a few that were outside its boundaries, to ask questions, and to look at prices, sanitation, pawn, and credit practices.

The DNA was clearly against the trader, and its staff of young attorneys, most of whom were not from the area (and thus, in a Southwesterner's eyes, not familiar with the conditions of life), succeeded in putting the traders on the defensive. Never very close to their fellow Anglo-Americans, traders retreated behind their counters, unwilling to talk or to trust either Anglos or Navajos who asked questions. When the FTC investigators came around, they met a gruff resistance, an unfriendly silence, from the men and women running the posts, who were not particularly interested in talking to another set of strangers and not eager to justify their behavior to those who so clearly came to criticize them.

There was not only a difference in generation and geographic background between traders and investigators, but in attitudes. There was little common ground between them even in experience. A new point of view toward Native Americans had appeared. Many people in earlier decades worked for a situation in which Indians would have rights and autonomy, among them Oliver La Farge and John Collier, as well as anthropologists and other social scientists.[2] Traders, perhaps, had been less visionary but no less active in the practical daily concerns of bringing in new education, a new economy, and new work, and they had strong feelings for the old Navajo ways. But now a modern wave swept over the Southwest. Political activist groups such as the American Indian Movement were militant and anti-trader. To many who were less militant, traders seemed to be symbols of old ways, and they became in part scapegoats for the Anglo world and the Navajo position in it.

On August 7, 1972, at a press conference in Los Angeles, the FTC announced a plan to hold hearings on trading at the end of the month.[3] The hearings were to take place at Window Rock on August 28 and 29, at Kayenta and Shiprock on August 30, at Crownpoint and Tuba City on August 31, and at Chinle and Piñon on September 1. They were to be open sessions at which complaints could be heard from Navajos as well as testimony from the DNA and tribal officials and from traders. An economics professor from the University of Wisconsin, Adlowe Larson, was called to give expert testimony on the trading system's price structure and financial efficiency, and the former director of SID, Charley John, was called to give information on the separate investigation that group had carried out in 1969. A lawyer representing the United Indian Traders' Association, Austin Roberts, was called to testify on behalf of the traders. Traders were also called to testify. The investigating board included Louis Bruce, commissioner of Indian Affairs, Ernest Stephens (himself a Native American), director of economic development for the BIA, Sandy McNabb, director of engineering for the BIA, Alfred Cortese, the assistant executive director for the FTC, and two regional directors of the FTC, Richard Lavine and George Zerwas.

On Monday, August 28, the hearings at Window Rock began with questions about the practices that were being objected to. Peter MacDonald, the tribal chairman, was the first witness, and he laid out the complaints against traders: the holding of welfare checks, the artificially inflated prices, the high interest rates, violations of the Truth in Lending Act, false accounting procedures, too little protection for pawn. He was followed by a representative from the DNA, Peterson Zah, who listed the major abuses as credit saturation, payment of livestock by credit slips for purchases at the store, and the practices of pawn loans, which, he claimed, violated the Truth in Lending Act.[4]

The investigating board began to question traders. Ed Foutz, of Shiprock Trading Post, was asked about his markup. He answered that it was 25 percent on groceries and 40 to 45 percent on hardware. His gross sales for 1971 were $450,000, of which he estimated his profit to be $20,000 to $30,000. He paid the tribe 1½ percent of his gross, which came to $6,750. Foutz stated, "We, like a lot of other trading posts, still carry a lot of credit which is risky. Our living conditions are high and we also have to furnish houses for our employees." Another trader, J. L. McGee, gave his 1971 gross sales at $360,000, his payment to the tribe $5,250, and his profits about $40,000. Both traders said the BIA had never audited their records.

Saul Price was then questioned. Price was chairman of the board of Fedmart, Inc., the chain that operated the supermarket in Window Rock: "A different kind of trader," as the *Gallup Independent* put it. The trading post, Price felt, was no longer an important institution, though he granted that it might have a place as a supplier of credit. Fedmart did not give credit, although large items could be purchased by monthly payments. He added, "When I was doing a survey of the trading post situation before we established the Fedmart in Window Rock four years ago, I was amazed and shocked at the prices they charged." The fact that trading posts, despite high prices, continued to do a good business had been one of the reasons that he had believed that Fedmart could make a profit with competitive prices. Price added that Fedmart's lease agreement with the tribe stipulated that the prices charged must be the same as those at other Fedmart stores. Lack of a state sales tax on the reservation also resulted in lower prices. Price gave Fedmart's gross sales at $7.5 million in 1971, but he did not give the store's profit. He believed there was enough business on the reservation for one or two more larger stores like Fedmart and a dozen small grocery stores "about the size of the '7 to 11' chain outlets." He said, in addition, that he had approached the tribe for his own company, but it had not responded positively.[5]

The following day the Window Rock hearings continued. Adlowe Larson, the economist, commented on the high prices at trading posts, which he pointed out were 27 percent higher than those in most other American communities. In his opinion, delivery and credit costs should only account for a few additional cents to the price, and in a free enterprise system there should be no reason for such high prices. "It may be claimed that differences in volume of business or scale of operations account for differences in prices charged," Larson said. "However, operations at trading posts are not small volumes." He stated that inefficiencies could be found. Not all posts were self-service and many stores were not adequately stocked. "Gross inefficiency," he concluded, "may explain high costs, but it is not an excuse for them and possible high prices [*sic*]."[6]

Larson was followed by Dennis Banks, national director of the American Indian Movement. Banks recommended that the traders pay the tribe $10 million dollars a year for the next ten years as a fine for the money they had taken from the Indian. In particular he criticized the Babbitts, whose wholesale outfit in Flagstaff had supplied traders for years and who also owned several trading posts on the reservation. "As long as the Babbitts remain, there will never be free enterprise on the Navajo Reservation," he said. After his testimony came Charley John, formerly director of SID, who said that once some traders received a Navajo's welfare check they would refuse to give him any cash until he paid off his account. This, he claimed, made the Navajo a "slave" to the trader, since the only money he might receive was from his welfare check. Finally, Michael Benson, who worked for the Gallup Indian Community Center, spoke briefly: "Traders use their ill-gotten power to get into school boards, . . . to sit on the OEO board which currently controls our poverty programs, and they even dare to define what we Indian people are and were through the sacrilege known as the Gallup Inter-Tribal Indian Ceremonial. The traders are a bastard gentry begotten through the rape of Navajo society, they are no more, no less." He did not give particular details of the problems with trading posts, but his testimony was an example of the attitudes of the more militant activists.[7]

Another set of hearings took place at Kayenta on Wednesday, August 30. They were attended by about half a dozen Navajos and several traders: Brad Blair of Kayenta Trading Post, John Zufelt of Warrens Trading Post, as well as Mildred Heflin, though she herself was no longer a trader since Reuben's death three years before. By now the newspapers were getting into the swing of things: "A type of slavery still exists on the Navajo Reservation," began the *Gallup Independent* report of the Kayenta hearings. "The slaveholders are traders who secure possession of a Navajo's welfare check and then refuses [*sic*] to convert it to cash."

Mrs. Maggie Bizardi, who lived near Kayenta and shopped at Warren Trading Post, gave the investigating board an account of her problems. "I don't want to trade there but I have no choice," she testified through an interpreter. Her account at Warren's was outstanding, and the checks, which she received through the post, were all taken by the trader to put against her bill. Having no cash, Mrs. Bizardi had no choice but to continue shopping at Warren's and crediting her account. She thought the prices were high and the food not always fresh. Bread that she bought there had been moldy, cookies stale, meat spoiled.

Sandy McNabb, who had noticed that not all the scheduled Navajo witnesses had turned up to testify at the hearings, asked Mrs. Bizardi about this: "Could it be possible that some of the witnesses that have failed to show have done so because traders have told them that they will give them no more credit if they come here and testify?" She responded that this was probably so. McNabb assured her that such action would be handled by the commissioner, who would consider filing criminal charges against any trader who appeared to be taking revenge by refusing credit. The board then questioned Mrs. Bizardi on her bill. What happened if her welfare check was higher than her grocery bill? She would, she said, receive a piece of paper showing how much money she had to her credit. Could she read English? No, she could not. Then how did she know that the trader was putting down the right figures? McNabb asked "Is it possible that he is cheating you?" "Yes," replied Mrs. Bizardi, "that is probably so." She was followed by other witnesses, among them a man who complained that Stokes had lost his pawn.

The hearings at Kayenta also brought positive testimony. Witnesses said that "some traders are honest and treat Indian customers with respect," and they mentioned Brad Blair in this connection.[8]

By now the hearings had become front page news, not only in local papers, but as far away as Denver and Los Angeles; journalists came out to the reservation to cover the events. After the Kayenta meeting, Mildred met a young reporter for the *Los Angeles Times* and suggested that he visit her father. Such a visit, she thought, would be as good a way as any for him to see the real trading post in operation. She could not imagine that anyone who talked to Stokes would not see the whole picture. The reporter, Robert Jones, drove to Inscription House, and Stokes greeted him with his usual gruff humor, the line all traders took. When he learned what Jones was doing he laughed. "I've been cheating the Indians for fifty years," he said jokingly, as Jones took notes and looked around the store. The story that appeared in the *Los Angeles Times* took the words so literally as to twist their meaning to fit popular impressions, a misunderstanding that seemed deliberate. "Halfway up the road to Navajo Mountain, O. J. Carson lives an uneasy alliance with the Indians around him. He is a white trader in the Navajo world selling his goods from a one-room store that smells of old leather and dust. Now half crippled, an old man, he opened his first trading post in 1916. But the Navajos believe he has cheated them ever since, and Carson's era, a vestige of the American

Frontier, may soon end. Inside Carson's Inscription House trading post the Navajos say little as they buy food or pawn jewelry."[9] The story was syndicated and appeared in other newspapers. After that, no trader would contemplate talking to a journalist.

Meanwhile, at the Shiprock hearings on August 30, Ernest Stephens promised new regulations within sixty days after the hearings, to be translated into Navajo and made available in booklets to be distributed to Navajo consumers and posted in every store. An ombudsman would be appointed, and in the interim an enforcement officer would be in authority to deal with abuses. Stopped credit would be considered as intimidation and would be dealt with severely. Following Stephens at the hearing, Mary Weaver, who lived at Teec Nos Pos, testified concerning her problems with pawn. She had pawned a bracelet at Barnard's Trading Post in Shiprock and received a brass token with a number on it as a receipt, but on returning three months later she was told that the bracelet had been sold. Mrs. Weaver noticed another bracelet in the pawn shelf that she had pawned earlier, and she asked if she could buy this one back. She told the committee that the trader "threw her out of the trading post physically and told her never to come back." She recovered the bracelet with the help of the DNA legal services. She had pawned it for $15—it was, she said, worth $100—and got it back for $17.[10]

A caseworker for the San Juan County Welfare Department said that receiving cash was a problem since welfare checks were accepted only if they were to buy groceries or pay credit accounts. At one trading post, food stamps were received by customers at the store and the trader insisted they be used in that store. A customer from Fruitland said that the trader always kept the part of the pawn ticket with the interest rate on it, and the trader picked up her checks from the post office and took them to the trading post. Ella Litson of Red Rock came to the stand to say that she had stopped trading at Red Rock because the trader was "always cheating me." She had bought $12 worth of groceries and found when she got home that he had added $20 to the bill; it was not, she said, the first time he had added to her bill. The food was often moldy there, and she would have to take it back. Though the trader replaced a loaf of bread for her, when she told him on another occasion that he often sold moldy oranges and tomatoes "he simply laughed." On the other hand, he did list the interest amount on the pawn ticket.[11]

The Crownpoint hearings on Thursday, August 31, took testimony from a trader named W. A. Palmer. He said that he always replaced spoiled food when a customer brought it back. In answer to a charge earlier in the day from a customer that he had lost or sold her pawn, he stated that he almost never lost pawn and he did not like to see it leave the area, and so preferred not to sell pawn. Asked about his markup, he said it was 25 percent on most products, 100 percent on some items. His store grossed less than $500,000, and his profit was on file with the BIA where anyone could check it. Most traders, he claimed, tried to do a good job, but most were vague on the specifics of the regulations that he felt—and it seemed that everyone felt—needed to be revised. A better understanding of regulations was needed, in his opinion, by both traders and customers.[12]

Meanwhile, at Tuba City, new regulations were also the major topic. Sandy McNabb pointed out that they would protect everyone, and that it was not the intention of the BIA to prevent the trader from making a fair profit. He repeated that he wanted the regulations translated and available to Navajos. McNabb was followed by a Navajo employee of the Tuba City trading post, who voiced complaints that stemmed from work at a post. He claimed there was no extra money for overtime, only minimum wages, no fringe benefits—sick leave and paid vacations came only after five years of working—and no discounts on purchases made at the store. He added that the store employees' paychecks were used to pay their accounts, with only the balance given to them in cash. What was more, the trader's wife would add to the bills of anyone she did not like.[13]

The hearings ended with simultaneous sessions at Piñon and Chinle. George Vlassis, a general counsel for the tribe, had been subpoenaed to answer questions on a possible conflict of interest between his law firm and the tribe, since a member of his staff, Bruce Babbitt, was related to the Babbitt Brothers trading firm. Vlassis stated that Babbitt held no stock in the trading firm. Further, Vlassis pointed out that the Department of the Interior, of which the BIA was a division, had a built-in conflict among its responsibilities to the Bureau of Land Management, to the Bureau of Reclamation, and to other federal agencies, all of whose interests were in opposition to those of the Navajo. The investigating board asked him who should draw up and administer trading regulations. He suggested that the tribe be responsible. How could that be, he was asked, "when the Tribe has not been very effective in enforcing the present regulations?" Vlassis replied that the tribe had been told by the BIA that it had no jurisdiction over traders. He was, in fact, tart, and he added that the hearings "in their zeal to root out evil had displayed a reckless disregard for the facts."[14]

With the end of the hearings, there was a general consensus that new regulations were needed. That there were problems in trading was obvious, and the major one seemed to be the cashing of checks, or rather the failure to do so, and the traders' insistence that checks be used to pay off accounts. Pawn and prices, spoiled food, lack of respect, hiring practices, and employment were all matters for complaints. With changing times, the Navajo, especially the younger ones, recognized that the trading post system was not the way of the rest of America, and they put in a claim for equal goods, and equal treatment, for automobile dealers and 7–11 stores, for supermarkets and Truth-in-Lending laws. Traders, on the other hand, were faced with the problem of credit. The Navajo, like the rest of America, found it easier to spend money on credit than to pay their bills, but unlike the rest of America they had less opportunity to earn the money they needed. Both welfare and employment checks had been handled rather like commodities and were exchanged for goods or as credit for goods. No doubt this had suited both Navajos and traders in the past, until there developed a variety of stores that Navajos could reach by automobile to purchase new goods, but for which money was needed. The trader was then in competition for the dollars that had once come almost exclusively to his store. The Navajo wanted checks converted to cash. The trader fought for the payment of his bills. The tactics employed by both were not always fair, but the access to the post office gave traders the upper hand. The Navajo, in return, shook a pound or two of salt into damp wool to increase its weight, and let their sheep go thirsty until just before sale, when they would be given water, for the same reason. Many Navajo complaints came from misunderstandings, and others came from justified resentment of a trader's arrogance. The hearings provided people with a forum for criticism, and they used it.

Traders were accused of hiring those who shopped at their store or who had large bills or pawn. The traders themselves found this an illogical charge, since outstanding credit indicated need. For the traders, need and some knowledge of a Navajo's reputation and reliability were sufficient criteria for hiring. Furthermore, Navajo society ran on networks of kin and clan rather than by the Anglo system, in which an attempt was made to regulate relations (as existed, for example, in work) between people who were essentially strangers. The networks with which a trading post was able to tie itself to the community were in no small degree a reason for its survival. Times were changing, however, and upon the realization that the Anglo world operated differently, Navajos found fault with the trader system. Over and above the justified complaints was the political statement of the Navajo. The hearings constituted a show of strength, a maneuver for equality.

A few weeks after the hearings were over, Stokes received a summons to appear before the FTC investigative committee in Gallup. He was to answer the charges that had been made against him concerning a piece of pawn, and to submit to questions regarding his business practices and procedures. As far as Stokes was concerned, the summons itself constituted a charge of wrongdoing, a criticism of his way of life, and he took it very hard. The Navajo Agency had never taken action against him, and he had been left alone to deal as best he could with the vagaries of trade. He did not understand the bold new radical tide that swept the country. His response had to be with specific and personal details. He brought out his books, his tax returns, his pawn tickets, and with a lawyer from Farmington went over the store's paperwork. The family gathered around to give him support. Marie had been staying at Inscription House, off and on, to help her parents (Willard had died in 1959); Jessie could no longer see very well and Stokes had taken over the bookkeeping. Jo came to drive him to Gallup, and Mildred and Chin came over to console Jessie at Inscription House.

The little party, Stokes, Jo, Marie, and the lawyer, drove to Gallup the day before his interview. Stokes had more trouble getting around, as a result of his bad knee, and he used a metal walker. However, he rarely took it on his infrequent trips to town, and he did not take it now. Mildred watched him climb stiffly into the car, dignified and still handsome at eighty-five, but grim and serious, dreading the ordeal as one might dread a jail sentence.

The federal building, newly completed, sat on a hill at the center of Gallup, next to the McKinley County courthouse. The courthouse had been built in 1938, a red stone building with halls lined in gay colored tiles, hung with tin lanterns, decorated with beams, carved wooden finials, stained glass—the details of Southwestern architecture that earlier public buildings loved to use. The new federal building was gleaming and modern, made of polished stone, concrete, steel, and glass, though its interior was plain, the only decoration the doors along the corridors. The Department of Agriculture, the Forest Service, the Railroad Retirement Board, and the BIA all had offices here. The Carsons and their lawyer were taken to a room where Stokes was questioned minutely by an investigatory committee lawyer. The lawyer asked questions about Stokes's methods, his sales and profits, his practices with pawn and with purchases, with hiring and pricing—the same questions other traders had been asked during the hearings. The questioning was unemotional, dry, and straightforward, far less of an ordeal than the family had expected. When it was

173

over, Jo took her father back out into the warm streets to the car. The trains rattled through the railway yards at the foot of the hill; it was another ordinary autumn day for Gallup. The Carsons drove to Farmington with a sense of relief.

Several points can be extracted from the hearings, apart from the political aspect. Trading had acquired a dubious reputation. Following the increase in tourism from the 1940s on, a host of so-called trading posts had sprung up along major off-reservation routes, thus avoiding the problems and no doubt the unprofitability of licensing, bond money, and regulations of regular posts. Such stores used the appeal of the phrase *trading post* and the vague knowledge among visitors that such stores existed in "Indian country" to attract Indians, from whom they accepted pawn, and tourists. They were not bound by BIA regulations, which those Navajos who went there to pawn may not have realized, nor did they have the means of contacting or informing pawn clients of impending due dates. Imitation jewelry was usually sold also, at very real prices. As mentioned earlier, trading posts in and near Gallup and other border towns, which had no community in the old sense and no dealings in wool or lambs, had become more involved in the pawning that went on in proximity to large towns and had suffered increasing competition from other stores, which, giving no credit, were first to receive a Navajo's cash. The situation on the reservation borders was always more tenuous, more fraught with problems between Anglo and Navajo. Many attempts had been made over the years to deprive Navajos of land allotments.[15] These problems were not necessarily all instigated by traders, but nonetheless traders were Anglos and thus suspect.

As for on-reservation trading posts, trading regulations had always existed, but were not administered with stringency. The BIA tended to leave traders alone, and though there existed a system both through the BIA and through the tribal trading committee for making complaints, it was not much used by Navajos, either because of distance, reluctance, or plain misunderstanding of the system. In one sense, the hearings were part of an internal dispute between government agencies: criticism of the BIA by the DNA (no less a government branch despite its activities at Window Rock against the BIA), investigated by the FTC. The DNA lawyers pointed out that the BIA had the legal responsibility of overseeing trade with all Indians. The FTC had little or nothing to do with such matters but had been called in by the BIA for their knowledge of business in the increasing complexity of twentieth-century trade. At the same time, the hearings were used by Navajos to bring a sense of accountability to the Anglos with whom they had dealings, whether or not those Anglos were responsible for unfair practices.

Trading had begun in a frontier mode, and the independent attitudes and behavior of frontier people had made trade with the Navajo possible: a disregard for possible danger, and an ability to struggle along on a shoe-string budget and to build and mend and barter in a different language. Technically the frontier had disappeared with the nineteenth century. Frontier attitudes of independence (most especially in the matter of debt collection) continued into the third quarter of the twentieth century and played a part in making the cross-cultural trade possible. Individualistic entrepreneurs, however, were no longer seen as commendable. Once barter decreased and welfare checks increased, the situation between those Navajos who could not read English and the traders and postmasters who could became fraught with temptation. Not all traders resisted it. The matter of checks was clearly in need of some firmer control.

Adams's study of trading had seen the trader as a dominant colonial figure resisting change and attempting to maintain dependency in his customers, which gave him power. Probably, however, most traders did not have such a clear goal. Rather, they attempted to manage trade, stay solvent at least, if possible make a profit, and somehow balance the rewards and drawbacks of trading life. Perhaps the idea of profit, especially if made from a less privileged group, did not sit well with the ideals of many of the reformers.

Traders had, moreover, an ambivalent relation with their own society. Their relations with the Navajo were in some ways closer than those with other Anglos. The life of traders lay in the Navajo community, despite their ability to move about, even to change trading posts. Many traders, or their sons, married Navajo women. The militant spirit of the 1960s and 1970s misunderstood traders, both their position between two cultures and the specific problems of their lives. The ideals that were being fought for lay beyond the compromises of daily life that traders lived. And traders, like many others in America as well as among the Navajo, were not comfortable with quick change and tended to be conservative. Though this was seen by Anglos as an admirable attitude among Native Americans, it was not approved of by the young in their own elders.

New regulations, however, were overdue. The last revisions dated from 1949 and had faded in everyone's memories, including those of the BIA officials. During the hearings, a former area director for the Navajo Service, Graham Holmes (who now worked for the tribe), was asked whether he had ever received complaints during his five years with the BIA. He said that he had, and that his response had been to write and talk to the trader concerned. He had closed down one post for not complying with the sanitation code, but he felt that the regulations were too vague and gave the BIA too little authority to close down stores that were in violation.[16] Traders questioned during the hearings regarding the enforcement of regulations answered that the BIA officials often told them that they were at their trading post "by the invitation of the Indians." The lease reminded them of it, had they forgotten. Though the last leases granted were for twenty-five years (dating from the mid-1950s, this left about eight years on the leases), there was no provision for renewal, and rumor had it that when the leases expired, the buildings and equipment would revert to the tribe. This impermanence, with its vague threat to the investment of traders in their leaseholds, added to their sense of insecurity and their reluctance to modernize. With no visible reinforcement of new business practices, trading had not moved with the times. Not infrequently, the old-fashioned aspect of trading posts was what made elderly Navajos feel at home, but the antiquated equipment and its failures also created old-fashioned problems.

17

Aftermath

After the FTC hearings, traders went back to their posts and business continued. Some were resentful, others took it in stride. A few customers who had testified came to tell them they had been "pushed" to do it, but whether that was true or merely a means of avoiding trouble would be hard to determine. In the months following the hearings, the BIA worked on new regulations, which, it was stressed, were not meant to discourage traders, nor to prevent them from making a fair profit. The FTC published a staff report, *The Trading Post System on the Navajo Reservation*, in June 1973. It was not complimentary: "The anachronistic trading post continues to exert significant influence on the Navajo reservation. The trader engages in abusive practices, detailed below, which in turn permit him to maintain his monopoly."[1] The report was not only negative toward traders, it criticized the BIA and the Navajo Tribe for not enforcing and revising regulations, for not controlling trade more carefully.

After a brief history of the Navajo and of trading, the report turned to abusive trading practices, beginning with the position of the trader in the community: "To the unsophisticated Navajo consumer," explained the report, "the trader represents dominant white society. He offers the hallmarks of an industrial economy; he understands how this economy functions. In contrast, many Navajos do not even know how to read numbers."[2] The prices charged at trading posts were, it stated, "unconscionable," and practices monopolistic. The report went on to say that "the trader maintains his monopoly through the geographic isolation of Navajo residents. . . . Despite the mobility of some Navajos, however, great distances create a dependence on the local trader for day-to-day purchases.

"The most formidable method by which the trader attains a monopoly over the Navajo consumer community is through credit saturation. This term refers to a practice whereby the trader extends credit up to his customer's known periodic income. By being constantly indebted to the trading post, the Navajo consumer exists in a state of economic indenture.

"The Navajo trader recognizes that his future prosperity is contingent upon reducing alternative markets available to his patrons. Various unfair, abusive and deceptive practices are employed to preserve the trader monopoly and to maintain the economic captivity of these people. These practices concern virtually every facet of the trading post operation.

"Many traders are honest and conscientious business men who contribute to the welfare of their communities. Even some of these traders, however, engage in questionable practices which impede economic alternatives to the Navajo consumer."[3] These practices included defrauding customers, adding to their accounts, and enlarging their shopping totals. Since prices were unmarked, customers could not compare the value of different articles.

The report criticized pawning heavily, claiming that "some of the most offensive trader practices involved pawned Navajo items." The formula for redeeming pawn was confusing and the pledgor did not receive the market value for the pawn piece. When pawn went dead, the trader "pockets any excess over the amount borrowed." "Many traders never sell pawned items and retain pledges for years," commented the report. "Traders assert that the sale of pawn, whether forfeited or not, created needless ill-will in their communities. Unfortunately, other traders do not adopt this altruistic attitude. Pawn is commonly sold before expiration of the redemption period."[4]

Sanitation was insufficient, the report continued, and not every post refunded spoiled goods. Weights and measures were suspect. The purchase of rugs, wool, and livestock exploited the Navajo, and as employees they were consistently underpaid. Last, the trader, as an employment agent for the community—a powerful position—"often prefers those having credit accounts or pawned items at his trading post. The trader then sells the chosen employee the clothing and supplies demanded by the position and sometimes even transportation to the job. When the job is completed, the Navajo is expected to return to the post with his check. If he does not, he may expect not to be hired again." Trading posts themselves hired

Navajos, but often the trading post ran its operation with help from the trader's wife, children, or relatives.[5]

The report completed this detailed account of problems by commenting on trader attitudes: "Navajos complaining about abusive trading practices often assert that traders lack respect for them or for the Navajo people. When complaints are directed to traders, the Navajo is silenced by the perennial, curt reply: 'If you don't like it you can go to the store across the street.' The nearest store is typically located twenty miles down a rutted dirt road."[6]

That the report was, though unintentionally, uncomplimentary to the Navajo as well, depicting them as dupes to the traders' dishonesty through ignorance, illiteracy, and naivete, went unnoticed. Describing the trader monopoly, the report read "First, the trader's monopoly rests upon ignorance and poverty. Many Navajos are illiterate; most are unsophisticated in commercial transactions. A debilitating cycle of Navajo destitution and naivete permits the trading post to attain monopolistic stature. The monopoly is then perpetuated by exploiting the Navajos' indigence and privations."[7]

It is certainly worth asking whether such indigence and naivete existed among the Navajos in the second half of the twentieth century. Traders had come to have a healthy respect for the quick wits, the understanding of exchange and trade, the persistence, and the general unruffled, even bold, behavior of their customers. By the 1960s there were few Navajos who could not add, subtract, and understand prices. Although the traders always had the upper hand, and although relations between traders and Navajos were anything but perfect, a Navajo had the ability to make a trader feel the limits of his power. A trader could be laughed at in ways that reduced his stature. Because he was an outsider, cheating was considered fair game, and sheer persistence worn down many a trader's patience and resolve, whether to keep his peace or to refuse a loan. But in an escalation of bad feelings the trader had the upper hand.[8] If the FTC achieved anything, it brought about a shift in power, a change of atmosphere at the trading post. This was due in no small part to the Navajo themselves, who by their testimony at the hearings had made a political statement.

Stokes returned to Inscription House and the daily routine. No further charges came out of the hearings. The FTC's report on the traders and the BIA's revision of regulations were considered sufficient. Though the new regulations were pored over by other traders, Stokes had other preoccupations. His health was deteriorating, and doctors diagnosed throat cancer. He received treatment and for a while felt better, and he could enjoy the fact that two of his grandchildren were beginning to learn the business of trading. Chin's daughter, Wy, married a young trader, and Jo's son, Raymond, began to work at Shonto after finishing college. If traders were on the way out, to be replaced by supermarkets and convenience stores, it would not happen immediately.

The new regulations for trade on all reservations included several revisions. A trader was still required to obtain a license from the Indian commissioner costing between $50 and $300 depending upon gross receipts, and to post a bond of $10,000. The new provisions required insurance on the value of buildings and average inventory. The trader had to win the approval of the local chapter before being granted a lease. The chapter could hear any customer complaints and refuse to give formal approval for the trader's lease. Furthermore, traders had to attend semiannual public meetings at the local chapter to hear and answer complaints.

Prices had to be marked. Sanitation must meet approved standards, and health regulations covering food handling must be observed. The trader, his manager, or an employee authorized to "conduct business"—presumably the buying and selling of products, the granting of loans and credit—had to be available on the premises. Checks brought by Navajos to be cashed at the post had to be paid in full, with no holding back of any amount to pay bills, though the trader could advise the customer on the amount of his debt. Payment for crafts or services could not be made by trade slips, only by cash or check. A statement of ownership of the lease had to be displayed in the trading post. Mail could not be withheld. Imitation native crafts could not be sold. Traders were to make no contributions to tribal politics. They could not retaliate against customers who complained. BIA personnel, as before, could have no involvement in trading. The trader could not give gifts to Indians, either to individuals or at a Sing.

Furthermore, the regulations required an additional license for a trader to deal in livestock. In order to give credit, the trader had to obtain an application form filled out by the customer on which was stated the maximum amount allowed, the conditions of any finance charge, and any minimum monthly payments. If monthly payments *were* required, the trader had to send monthly statements showing the finance charge and the dates of payment. All this had to be in writing, the regulations stated firmly, regardless of the customer's ability to read or speak English. For Anglo law to support the customer, an Anglo system of records had to accompany the transaction. The regulations themselves covered Indian customers, but the law to which customers could turn—specifically, the regulations mentioned the Truth in Lending Act—was U.S. law. Last, the finance charge could not exceed 24 percent.

Trading post audits had to be carried out by the commissioner of Indian Affairs, and a price survey done regularly on flour, sugar, eggs, lard, coffee, ground beef, bread, cheese, fresh milk, canned fruit, and other goods, with the result printed and sent out by the BIA and displayed in the store. The commissioner had the power to order any exorbitant prices lowered. Records had to be kept according to standard accounting practices, but a "model bookkeeping system" could be suggested at a later date. This, at any rate, was unchanged from earlier times. No one had yet been able to come up with such a model system. Account and records should be filed with the BIA and the Navajo Tribe.

The new regulations gave lengthy attention to pawning because the subject had aroused the most consistent complaints over time. To pawn, a trader had to have a pawnbroker license, in addition to his trading license, and further bond for $25,000 over and above his trading bond. Every pawn transaction had to be accompanied by receipts recording such data as names, dates, census and social security number of the pawner, value and description of pawn, the loan amount in cash or credit, the finance charge, the amount financed, and the dates and amounts of payments to be made. Pawn had to be held at least twelve months and could not be sold for thirty days following the end of the twelve-month period. If the pawn was going dead, the fact had to be made public and notices of default mailed. When the pawn was sold, the name and address of the purchaser and the amount received from the sale had to be noted, and any surplus over the loan and finance charge (minus any costs of the sale) returned to the original owner. Pawn could be redeemed (if all charges were paid) up to the day of the sale and could not be sold after twelve months from the date of notice of the sale; in other words, if no one came to buy dead pawn, the pledgor could still redeem the piece. Lost pawn tickets were not to constitute a problem or create any extra charges.

To a man, traders ceased to deal with pawn. Pawning had been a daily activity, as Chin Smith's account of a day at Oljato in 1957 witnessed (see Chapter 15). Accepting pawn had often been a convenience to the customers. As W. A. Palmer had testified at the hearings, many traders felt reluctant to let pawn jewelry go out of the community and held pieces long after dates of expiration. Much recent pawn was not valuable jewelry but small bracelets or rings, even Timex watches, old Pendleton blankets, rifles, saddles, cradle boards, and dimestore beads, a point not entertained by the hearings. The newly required paperwork of pawn seemed onerous, and traders felt that it was still possible for problems to arise for which they would be held accountable. The DNA assured them that they could legally charge 120 percent, as pawnshops in New Mexico did. To the Navajo the cessation of pawn transactions was a startling and unexpected result of the regulations, and many must have assumed it was revenge. Pawn did not cease, but it moved off the reservation to trading posts and pawnshops that had no ties to a community. The DNA briefly considered suing the traders for conspiring against their customers but dropped the idea. Credit continued, though a few trading posts, including Oljato, ceased that too. Livestock was becoming far less prevalent, and the tribe now had a livestock-purchasing program. Wool and crafts continued to constitute an important part of the daily business.

Stokes's lease still had about six years left on it in 1974, but he would not need them. Overtaken by illness, he finally entered a hospital in Tuba City. He died on October 14, 1974, at the age of eighty-eight. Jessie lived another six months. She had had what the family realized were a series of small strokes, and her memory failed. Jo and Mildred in turn took care of her until her death on April 12, 1975, and she was buried beside Stokes in a graveyard in Farmington.

Part V

1983

18

Epilogue

Some fifteen years have passed since the dramatic investigation of trading. The reservation had changed, but trading posts are still in business in remote areas. Professional careers as well as wage work are more prevalent, but the traditional economic resources of sheep, wool, rugs, blankets, jewelry, pottery, and other crafts continue. Modern life is slowly creating visible change, although the less attractive aspects, billboards and neon, traffic jams, concrete, are still absent from the landscape. Tourists come in thousands. The landscape swallows them up, and they visit trading posts frequently and assure the purchase of crafts.

Convenience stores have grown up along major routes, providing cheap gasoline and a limited inventory of useful goods. Their prices are no lower and often higher than those of trading posts, and they give no credit or service. The corporations owning the stores have agreed to train Navajos, over time, as managers. All stores—trading posts, convenience stores, gas stations, fast-food chains—hire Navajos. Supermarkets did not immediately take up the challenge of Fedmart's chairman to move onto the reservation. The next supermarket, Bashas', was built in Chinle in 1981, almost ten years later. Bashas' is large, has an inventory that goes from Chinese food to watermelon, and has prices among the lowest on the reservation. In 1983 the finishing touches were put on another supermarket in Tuba City, one belonging to the same chain. What this will do to competition, and thus prices, remains to be seen.

In the meantime, trading posts have grown larger. The stores have been increasingly rearranged into self-service units, the high counters have been removed or replaced by lower ones, and modern heating and cooling systems have been installed. Most posts keep a stove for extra heat and for customers to stand by for warmth. Very little has changed in the external appearance of old posts. They are still to be recognized by their unmistakable architecture—square, rambling, with additions in various styles or materials, surrounded by corrals of weathered, gray cottonwood fences. Newer stores range from handsome local stone to modern prefabricated materials. One trading post, Baby Rocks, put in the 1960s, has exceptionally handsome architecture. Built out of large, irregular slabs of local stone in the form of a double hogan—a figure eight—it both captures the eye and blends into the red cliffs that rise behind it. But at all posts the sign, if one exists at all, is small. The gas pump is the single obvious distinguishing feature, often accompanied by a soft-drink-dispensing machine. A board may announce the purchase of lambs or wool, or list some of the goods, especially building materials, that are sold.

Kayenta and Shiprock trading posts are now virtually supermarkets, with large and varied inventories, many brands, and good butchers. Only the aisle that displays homespun wool and the counter full of jewelry and baskets hint at the other trading operations. Smaller posts still provide a wide range of traditional items of trade such as velvet, rawhide, tin cookware, kerosene, and lamps and stoves—but they also stock car parts, bed linens, radios, crock pots, yogurt, and sandwiches. A few can no longer survive the competition and struggle—or seem content to fade away—with an inventory that consists of gasoline, Pampers, ice cream, and a few canned goods. Undoubtedly these tiny stores provide some services, buying lambs and wool or cashing checks, but they provide little else. Other posts, though small, try to attract customers, and in order to do this they have special sales, novelty goods, or an inventory solid in some items, like car parts, which the trader has discovered the community needs. Two Gray Hills and Nazlini (by now probably others) have installed video games. Some trading posts offer furniture and most sell, or will order from their suppliers, stoves or large household appliances. Posts still provide most of the services rendered in the past: credit, loans, the purchase of commodities, the connection to a few jobs. One large trading post in Tuba City takes pawn, but it is the only place on the reservation that will.

Mildred has retired to Flagstaff, and Marie to Farmington, though she still holds the lease on Two Gray Hills and spends time there. Derrold Stock, Marie's long-time partner in the post, died a few years ago, and now a young couple who had worked at Shonto and at Many Farms Trading Post manage it. In 1983 Joe and Sam continue to run Carson's; Chin and Ed remain at Oljato.[1] Gouldings, on the other side of the mesa, is now a pleasant motel, and the old store is a crafts shop selling rugs, jewelry, and other Southwestern goods to tourists. The Gouldings themselves retired to a trailer park across Lake Powell several years ago, and when they did so they sold the store to the University of Illinois with the idea of using the profits to create scholarships there for the Navajo students. However, the university sold the store, which is now a motel and craft shop.

Freddie and his wife, Alice, also retired to Farmington, though that is hardly the word to describe their busy life: Freddie works at the Russell Foutz Indian Room, which carries fine rugs from many parts of the reservation, baskets, belts, "sandpaintings"—the commercial paintings made with colored sand that now constitute a genre of Navajo artistic work—jewelry, and raw materials for use by Navajo silversmiths. Freddie sees many people that he recognizes from his trading years, though it is more often they that recognize him; many were children when he last saw them.

Window Rock is rapidly expanding. A large shopping center surrounds Fedmart. New tribal buildings have been added to the stone administration buildings of the New Deal and the ubiquitous trailers that are stopgap offices for a rapidly expanding Navajo bureaucracy. There is also a new tribal museum, with exhibits labeled in Navajo and English that show the land, the early Navajo history, the period at Bosque Redondo, the farming methods and tools, the clothes worn, and the means of transportation. In one corner stands a life-size display of a trading post, with high counter and shelves of boxes and tins and bottles, all the old brands, Arbuckle's Coffee, Mentholatum. Bolts of calico, an antique cash register, are all there, as well as examples of *seco*—the metal counters that many trading posts used at the turn of the century. Goods hang from the ceiling. There is even a white papier-mâché model of a trader leaning on the counter. The trading post is part of Navajo history, Navajo in its surroundings, its customers, its goods and exchanges, though not in its ownership.

Trading posts no longer monopolize contracts between Anglos and Navajos; in fact, they have not done so for at least twenty-five years. Chapter houses and federal and tribal officials, schools, and clinics provide new links between the two cultures.[2]

Carson's Trading Post is much the same, perched on the sandstone slope above Gallegos Wash, buffeted by the dry winds that bothered Jessie Carson. Farmington supermarkets are close, and cheap, and thus food has become a less important item at Carson's except as a convenience. A Circle K seven miles away sells food, magazines, gas, and liquor; its prices are high for everything except gas. Carson's survives on its services and goods, on its continuity with the past. The constellation of goods and services it provides are less easily obtained elsewhere: credit, mail, gas, specific items of hardware, wool cards and dyes, hats, shoes, and shirts that are especially liked, good bacon, a certain kind of sausage that Sam has always stocked. Sam buys wool but no sheep. The tribe runs an auction of sheep, goats, and cattle each spring at the Huerfano chapter house behind the post. The Navajo Irrigation Project, a large agricultural enterprise begun in the 1960s with irrigation from the San Juan River, now comes to the edge of the dirt road running past the store: huge fields of corn and alfalfa bordered by miles of straight paved roads.

The rugs at Carson's have improved in quality because Jo encouraged weavers, watching local families grow up and learn the craft, seeing the quality of their weaving improve with time and practice. New designs or new colors crop up; currently a clear red, obtained from pulverizing a particular rock, appears in some Carson rugs. Old patterns are repeated—some copied from rugs that Jessie bought, that still decorate the house. Several of the old rubs have designs of animals—rabbits, goats, sheep—and recent weavers have taken up the theme. A particularly unusual rug brought in for sale in the winter of 1982–83 had three pigs woven on it, and in the corner a half-eaten apple core.

Stokes's granddaughter Wy and her husband, Al Townsend, went to Inscription House Trading Post to manage it for their aunts, who took over the lease. When it came time, the Townsends renewed the lease in their own name. None of Mildred's daughters went into trading, but Nina worked for the Navajo Tribe and, following in her father's footsteps, became manager of the Window Rock Motor Inn, which is owned by the tribe. Raymond Drolet stayed at Shonto. He was married in 1979 to Melissa Kaplan, who had also been at St. Johns College, and Shonto Trading Post continued to be managed by a resident family. Like Stokes, Raymond appreciated saddle blankets; unlike Stokes, he did not appreciate sheep. Inscription House still deals in sheep, but Shonto does not. Both deal in wool.

Shonto remains a busy post in a good-size community. Pickup trucks and cars come and go all day, and though the trading post is open from 8:30 A.M. to 5:30 P.M. and closed at lunch, people come before the store opens and after it closes to use the pay telephone, the soft drink machine, to ask to buy gas or to borrow money, and if they live very close by and have forgotten items, to shop. In emergencies no one will hesitate to wake the Drolets—the emergency may be a request for gasoline at 3 A.M., or more rarely a death or an accident.

Snow comes at Thanksgiving and disappears in March, and in the summer the canyon is cool, shaded by the same cottonwoods the CCC planted, now a tall, dense grove. Trade comes from all around, and the BIA boarding school on the north rim of the canyon brings families in to visit their children and shop. The Peabody Coal Mine on Black Mesa is a few miles south, and men from Shonto work there and cash their paychecks at the store. There is still no bank nearby. Keeping enough cash in the till—the Peabody paychecks are not small—is a process of juggling cash, since money is usually ordered by mail from Page, sixty miles away, and arrives the next day. The telephone, however, is more of a problem than the mail. For reasons no one, least of all the telephone maintenance men, can fathom, it works when it pleases. Goats perhaps chew on the wires above the roof of the store, or winds tangle them. In the event of telephone failure coinciding with payday at the mine, Drolet or a clerk drives to the bank in Page.

Delivery of goods now comes on a regular basis, though supplies can run suddenly low. The UPS van comes daily, bringing mail-order purchases for Navajo customers to the trading post—the store is a convenient central place for deliveries.

The store at Shonto has been enlarged since Reuben Heflin's day, and the later additions are no longer in hand-hewn sandstone, but in boards and cement block. The walls of the grocery section are lined with refrigeration units, but storms still cause power failures that occasionally spoil the store's supply of milk and cheese, and thaw out the large supply of meat and ice cream. The west end of the store holds dry goods, a toy counter, hardware, and pharmacy goods. Outbuildings include the wool barn and a shed for tire repairs and for weighing wool and piñon nuts. The corrals behind and in front of the store are empty except for bee weed, tall grasses, and a few old cans and bottles. The guest hogans are used for storage.

Early on a cold March day, despite the icy sand in front of the post, five pickup trucks wait for the store to open. The morning begins with the arrival of the store employees, all of whom are Navajo: Floyd Talker, Sr., had worked at Shonto for years; his son Floyd Talker, Jr., is the fourth of his children to work at the store. After the Talkers comes Grace Brown, the head clerk, who lives in a trailer in the *rincon* just beyond Shonto's barn. Grace is followed by Drolet, jangling keys—keys to cash registers, ice chest, and drawers, keys to cabins and long-lost padlocks. The walk-in safe, which is also an office, is opened. Cash registers and lights are turned on, shelves are straightened, customers are let in. With the customers come Bill and Mary Brown and Ruby Clitso. Ruby and Mary are sales clerks, and Bill deals with gasoline, fuels, automobiles. Pumping gas is a full-time occupation, and the waiting pickups usually want gas to get to work. Bill Brown is hardly ever to be seen first thing in the morning; only the peak of his cap is visible behind a string of pickups. He keeps a tally of gasoline bought, and the cash or credit and payments, as well as the occasional purchase on account.

Mornings are busy, especially Mondays and Fridays. There are many mothers and children, many older men and women. Greetings and conversations in Navajo fill the store, but there is not a Navajo at Shonto under thirty and over six who is not bilingual. Small children hang like mosquitos over the candy counter and lay their change down with precision. The younger children stare in awe at their seniors, and given a few minutes they too will point and claim a sucker or a peppermint stick, though not all the smaller children speak English.

Meanwhile their mothers and grandparents shop. Shopping baskets and hand carts are slowly filled with flour and cheese and soda pop, frozen chicken and fresh mutton, laundry soap (the chapter house and Shonto Boarding School have laundromats).

The major part of the store is the dry-goods section. There are racks of blouses, shelves from floor to ceiling for fabrics, more shelves for jeans and shirts and hats both straw and felt, a small room for shoes. Leather and saddle tack hang from the ceiling. A corner is taken up with clothes for small children and baby gear. Pendleton blankets are folded into thick squares, their colorful edges brightening a high shelf. All the dry goods are ordered by Grace Brown. Salesmen bring in their wares for her to choose, and she selects, with a sure eye, the style, range, and quantity of each size of clothes, shoes, and variety goods that the store will stock.

A woman comes in with a small bundle, wrapped in a pillowcase, under her arm. She catches Melissa's eye as she emerges from the office. Melissa takes the lady and her bundle into the room behind the store— the rug room—to look at her handiwork, a wedding basket. Traditionally these were made by Paiutes and were traded and used by Navajos for wedding ceremonies; hence the name. In even earlier times Navajos made their own baskets and are again doing so. When a wedding basket is brought for a ceremony, it is preferred that it be a used one, and Navajos will sell and buy old baskets at the store and from each other. Both Ray and Melissa speak Navajo, Raymond quite fluently; but children often come with their relatives to translate or to make sure all is understood.

Another woman comes in with a double saddle blanket, also carefully wrapped, and she stands in the doorway waiting for Melissa to finish. The blanket is thick and straight and has red and black stripes separated at intervals by bands of white. When times are hard, such as they were in 1981 and 1982, weaving is still an economic failsafe, and good traders will buy rugs, at least until they themselves are suffering. At that time, Shonto's inventory increased to the point where rugs, piled high on wooden pallets around the rug room, overflowed into the room beyond. A large portion of the inventory consisted of saddle blankets: fluffy ones, smooth ones, brilliantly colored, or the colors of sheep or of vegetal dyes, saddle blankets of every variety and pattern. Soon the post's own economy grew tight and the purchase of rugs diminished until the inventory fell to more normal size. By then, the financial situation everywhere was less stringent, and tourists, who had been fewer and less ready to buy, reappeared.

Besides the baskets and rugs there are the usual borrowings and payings. One family comes in to ask for $200 for a funeral. Whatever they want will be approved, as will further requests over the next few days. Community ceremonies—deaths, births, the traditional dances and sings—bring requests for loans or for large additions to accounts, requests that are usually honored.

Around 11:00 the mail will be ready at the small post office across the wash, and Raymond, Melissa, or, if they are busy, someone else will collect outgoing mail from a small wooden mailbox on the counter and go across the wet slick sand, over the iron bridge, to pick up the store mail, including mail for many of their customers who use the trading post as their postal address.

At 12:30 the store closes for lunch, and when it reopens an hour later a woman comes in asking to put goods on her husband's account. Though accounts may include family members, often down to grandchildren, traders must be certain that permission of the customer responsible for the account covers everyone. In this particular case, the woman is separated from her husband, who gives her generous child support via the trading post ("Just let her run up to $400, Ray; just so long as I don't have to see her.") But she has already reached the limit for the month, as Raymond tells her in Navajo and which she undoubtedly knows. Only the very elderly are unable to cope with much counting. The era of inability to deal with figures went long before Stokes did, and the clerks are all faster than the adding machines they use.

Chapter 18

A very tall, very polite young man of about sixteen comes into the store to buy a watchband. He is Helen Hudgens's grandson. Helen still lives not far from Shonto and occasionally comes to the store. Her grandson is struggling to get the watchband pin into the holder on his watch. The pin is recalcitrant and keeps flying across the counter. The young man finally laughs and says he will take it anyway, and if it doesn't fit he will bring it back. He departs cheerfully after putting it—as his purchases are always put—on the account of his other grandmother. Grace has been watching, amused, and shakes her head and the long dark hair that falls to her waist.

Grace has worked at the store about fifteen years, and she commands respect. Though she is probably a little older than Raymond Drolet (himself in his mid-thirties) and has a face that looks younger, she has a presence. Grace does not get flustered, or impatient, or annoyed, or if she does she never reveals it. There may be one customer or five waiting at her dry-goods counter. She waits on them all in turn, showing velvet, cotton, satin, and waiting for the choice, reaching with a long hooked pole for baby goods from the top shelves, selling money orders, bringing customers shoes in different styles and sizes.

Mary and Ruby, down at the second register among the groceries, are no less busy. The adding machines stutter away, the cash register, a sophisticated electronic machine, rings busily in a more subdued tone than the old-fashioned register bell, but not less frequently. Bill Brown, in a temporary lull between requests for gas, enters the cash into the register and tallies his receipts and credit card slips, while Floyd Talker, Jr., restocks the canned goods, labeling each can with the price.

As in earlier times, the railroads hire many from Shonto as well as other communities, and Drolet, like his father and grandparents, is a railroad agent, empowered to sign up those who go out on jobs and those who have been laid off. These records consist of cards, countersigned by the workers, that go to the Railroad Board, which then pays the workers' salary if they have been hired or unemployment benefits if there is no work. The men, all ages from twenty to sixty, come in every two weeks to sign in.

Men who work at the Peabody Mines come in to cash their paychecks. They pay off their bills at the same time, but the transaction is a formal one. First the cash is counted out, then Grace or the Drolets bring out the account book and total the amount, and the bill or part of it is paid by the customer from the cash they have just received. The store account will often be one of several bills, such as utilities, Fingerhut or Sears mail orders, a charge account at a store in Flagstaff or Page, magazine subscriptions. These are usually paid by money order, though payment by personal check is becoming more common. The trading post, in the absence of checking accounts, or banks for that matter, continues to give many services.

The afternoon is quiet for an hour or two. A woman comes in, dressed, as all the older women and a few younger ones still are, in a long satin skirt and velvet blouse, in dark blue and green. Mary Bedonie buys a carton of milk, a bag of cornmeal, and a candy bar. A trip to the store is, as much as anything else, a break in the routine, a chance to visit people. A couple of younger men come in, buy a Coca Cola and sandwiches, and leave quickly, since they are probably working or on their way to work. An old man limps in, greets Mrs. Bedonie, and buys a soda pop. Two other older men come up and stand and talk quietly, falling silent occasionally, glancing out at the graying afternoon, the bare branches waving in the cold wind. For them too the store provides a diversion from home.

There is a surge of shopping before closing time. Many mothers and children come in after school, or after work, or if they are on their way to meet their husbands. Shopping carts are wheeled up to the cash registers, food stamps are pulled out of handbags. The tribe's social welfare program provides benefits to mothers with small children in the form of checks that specify on a form attached what food items (cheese, cereal, milk, etc.) the mother may buy and how much of it. The cashier rings up the purchases, following the list carefully, and fills in the amount on the check, which the customer signs. Small children are back for more candy, and pickups are beginning to file out of the parking area.

The day has almost ended. In the evening Melissa will make up a deposit, record checks, update various records on rug buying and selling. The late requests for gas or loans come less often in the winter and the evening will be quiet except for the dogs barking at the cattle that graze in the cottonwood grove. The post has a cohort of dogs—four at the moment—that create a great clamor when anyone arrives at the house. Stray puppies are left or abandoned at the store, partly because people know that the Drolets will not shoot strays, partly because there is always food around and if a puppy is tolerated by the other dogs it will be fed, along with the chickens, the cats, and the tortoise (another stray). This is hardly a serious aspect of trading, and yet it is indicative of a common characteristic of trading post life, namely, the acceptance of dealing with irregularities.

The exchange between Navajo and trader is not exactly irregular; indeed, after one hundred years it has some very regular aspects. The FTC, the BIA, the DNA, and the Navajo Tribe have each tried to ensure that it *is* regular. Yet it is not a store like any other. A Navajo, asked the reason why he or she shops at a trading post, will give a number of answers, both practical and personal. The trader may pay good prices for rugs, or give credit, or know of a job, or the store may be convenient and may carry necessities. In addition, the trader may be liked, or the store may be a good place to meet other Navajos, avoid non-Navajos, remain within the Navajo world.[3] The Anglo trader does not become Navajo by living in the Navajo world, but he usually becomes familiar, constant, and predictable.

Stokes Carson traded for fifty years during a period of visible change in both Navajo and Anglo culture. He saw the growth of Navajo tribal government and the activities (both in the 1930s and the 1960s) of Navajos who had been educated in Anglo schools and had taken up leadership among the people. He saw changes on the community level in burial practices, health, in modes of dress and means of transporation, in work, and in purchases. Stokes's observations did not cover only the Navajos but his own society as well, through financial panic, the radical New Deal, two wars, and the increase in government regulations. Technological changes had occurred that made life easier, and welfare programs had made life better, for those who had very little. The Navajo had been the recipients of some of these advances. The traditional life, with which Stokes was so familiar, had continued in the face of change, and he respected it. He never underestimated the Navajos. Indeed, the FTC hearings had shown the Navajos' ability to grasp a situation and turn it to their political and psychological advantage. Stokes took the hearings as a blow to his reputation as a good trader, though he quickly recovered his good humor and his involvement in trading. From his hospital bed in Tuba City, before his death, Stokes would ask his visitors about the piñon crop, due to be a bumper one the autumn of 1974. To the end he remained a trader inextricably bound up with the resources from which both he and the Navajo made a living.

Notes

1. For a discussion of trade networks of the Spanish and early traders, see McNitt (1962:44–67).

2. Amsden (1934:133) quotes Don José Cortez, an officer of the Spanish royal engineers in 1799, who mentions that Navajos "go to the province of New Mexico with the surplus and there exchange their goods . . . for the implements they need." David Brugge (personal communication, 1982) also confirms trade in the early eighteenth century.

Chapter 1

1. On early settlers of Farmington, see MacDonald and Arrington (1973:13–14), Furman (1977). The population of Farmington in 1890 was 336; in 1900, 548; in 1910, 785 (Coan [1925:460]).

2. See MacDonald and Arrington (1970:87–90). Jessie Smith's time at the mission is also described in Kildare (1974).

Chapter 2

1. Amsden gives the first reference to Navajos as that in the *Relaciones* of Father Gerónimo Zarate-Salmerón, which gives a history of the Spanish in New Mexico between 1538 and 1626. The history gives the name "Nabaho" as well as Navajo. Amsden also quotes from Edgar L. Hewett: "Fray Alonso de Benevides, in his Memorial on New Mexico published

in 1630 . . . says: 'But these (Apaches) of Navajo are very great farmers, for that is what Navajo signifies—great planted fields.' " Amsden (1934: 126–27) quoting from Hewett, 1906, *Origin of the Name Navaho, American Anthropologist* 8:193.

2. On New Mexico's battle for statehood, see Larson (1968: Chaps. 9–17). Population of sheep from Coan (1925:516). Population of New Mexico in 1900 is given by Larson (1968:243) as 195,310. On the movement of sheep rearing west, see Cole (1926:74–75).

3. On land, religion, and language as issues, see Larson (1968:303–4); on Spanish and Anglo land titles, see Larson (1968:154).

4. For this very brief history of the Navajo, the following sources have been used: Aberle (1966); Amsden (1934); Brugge (1980); Kluck-hohn and Leighton (1962); Underhill (1959); Van Valkenburgh (1938, 1941).

5. Increases in reservation: Underhill (1956:148–49).

6. Population figures of sheep from Underhill (1956:215); of people, from Johnston (1966:137). In 1864 the Navajo population was 8,354; in 1865, 7,151. According to Johnson (1966) this was the count at Fort Sumner.

7. See Underhill (1956:155–56).

8. On early trade in rugs, see Amsden (1934:133). On early Navajo dress and weaving at Bosque Redondo, see Amsden (1934:96–98, 134). Navajo women's dress was two small blankets sewn together at the sides and shoulders and belted. The colors were usually black, with blue and red border designs. The garment closely resembled traditional Pueblo dress except that the latter had one shoulder bare.

9. See Amsden (1934:179).

10. See Hill (1948), who gives considerable detail on Navajo trading and points out that it was the Navajo who were active agents in the search for trade.

11. On early regulation of trading, see McNitt (1962:44–57).

12. This legislation is crucial. When, in 1969, opinion ran against the traders, a lawsuit was brought against the secretary of the Interior and the commissioner of Indian Affairs for not carrying out their responsibility to regulate traders. It was this suit that in part set in motion the ensuing investigation. See Chapter 16.

13. For history of the early Anglo traders, see McNitt (1962:68–115).

14. See McNitt (1962:163, 165). McNitt quotes Army, the Indian agent of 1875: "I would . . . respectfully suggest that a law be passed making it

a criminal offense for a white man to cohabit with an Indian squaw unless he is married to her under the laws of the United States and that when married they shall no longer live on the reservation."

15. See McNitt (1962).

Chapter 3

1. See McNitt (1962:298–301).

2. Yana-pah had woven, in a few of her rugs, a single large Yei figure—a figure from legend and ceremony—as part of the central design. This was unusual: most weavers believed that incorporating sacred figures into the rugs would bring them harm. Yana-pah was among the first to do it (McNitt [1962:298], Amsden [1934:106]).

3. See Brugge (1980:308).

4. On W. F. Hunter, see Bailey and Bailey (1982:280–81). Building on the bridge was begun by the traders, but it was washed away by high water before completion.

Chapter 4

1. On the treaty of 1868 and subsequent settlement of the Navajo, see Brugge (1980:49–55); Underhill (1956:144–56). On the Checkerboard area, see Kelly (1968:20).

2. Brugge (1980:63–64).

3. See Brugge (1980:106–8, 121–29); Kelly (1968:16–32).

4. On Navajo legends and oral histories of their origin, see Kluckhohn and Leighton (1962:122–25).

5. McNitt (1962:331–33); Brugge (1980:305). The Carson family have letters Pat Smith wrote a few days before his death, which Jessie kept. They were found after she died. Pat's body, such as it was, was collected by his brother Bob for burial in Farmington.

6. Brugge (1980:306–7).

7. Brugge (1980:305) suggests that these sporadic acts of violence stemmed from the frustration over the land situation in the Checkerboard region. McNitt (1962:331) attributes the violence to an influenza epidemic, but Brugge points out that this followed Pat's death.

8. See Brugge (1980:314) and Bailey and Bailey (1982:207–8). Indian agent Stacher also mentions this event in a newsletter (NPS: CCNHP).

Chapter 5

1. Amsden (1934:234 plate 123) and Underhill (1956:194) both suggest that the style that is now seen as "traditional" Navajo dress stemmed from the Civil War, at least for the women, which they would have encountered at Bosque Redondo. Underhill speculates that velvet was a surplus commodity in the east which found a market among the Navajo. She suspects that there was also an influence from Spanish women's dress, which was not unlike that of the Civil War period in the United States.

2. Milton Jackson photograph, Maxwell Museum, University of New Mexico, photo archives.

3. From Blinken (1948:32), who gives the amount of wool used as increasing from 293 million to 509 million pounds.

4. On early pawn and its problems, see Brugge (1980:127, 194–95); McNitt (1962:56). Richard Wetherill was charged by a Navajo with having sold a belt that the Navajo had pawned to Wetherill's brother at Two Gray Hills Trading Post. The Navajo recognized his belt on a Navajo in Chaco Canyon and was most upset (Brugge 1980:195).

5. See Frisbie (1977).

6. On credit as a competitive edge, see Brugge (1980:294). Indian agent Stacher thought that there was enough competition to keep prices reasonable.

7. Brugge (1980:354–55).

Chapter 6

1. On the upgrading of Navajo sheep, see Brugge (1980:69, 267). Data on wool growing, wool use, and importation is taken from the following sources: U.S. Tariff Board (1912); U.S. Department of Agriculture (1949); Wright (1910).

2. For information on the churro, see Kupper (1945:155).

3. Underhill (1956:155–56) gives Sam Day as her informant on the kind of sheep given out to the Navajo. Day told her they were the old churro breed. She also mentions sheep as belonging to women (p. 60). However, Amsden (1934:198) writes that Robert C. Prewitt, "merchant of forty years experience in the Southwest, told me he read in some old Government source that the sheep furnished under the treaty were Kentucky Cotswolds." Amsden could not locate this source.

4. Amsden (1934:199–200), Underhill (1956:156), Parman (1976:10).

5. The details and description of different breeds of sheep are given in

Chapter 9

Coffey (1918). The many photographs in this volume showing typical animals of each breed were compared with modern-day animals at the New Mexico State Fair in Albuquerque in September 1982. The breeds did not appear to have changed appreciably in the intervening sixty-five years.

6. For weights and cost of lambs in 1926, see Brugge (1980:354–55); Bailey and Bailey (1982:224–25).

7. See Parman (1976:129–30).

8. Amsden (1934:200).

9. See Amsden (1934:199–200).

10. Parman (1976:33); Fred Nelson was talking at a Navajo tribal council meeting in Fort Defiance, March 12 and 13, 1934.

Chapter 7

1. *Farmington Times Hustler*, April 26, 1929.

2. See Brugge (1980:154).

3. From Coffey (1918).

4. See Brugge (1980:206, 305); for Anglo claims that Navajo sheep had scabies, see Brugge (1980:261).

5. See Amsden (1934:33).

6. In the 1950s, oil and gas exploration and discovery around Carson's brought the families of those Navajos who had land considerable royalties.

Chapter 8

1. See Kluckhohn (1944) for an account of Navajo witchcraft.

2. On schooling of Navajos in this period, see Boyce (1974), Young (1978).

Chapter 9

1. On the discovery of oil, see Kelly (1968:48–58), Young (1978: 55–58), Parman (1976:16).

2. Price of lambs is from Kelly (1968:113), Brugge (1980:371). On barter among the Navajo, see Brugge (1980:376). Discussion of wages and subsistence is in Bailey and Bailey (1982:374). One bank, the McKinley County Bank, failed in Farmington in the late 1920s, but it is not clear if it was related to the depression (*Farmington Times Hustler*, April 18, 1930).

3. On the winter and government relief, see Brugge (1980:386–87).

4. Newspaper comment on overgrazing is from an unidentified clipping in the Carson family files. Navajo population in 1930 is given as 39,000 by the U.S. Census; the BIA had figures of 48,858 (Johnston 1966:137). The sheep population in 1930 is from Coan (1925:515); Parman (1976:53) gives a figure of 1,152,000 from sheep dipping records from 1933. Many sheep died in the winter of 1931–32.

5. On stock reductions, see Parman (1976:50–52).

6. See Young (1978:77–78).

7. See Navajo Community College Press (1974). According to Parman (1976:64) in 1934 Carl Beck, a government stockman, shot a herd of sheep and goats he was taking from Navajo Mountain to Tuba City. He had reached Inscription House, but in the drought of that year he thought the animals could not make the forty-five miles. There may be other, undocumented, incidents.

8. See Counselor and Counselor (1954), Parman (1976:150, 153).

9. On chapter houses and local leaders, see Young (1978:17–20, 66–68); Brugge (1980:442).

10. Very little violence occurred on the part of the Navajo toward the government employees who came to take their sheep. One range rider was beaten on his return from the weary business of handing out grazing permits to the hogans in his district, and his horse was taken, so that he had to walk home. He walked right out of the job (Ward [1951:77–78]).

11. Slightly different vote counts are found for the Wheeler-Howard Bill: Young (1978:86) gives 7,608 for, 7,992 against; Parman (1976:76) gives 7,679 for, 8,197 against; Kelly (1968:169) gives figures from the *Albuquerque Journal* (June 17, 1935) of 7,995 for, 8,215 against.

Chapter 10

1. Figures from Bailey and Bailey (1982:217).

Chapter 11

1. See McNitt (1962:271).

2. On founding of posts, see McNitt (1962): Beclabito (p. 301); Chilchinbeto (p. 251); Dinehotso (p. 295); Mexican Water (p. 343); Teec Nos Pos (pp. 341–42).

3. The author learned this in an interview with the Gouldings (June, 1979), but see also Klinck (1953).

4. See Parman (1976:217–31).

Chapter 13

5. See Parman (1976:427–29).
6. *Farmington Time Hustler,* October 17, 1941.
7. Interview with Bob Cooke, 1979.

Chapter 12

1. *Farmington Times Hustler,* July 12, 1940.
2. On the Navajo Code Talkers, see Parman (1976:287).
3. Elizabeth Compton Hagemann's book, *Navajo Trading Days* (1963), is the best and most delightful firsthand account of trading in the 1930s. Elizabeth Compton came from a well-to-do Midwestern family and married Harry Rorick; together they ran Shonto Trading Post. She knew everyone, from the wives of cabinet ministers to the Shonto Navajos, and she liked to mix both worlds. She and Harry Rorick parted ways, in her words, and Rorick remained at Shonto until the Helfins bought it from him.
4. For more information on Two Gray Hills, see McNitt (1962:259–61). Two traders, one at Two Gray Hills, one at Toadlena, were responsible for encouraging fine weaving in this area in the 1920s. Toadlena Trading Post, two miles from Two Gray Hills, was built in 1909 by Merritt and Bob Smith, Jessie Carson's brothers. They sold it in 1911. It is an unusual-looking trading post, built of brick and two stories high.

Chapter 13

1. See the following newspapers: *Gallup Independent, Farmington Times Hustler, Denver Post* for the years 1947–48. These would have been the newspapers most available to reservation residents. The House Un-American Activities Committee was active, and actively reported on the front pages, during these years also. See, for example, the *Gallup Independent,* July 8, 1948 and July 21, 1948.
2. On the contents of the boxes to Navajos, see the *Desert Magazine,* March 1948.
3. *Gallup Independent,* March 22, 1949; according to Mildred Heflin's letters of the period, the Red Cross was bringing aid long before this.
4. On the wheat scarcity, see the *Gallup Independent,* October 1947; the *New York Times,* October 1947.
5. Parman (1976:129–30) comments that the Navajo were humiliated by the "dole."
6. On Norman Littell, the refusal of funds to the tribe, and the BIA postwar planning report on rehabilitation, see Young (1978:124–27).

7. The two specific reports, Drefkoff's, entitled *An Industrial Program for the Navajo Indian Reservation,* and Professor G. I. Chávez's, entitled *The People: A Study of the Navajo* (on education), were incorporated in the final report of Interior Secretary Krug.

8. Drefkoff's comment on traders and missionaries is from the *Denver Post,* October 10, 1947. Other comments on Drefkoff can be found in the *Gallup Independent,* March 12–19, 1948. On the United Indian Traders' Association, with Carr as their attorney, see the *Gallup Independent,* April 20, 1948. On the issue of rent for traders, see U.S. Bureau of Indian Affairs (1949).

9. *Denver Post,* October 29, 1947.

10. On tribal welfare programs and scholarships, see Young (1978:153, 157–62). The population data on the Navajo in 1948 are from the *Denver Post,* October 10, 1948. Underhill (1956:253) gives figures of 55,000 for 1947. The Navajo yearbook of 1946, quoted in Johnston (1966:137), gives 59,997. The figures for 1950 are given as 54,997 on the reservation and 62,167 "in the service area" by the BIA, and as 64,274 (total) by the U.S. Census. Many Navajos lived outside the reservation, and an increasing number began to move to larger southwestern cities as well as to California.

11. See Brugge (1980:276).

12. See Adams (1963:226–27).

13. The remarks of Horace Boardman (who had once been a trader himself) are from a tape transcript of a White Rock radio broadcast, of 1935.

14. U.S. Department of Agriculture (1935).

15. U.S. Bureau of Indian Affairs (1949).

16. Ibid.

Chapter 14

1. See Luckert (1977:5–12) for the history and religion of the Navajo Mountain area.

Chapter 15

1. Adams (1963:22).
2. Adams (1963:307).
3. Adams (1963:24).
4. Adams (1963:26).

5. Richard Mike, of the education division of the Navajo tribal government, suggests that the explosion of Watts began the activist movement among all minorities, a movement that reached the Navajo Reservation by the late 1960s and took several forms. The fight against economic exploitation and for more autonomy and equality came out of this movement. Mike mentions, in this context, the demonstrations at the Gallup Ceremonial and the actions against the then director of the DNA.

6. On the motel opening, see the *Gallup Independent*, May 3, 1965.

7. On oil and gas royalties, see the *Gallup Independent*, March 3, 1965. On the financial chaos of the tribe and criticism of BIA management of tribal funds, see the *Navajo Times*, January 27, 1966. Young (1978:13) discusses the discord between Nakai and the "old guard."

8. On the OEO antipoverty grant and the establishment of the ONEO in 1965 (Peter MacDonald was executive director), see the *Gallup Independent*, May 3 and May 6, 1965.

9. Adams (1963:270) discusses off-reservation trading posts. Richard Mike also drew the author's attention to the difference between trading posts on the reservation and those outside it. See the *Gallup Independent* of January 11, January 27, and February 11, 1969 for accidents and violence. See also Iverson (1981:173–74) on border town tensions and violence.

10. On the electricity station at Kayenta, see the *Navajo Times*, April 14, 1966. The Navajo Tribal Utility advertisement was in the *Navajo Times*, July 27, 1969.

11. Gilbraith (1973:59–78). The tribe tried to encourage cooperatives and Navajo traders and small business but only in the 1970s (no doubt due to the economic climate) did Navajo entrepreneurs begin to flourish: see Iverson (1981:170–72). In 1979, an informal check revealed one Navajo trader, though there were many others in partnership and in responsible positions in the posts.

12. For details on the DNA, Theodore Mitchell, and Normal Littell, see the *Navajo Times*, May 29, 1969, June 5, 1969, August 21, 1969, September 4, 1969, October 23, 1969, and October 30, 1969; see also Iverson (1981:91–100).

13. See the *Navajo Times*, August 28, 1969; Young (1978:143–46).

14. On the Gallup Ceremonial demonstrations and ensuing court action, see the *Navajo Times*, September 11, 1969, September 18, 1969, September 25, 1969, August 13, 1970 and August 20, 1970, and the *Gallup Independent*, February 21, 1969 and December 11, 1970.

15. *Navajo Times*, June 12, 1969. It is worth noting that the pawn

regulations are so confusing at this time that from the wording of the article it appears to state that the pawn must be held indefinitely if *no* payment is received.

16. On the DNA case report, see the *Navajo Times*, August 28, 1969; and DNA Brief No. 25437, U.S. Court of Appeals. John Rockridge and Henry Zah v. Graham Holmes, Bureau of Indian Affairs Area Director, Walter J. Hickel, Secretary of the Interior, and Louis R. Bruce, Commissioner for Indian Affairs. June 1970.

17. Southwestern Indian Development, Inc. (n.d.:7)

18. Southwestern Indian Development, Inc. (n.d.:8)

19. Southwestern Indian Development, Inc. (n.d.:7); they give Adams as the reference for the quote.

20. Southwestern Indian Development, Inc. (n.d.:i).

Chapter 16

1. An FTC report of 1973 quotes a letter from Louis Bruce, commissioner of Indian Affairs, to Miles Kirkpatrick of the FTC, dated April 7, 1972. On DNA suits, see the *Gallup Independent*, August 28, 1969, and October 9, 1969.

2. Oliver La Farge formed the American Association on Indian Affairs in the 1930s and worked with both Howard Gorman, former tribal chairman, and Moris S. Burge (who wrote the 1948 report on traders). La Farge was active on the Navajo behalf during the New Deal. Parman (1976:153–54).

3. The FTC press conference was covered in the *Los Angeles Times*, August 8, 1972 and the *Navajo Times*, August 10, 1972.

4. On MacDonald and Zah, see the *Gallup Independent*, August 29, 1972.

5. On Foutz, McGee, and Price, see the *Gallup Independent*, August 29, 1972.

6. *Gallup Independent*, August 30, 1972.

7. *Gallup Independent*, August 30, 1972.

8. The Kayenta hearings are covered in the *Gallup Independent*, August 31, 1972. Brad Blair was in the audience, and so was John Zufelt. From all accounts, Blair was a fine trader; his funeral in 1983 was attended by many people from the community, and included a moving eulogy given by a Navajo. His wife was Navajo, which undoubtedly helped to bring him closer to the community.

9. *Los Angeles Times*, September 4, 1972; *Las Vegas* (Nevada) *Review*

Journal, September 10, 1972. When the author visited Inscription House in 1979, without an introduction, the trader, Stokes's granddaughter, remembering earlier twisted accounts of traders, was not enthusiastic about being interviewed until she had made sure the author was not a journalist.

10. *Gallup Independent,* August 31, 1972.

11. *Gallup Independent,* August 31, 1972.

12. *Gallup Independent,* August 31, 1972.

13. *Gallup Independent,* September 1, 1972.

14. *Gallup Independent,* September 2, 1972.

15. Attempts to move Navajos off land began in at least the 1920s. In the 1970s Navajos, with the aid of DNA, began to fight back through the courts, a long-drawn-out, often unresolved, battle: see Euler (1949); Johnston (1939); NPS File #L3019 (NPS, WNM); also *Flagstaff Daily Sun,* May 12, 1970; *Gallup Independent,* May 13, 1970; and the *New York Post,* May 12, 1970.

16. *Gallup Independent,* September 2, 1972.

Chapter 17

1. U.S. Federal Trade Commission (1973:15).

2. U.S. Federal Trade Commission (1973:15–16).

3. U.S. Federal Trade Commission (1973:15).

4. U.S. Federal Trade Commission (1973:22–26).

5. U.S. Federal Trade Commission (1973:28–29).

6. U.S. Federal Trade Commission (1973:29).

7. U.S. Federal Trade Commission (1973:15).

8. Rumors of violence among traders are hard to substantiate, but they are heard, usually in reference to the past (and occasionally among themselves; see the *Gallup Independent,* February 23, 1953). Jack Anderson wrote a column in connection with trader-Navajo relations, describing two incidents: one in which a woman claimed a trader had forced her at knifepoint to endorse her welfare check; another in which a second woman claimed she had been forced to go in a small plane (a terrifying experience for her) to talk to a lawyer concerning a charge she had made against the trader (*Albuquerque Journal,* February 1, 1970). The SID report attached a copy of the column in the appendix.

Chapter 18

1. In September 1985 Jo Drolet and Chin Smith died in an automobile accident. Ed Smith died four months later. Sam Drolet is still running Carson's Trading Post.

2. While Adams in 1957 noted that the main current of Anglo-Navajo relations flowed through the trader, by 1963 Aubrey Williams, an anthropologist working for the Navajo Tribe on a land claims case, found that cooperation of chapter officials was instrumental for interviewing local Navajos. See Williams (1970).

3. These responses were given by Navajos to the question, Why do you shop at a trading post? in a survey done by National Park Service employees at the Hubbell Trading Post. Jim Ostler, personal communication.

Bibliography

Aberle, David F. 1966. *The Peyote Religion Among the Navajo.* Chicago: Aldine.

Adams, William Y. 1963. *Shonto: A Study of the Role of the Trader in a Modern Navajo Community.* Smithsonian Institution Bulletin 188. Washington, D.C.

Amsden, Charles Avery. 1934. *Navajo Weaving: Its Technic and History.* Santa Ana, Calif.: Fine Arts Press. (reprinted by the Rio Grande Press, Glorieta, N.Mex. 1974)

Bailey, Garrick A., and Roberta G. Bailey. 1982. *Historic Navajo Occupation of the Northern Chaco Plateau.* Tulsa, Okla.: Faculty of Anthropology, University of Tulsa.

Bernheimer, Charles L. 1929. *Rainbow Bridge: The Expedition of 1929.* Garden City: Doubleday, Doran and Co.

Billington, Ray Allen, ed. 1966. *The Frontier Thesis: Valid Interpretation of American History?* New York: Holt, Rinehart and Winston.

Blinken, Donald M. 1948. *Wool Tariffs and American Policy.* Washington, D.C.: Public Affairs Press.

Boyce, George A. 1974. *When Navajos Had Too Many Sheep: The 1940s.* San Francisco: Indian Historian Press.

Brugge, David M. 1980. *A History of the Chaco Navajos.* Albuquerque: National Park Service.

Chisholm, James S. 1981. "Social and Economic Change Among the Navajo: Residence Patterns and the Pickup Truck." *Journal of Anthropological Research* 37:148.

Coan, Charles F. 1925. *A History of New Mexico*, vol. 1. Chicago: American Historical Society.

Coffey, Walter C. 1918. *Productive Sheep Husbandry.* Lippincott's Farm Manuals Series. Philadelphia: Lippincott.

Cole, Arthur H. 1926. *The American Wool Manufacture*, vol. 2. Cambridge, Mass.: Harvard University Press.

Counselor, Jim, and Ann Counselor. 1954. *Wild, Woolly, and Wonderful.* New York: Vantage Press.

Downs, James F. 1964. *Animal Husbandry in Navajo Society and Culture.* Berkeley and Los Angeles: University of California Press.

Euler, Robert C. 1949. "An Economic Study of the Navajos in Wupatki Basin, Arizona." Unpublished manuscript on file, NPS, WNM.

Frisbie, Charlotte J. 1977. "Navajo Medicine Bundles or Jish—and the Question of Pawn." *The Master Key* 51(4):127–39.

Furman, Anges Miller. 1977. *Tohta: An Early Day History of the Settlement of Farmington and San Juan County, New Mexico 1875–1900.* Wichita Falls, Tex.: Nortex Press.

Gilbreath, Kent. 1973. *Red Capitalism: An Analysis of the Navajo Economy.* Norman: University of Oklahoma Press.

Gillmor, Frances, and Louisa Wade Wetherill. 1934. *Traders to the Navajos: The Story of the Wetherills of Kayneta.* Boston: Houghton Mifflin. Reprinted 1953, Albuquerque: Unviersity of New Mexico Press.

Gregg, Josiah. 1954. *The Commerce of the Prairies.* Norman: University of Oklahoma Press.

Hegemann, Elizabeth Compton. 1963. *Navajo Trading Days.* Albuquerque: University of New Mexico Press.

Hill, W. W. 1948. "Navajo Trading and Trading Ritual: A Study of Cultural Dynamics." *Southwestern Journal of Anthropology*, 4:371–96.

Iverson, Peter. 1981. *The Navajo Nation.* Westport, Conn.: Greenwood Press. Reprinted 1983, Albuquerque: University of New Mexico Press.

Johnston, Dennis Foster. 1966. *An Analysis of Sources of Information on the Population of the Navajo.* Smithsonian Institution Bulletin 197. Washington, D.C.

Johnston, Phillip. 1939. "Peshlaka Atsidi." *Plateau* 12(2).

Kelley, Klara B. 1977. "Commercial Networks in the Navajo–Hopi–Zuni Region." Ph.D. thesis, University of New Mexico, Albuquerque.

Kelly, Lawrence G. 1968. *Navajo Indians and Federal Indian Policy 1900–1935.* Tucson: University of Arizona Press.

Kennedy, Mary Jeanette. 1965. *Tales of a Trader's Wife.* Albuquerque: Valiant.

Keur, Dorothy. 1944. "A Chapter in Navajo–Pueblo Relations." *American Antiquity* 10(1):75–86.

Kildare, Morris. 1969. "The Last Navajo Traders." *Western Digest*, May.

———. 1974. "Girl on a Strange Frontier." *True West*, June.

Klinck, Richard E. 1953. *Land of Room Enough and Time Enough.* Albuquerque: University of New Mexico Press.

Kluckhohn, Clyde. 1944. *Navajo Witchcraft.* Peabody Museum Papers, vol. 22, no. 2, Cambridge, Mass.: Harvard University. (Reprinted 1970, Boston: Beacon Press).

———, and Dorothea Leighton. 1962. *The Navajo.* revised ed. Garden City: Anchor Books, Doubleday.

Kupper, Winifred. 1945. *The Golden Hoof: The Story of the Sheep of the Southwest.* New York: Knopf.

Larson, Robert W. 1968. *New Mexico's Quest for Statehood 1846–1912.* Albuquerque: University of New Mexico Press.

Levitan, Sar A., and Barbara Hetrick. 1971. *Big Brother's Indian Programs with Reservations.* New York: McGraw-Hill.

Luckert, Karl W. 1977: *Navajo Mountain and Rainbow Bridge Religion.* American Tribal Religions, vol. 1. Flagstaff: Museum of Northern Arizona.

MacDonald, Eleanor D., and John B. Arrington. 1970. *The San Juan Basin: My Kingdom Was a County.* Denver: MIDO Printing Co.

McNitt, Frank. 1962. *The Indian Traders.* Norman: University of Oklahoma Press.

Navajo Community College Press. 1974. *Navajo Livestock Reduction: A National Disgrace.* Chinle, Ariz.

———. 1977. *Stores of Traditional Navajo Life and Culture,* by twenty-two Navajo men and women. Tsaile, Navajo Nation, Ariz.

Otero, Miguel Antonio. 1939. *My Life on the Frontier.* Albuquerque: University of New Mexico Press.

Parman, Donald L. 1976. *The Navajo and the New Deal.* New Haven: Yale University Press.

Phelp-Stokes Fund. 1939. *The Navajo Indian Problem.* New York.

Reeve, Frank D. 1946. "A Navajo Struggle for Land." *New Mexico Historical Review* 21:2–21.

Reichard, Gladys. 1950. *Navajo Religion: A Study of Symbolism.* Bollingen Series 18. Princeton: Princeton University Press.

———. 1936. *Navajo Shepherd and Weaver.* New York: J. J. Augustin.

Sasaki, Tom. 1960. *Fruitland, New Mexico: A Navajo Community in Transition.* Ithaca: Cornell University Press.

Schmedding, Joseph. 1951. *Cowboy and Indian Trader.* Caldwell, Idaho: The Caxton Printers.

Southwestern Indian Development, Inc. 1969. *Traders on the Navajo Reservation: The Economic Bondage of the Navajo.* Window Rock, Ariz.

Underhill, Ruth M. 1959. *The Navajos.* Norman: University of Oklahoma Press.

U.S. Bureau of Indian Affairs. 1949. Report to the Commissioner of Indian Affairs on Navajo Trading, prepared by Moris S. Burge. Washington, D.C.: Government Printing Office.

U.S. Congress, Senate Committee on Indian Affairs. 1936. *Survey of Conditions of the Indians of the United States, Hearings before a Subcommittee of the Committee on Indian Affairs.* 75th Cong., 1st sess., Pt. 34. Washington, D.C.

U.S. Department of Agriculture, Bureau of Agricultural Economics. 1949. *Wool Statistics Including Mohair and Other Animal Fiber.* Washington, D.C.: GPO.

U.S. Department of Agriculture. 1935. *Navajo Trading: A Report,* prepared by Bonney Youngblood. Washington, D.C.: GPO.

U.S. Federal Trade Commission. 1973. *The Trading Post System on the Navajo Reservation.* Staff Report to the Federal Trade Commission. Washington, D.C.: GPO.

U.S. Tariff Board. 1912. *Wool and Manufactures of Wool: Message of the President of the United States transmitting a Report of the Tariff Board on Schedule K of the Tariff Law.* Washington, D.C.: GPO.

Van Valkenburgh, Richard. 1938. "A Short History of the Navajo People." Mimeograph, U.S. Indian Service, Window Rock, Ariz.

————. 1941. *Dine Bikeyah.* Edited by Lucy Wilcox Adams and John C. McPhee. Window Rock, Ariz.: Navajo Service.

Ward, Elizabeth. 1951. *No Dudes, Few Women: Life with a Navajo Range Rider.* Albuquerque: University of New Mexico Press.

Water, L. L. 1950. *Steel Trails to Santa Fe.* Lawrence: University of Kansas Press.

Williams, Aubrey W., Jr. 1970. *Navajo Political Process.* Smithsonian Contributions to Anthropology, vol. 9. Washington, D.C.: Smithsonian Institution Press.

Wright, Chester Whitney. 1910. *Wool Growing and the Tariff: A Study in the Economic History of the United States.* Cambridge, Mass.: Harvard University Press.

Wyman, Leland C. 1957. *Beautyway: A Navajo Ceremonial.* Bollingen Series 53. New York: Pantheon Books.

Bibliography

Young, Robert. 1978. *A Political History of the Navajo Tribe*. Tsaile, Navajo Nation, Ariz.: Navajo Community College Press.

——, and W. Morgan. 1969. *The Navajo Language*. Salt Lake City: U.S. Indian Service.

Archival Sources

National Park Service (NPS)
    Chaco Culture National Historic Park (CCNHP) files
    Wupatki National Monument (WNM) files
Dinebeiina Nahilna Be Agaditahe (D.N.A.)
Letters and Journals of the Carson family
Letters of C. E. Purviance
Interviews: Douglas Anderson, Bruce Barnard, Harry Bachelor, Bob Cooke, Jo Drolet, Melissa Drolet, Sam Drolet, Raymond Drolet, Harry and Mike Goulding, Mildred Heflin, Nina Heflin, Marie Leighton, Luther Manning, Richard Mike, Walter Scribner, Chin Smith, Ed Smith, Maurice Tanner, Allan Townsend, Wyona Townsend.

Newspapers

Denver Post, Denver, Colorado
Farmington Times Hustler, Farmington, New Mexico
Flagstaff Daily Sun, Flagstaff, Arizona
Gallup Independent, Gallup, New Mexico
Las Vegas Review Journal, Las Vegas, Nevada
Los Angeles Times, Los Angeles, California
The New York Times, New York City, New York
New York Post, New York City, New York

Index

213